FRINGE AND FORTUNE

FRINGE AND FORTUNE

THE ROLE OF CRITICS IN HIGH AND POPULAR ART

WESLEY MONROE SHRUM, JR.

PRINCETON UNIVERSITY PRESS

PRINCETON, NEW JERSEY

Copyright © 1996 by Princeton University Press
Published by Princeton University Press, 41 William Street,
Princeton, New Jersey 08540
In the United Kingdom: Princeton University Press,
Chichester, West Sussex

Library of Congress Cataloging-in-Publication Data

Shrum, Wesley, 1953–.
Fringe and fortune : the role of critics in high and popular art /
Wesley Monroe Shrum, Jr.
p.   cm.
Includes bibliographical references and index.
ISBN 0-691-02145-7 (cloth : alk. paper)
ISBN 0-691-02657-2 (pbk. : alk. paper)
1. Art and society.   2. Art criticism.   3. Popular culture.
4. Social classes.   I. Title.
N72.S6S47   1996   700'.1'03—dc20   96-4417   CIP

Tables 6.1–6.3 and Appendix B are reprinted with the permission
of the University of Chicago Press from the *American Journal of
Sociology* 97:347–75. Copyright 1991 by The University of Chicago.
All rights reserved.

This book has been composed in Galliard

Princeton University Press books are printed
on acid-free paper and meet the guidelines for
permanence and durability of the Committee on
Production Guidelines for Book Longevity
of the Council on Library Resources

Printed in the United States of America

10 9 8 7 6 5 4 3 2 1

10 9 8 7 6 5 4 3 2 1
(pbk.)

To Paula and Brittani

Now treasure is ticklish work; I don't like treasure-voyages on any account; and I don't like them, above all, when they are secret, and when (begging your pardon, Mr. Trelawny) the secret has been told to the parrot.
—*Robert Louis Stevenson,* Treasure Island

CONTENTS

ILLUSTRATIONS

PHOTOGRAPHS (following page 108)

Photographs 1–3 and 7–14 by Malcolm Cochrane,
4–6 by Wesley Shrum.

FIGURES

TABLES

PREFACE

WHEN I FIRST CAME to Scotland in 1973 I missed the Festival Fringe by a week. When I left my job at British Rail in 1974, it was a month too early to see the festival's first shows. And when I arrived for sabbatical in Edinburgh in 1988 the last thing I expected was to become engrossed for a period of eight years in the study of this massive effusion of modern performance art.

For a sociologist of science and technology, that may not be considered so surprising. Science is no longer viewed as an epistemically privileged enterprise, and students of science are more likely now to consider the wider field of culture as an appropriate topic of inquiry. The history of this work began with a narrow empirical question, Do critics matter? It seemed the issue could readily be addressed in the context of this most propitious of research sites, that infinitely exhilarating and highly organized chaos known as the Edinburgh Festival Fringe.

The study that emerged instead deals with a much larger and thornier theoretical problem: the nature of cultural hierarchy and its persistence. The main argument is that the difference between high art and low depends on the way our opinions about artworks are formed. It is a function of the discursive practices that mediate the relationship between art and its public, involving a transfer of judgment legitimated by reference to standards. As I watched and listened, analyzed and wrote, it became clear that conventional class distinctions were not the answer to questions about why performance genres such as theater and comedy were treated so differently by performers, spectators, and critics. The mediating role of the critic is a significant part of this story and forms the main subject of the present work.

The individuals most responsible for the evolution of this work are associated, one way or another, with Edinburgh and its Festival Fringe. My study began in the "third term" of Mhairi Mackenzie-Robinson and Trisha Emblem. Mhairi, the Fringe administrator, and Trisha, assistant administrator, were as close to a team as one ever sees in the administration of a large organization. When I first started thinking about spectators and critics, it was Trisha, sitting in the City Cafe, who intoned fatefully "sure, you can have the information"—words that have been the undoing of many a sociologist who did not know how much information there actually was. Mhairi and Trisha patiently answered two million questions about the operation of their office and the workings of the Fringe.

Since I do not address the issue in the chapters that follow, it is worth mentioning here that during the years of my study the full-time staff of the Fringe office has consisted almost entirely of women. Given the egalitarian nature of the Fringe described in Part Two, this is certainly grist for theories of the relationship between gender and democracy. Yet gender is not a convincing explanation for the organization of the Fringe. The feminization of the office is recent, while the structure of egalitarianism has been constant since the early 1970s. Mhairi was the first woman to administer the Fringe and the numerous innovations of her tenure are all consistent with the logic of the Fringe as a laissez-faire performance market. Jean Dickson undertook the design and programming of the database that computerized the Fringe, and her generosity allowed me to understand some of its esoteric aspects. Hilary Strong, the current administrator, explained recent developments in organization. The entire Fringe staff has been helpful beyond any call of duty, especially Laura Mackenzie Stuart and Kathleen Mainland. Several press officers, a role that was barely institutionalized when I began this work, have come to my aid, providing a great deal of conscientious guidance and insight about the actual behavior of critics, primarily Faith Liddell, Stuart Buchanan, and Alison Forsyth.

I am especially indebted to two publications. The *List* is the arts and entertainment magazine for Edinburgh and Glasgow. Alice Bain, editor in the late 1980s, initially invited me to review and publisher Robin Hodge has generously extended the invitation over the years, providing me the opportunity to act as a participant observer of critics. The physical layout of the *List*'s office makes it ideal for social interaction. I have profited greatly from my association with critics and members of staff, including Lila Rawlings, Andrew Burnet, Eddie Gibb, Alastair Mabbott, Bethan Cole, Kathleen Morgan, Thom Dibdin, Jo Roe, Ellie Carr, Nikki Turner, Georgette Renwick, Ross Parsons, Susan Mackenzie, Gill Roth, Jonathan Trew, James Haliburton, Paul Keir, Barrie Tullett, Stuart Bathgate, Iain Grant, Jo Kennedy, Lesley Lawrie, John Higgins, Philip Parr, and Tom Lappin. There have been many others, now gone on to other pursuits, but in particular I thank Mark Fisher, formerly theater critic for the *List* and editor of *Theatre Scotland*. He embodies what I take to be the ideal combination of seriousness of purpose, reflexive self-awareness, and attunement to audience that should characterize the modern critic.

The *Scotsman* has developed a particular and well-deserved reputation for criticism during the Festival. Arts editor Allan Wright lent encouragement during the early going. His "witches and warlocks"[1] have guided, entertained, amused, and terrorized spectators and performers for many years. Although an articulate band of critics might be considered unsurprising, it was my sheer good fortune to find such a beneficent and amiable group. Catherine Lockerbie, Joseph Farrell, Colin Affleck, Joy Hendry, Ellie Buchanon, Peter Whitebrook, Christopher Bowen, Juan Hyde, David Campbell, David Hamilton, Robin Dinwoodie, Honorah Perry, Ian Spring, Owen Dudley Edwards, and Joyce Macmillan illuminated the critical enterprise for me in a variety of settings. Hayden Murphy, an expatriate Irish poet, has been an invaluable companion, source of inspiration, and critic for me personally, not least for showing me the Edinburgh pubs suitable for writing.

There are many contingent factors that encourage the writing of a book, but one stands out in my mind. Michael Mulkay and Trevor Pinch invited me to speak at the University of York on social network approaches to the micro-macro problem. I was to present an essay I had worked on for several months. On my arrival, hearing of this new Fringe study, they asked me how I felt about taking a couple of hours to prepare a completely new talk on the sociology of criticism. Then at the beginning of the scheduled hour they invited the members of their department to vote for their preferred topic. I have been heeding their unanimous vote for a very long time.

On my return to Louisiana a director from the Royal Shakespeare Company moved just down the street. Such folk are rather thin on the ground in Baton Rouge and I took it as an auspicious omen. Barry Kyle and actress Lucy Maycock formed a professional repertory company in Louisiana. It was to be housed in an old agricultural building and called Swine Palace Theater. Barry allowed explicitly that his own work had been affected by critics—his RSC production of *The Taming of the Shrew* was a response to a specific critical "challenge" that a modern version of the play was "impossible." In addition, may thanks to Billy Harbin, Deb Brothers, Caroline Cromelin, Ginger Donaldson, Paul Clements, David Arrow, Don Hall, Jason Meyer, and Karin McKie serve as a proxy to all of the performers, directors, publicists, and artists that aided this enterprise.

It is much easier to identify those that have brought manuscript to book. I thank my editor Mary Murrell for her trust as much as for her splendid work, her colleagues Deborah Malmud and Molan Chun Goldstein, and my copy editor Brian MacDonald.

Shortly after I began the Edinburgh study, Dafna Goldberg kindly offered to collect what proved to be illuminating information at the Festival of Israel. The analysis is an important addition to the evidence in Chapter 9. Others who deserve particular thanks for helping scrape together bits and pieces of the larger puzzle are Jodie Rabelais, Dorothy

Armstrong, Dawn Deshazo, Janet Elrod, Mari Haget, Kim Hall, Kerri Hoyt, Lori James, Michelle Jones, Charlotte Kolder, Chinh Minh Le, and Krista Tullos.

Robert Wuthnow will always be my role model owing to both his humanity and his profound commitment to intellectual work. I thank him for his perusal of the manuscript, as well as my other readers, including Kenneth Zagacki, David Courtwright, Gaines Foster, Robert McMahon, Steve Fuller, James Catallo, Jack Beggs, Jeanne Hurlbert, and Gladys Lang. John Henderson was kind enough to publish his book on commentary at precisely the right time. John Henry, historian of science, and Lance Butler, who introduced me to the works of Samuel Beckett at the University of Stirling many years ago, provided energy and stimulation at each of our meetings in Scotland.

All readers should peruse the introductory chapter for an overview of what lies ahead. Those whose interest lies mainly in the theoretical analysis of cultural hierarchy might first read Part One, which outlines the argument for discursive mediation, and Chapter 10, which summarizes the empirical findings as well. For those who are fascinated, as I am, with the Fringe as a performance context, Parts Two and Three (but especially the former) tell most of the story. The process of criticism is the primary explanatory focus, with the most systematic evidence to be found in Part Three, and conceptual-historical background in Chapters 2 and 5. Spectators are examined primarily in Chapters 2, 6, and 9, while much of the information on performers is in Chapters 8 and 9.

Support for writing was provided in part by the Manship Foundation but mostly by the sheer hospitality of David and Barbara Edge, whose home has been mine as well each August. David, founder of the Science Studies Unit at the University of Edinburgh and editor of *Social Studies of Science*, has contributed greatly to my understanding of the critical review in academic life and has undoubtedly been a covert point of comparison for this study of the artistic mediation process. Barbara's contributions are too numerous to mention, apart from the fact that subscriptions to so many English and Scottish newspapers have made my job much easier than it should have been. Accepting the 1993 Bernal Prize of the Society for Social Studies of Science, Professor Edge thanked the members of the society for help "On Keeping Bouncing."[2] It is high time I offered David and Barbara such thanks as well.

August 1995
Edinburgh, Scotland

FRINGE AND FORTUNE

Introduction

A CRITIC'S NEW CLOTHES

A T THE 1989 Edinburgh Festival Fringe a new play opens in a small venue across from the Royal Lyceum Theatre. *A Grand Scam* proves to be an insightful and self-referential play about the relationship between performance art, criticism, and the public.[1] It is not well attended, but that is unsurprising, since more than a thousand other performances are held during the festival.

The audience that day numbers three and all are critics. I am writing for the *List*, a weekly arts and entertainment magazine for central Scotland. Beside me, waiting for the performance to begin, sat the reviewer for the *Scotsman*, Edinburgh's morning daily and the most important source of reviews during the festival.[2] Before long a third critic arrives, a well-dressed gentleman named Art King. He is anticipating a modern Noh play, as we can tell from his badinage with a custodian who is still sweeping the theater.

But as happens so often in Edinburgh, the lines between spectator, critic, and performer have been muddied. A performer has usurped the role of this third critic. By the time that Andrew Dallmeyer makes his appearance as Tristram Taylor, actor extraordinaire, we are not surprised to find that this third critic is not, or at least not "really," one of us.

Meanwhile, Art King finds, to his irritation, that he is mistaken as to the character of the promised performance. It is not a Noh play, but rather "no play . . . a play about nothing." The critic, seeking to avoid any more surprises, warns Taylor that he is notoriously difficult to please:

> Over the years I have remained indifferent to all but the choicest cuts from the dramatic delicatessen. My palate is jaded, my tastebuds are fickle, my appetite is dulled by overindulgence and many an inflated bubble reputation has been pricked by the tip of my poisoned tongue.

But Mr. King stays, witnessing a pause-laden soliloquy on the difficulties of doing a play without scenery, sound, lighting, costume, characters, plot, dialogue, or even meaning. Returning after a brief exit, Taylor apologizes and makes excuses for his performance. He winds up groveling at the feet of the critic, weeping and imploring him to praise the play.

To our utter surprise, Art King loves it—though it is never clear whether Tristram's bawling is a genuine outpouring of emotion, or simply the second act of his play. King applauds its "central core . . . the notion of something from nothing . . . because that, after all, is what all art is." He lauds it in his syndicated column and plugs it on television, turning the show into a smashing success. For the remainder of the run it plays to full houses and universal acclaim.

Until the last performance. Curiosity finally gets the better of the young Scottish custodian we had seen at the outset, a juvenile delinquent who has been detailed to care for the hall. He will stay, so he tells the great actor Tristram, "fur te see yir wee extravaganza fur masel." Instinctively offended by the theatrical mannerisms and by the conceptual, reflexive, aestheticist performance, it is not long before Tommy directs his fury at the audience:

> Surely te God ye must aw realise that ye've bin taken te the bloody cleaners. Ye've been conned rotten, skinned alive and shagged senseless. . . . Ye're like a flock o' bloody lemmings. Just because some big-shot American writes in the paper that he thinks its guid ye aw follow blindly along straight ower the cliffs.

Tristram, who has disappeared offstage, escapes with the cash. The critic, admitting he's been hoodwinked, offers to take Tommy to America for his "straight-talking presence" and "no-nonsense approach."[3]

The Emperor's New Clothes is a potent archetype for the distinction between high and low art. Dallmeyer's retelling for the stage raises most of the issues treated in the chapters to follow: the role of criticism, its effect on audiences, its taste-making function, and its relation to highbrow and popular art. The comparison between Emperor and critic is instructive.

In the original story, the Emperor's word is sacred. The flatterers who surround him, his tailors, and the mob that views his procession are awed by his majesty and power. Yet the crowd is there for the simple reason that he *is* the Emperor. His status is based on his illustrious social position. In *A Grand Scam* and in the competition for artistic recognition, there is no "natural" crowd for the performance. Sometimes there is no crowd until the critic solicits one, no audience for Art until the product is explained, evaluated, and legitimated for the public.

The child who exposes him by naively shouting that the Emperor has no clothes expresses a clear and readily observable fact. Everyone can "see" that the monarch is not exhibiting a *new* wardrobe, but rather no wardrobe at all. He has lost touch with common standards of decency and taste. He is beyond normal feelings of shame, misled by sycophants, perhaps expressing his own fantasy that he alone sets the standards. Whether or not there were nudists in the crowd, sincere in their enthusiasm, we are not told.

But the custodian of *A Grand Scam*, honest and plain spoken, is not merely a "boy," a childlike representative of some generalized anti-aesthetic viewpoint. He revels in the *Revenge of the Zombies*:

> the hero's drivin along in his car, ken, mindin' his ain business when aw o' a sudden this big darkie appears right in the middle o'the road. . . . then aw at once there's a bloody great bang o' a gun going off . . . and he's blown his brains oot aw over the windscreen, and they're spread right across like aw thick and lumpy. So the hero puts on the windscreen wipers but the brains are too thick so he has te get oot o' the car and scrape it aw away wi' his fingers. Magic!

What interests him especially are the technical means used in the creation of such effects. After much deliberation he settles on "porridge and raspberries."

The youth is an avid consumer of art, no less than the critic. He craves understanding of the genre, and cues whereby he can generate and support interpretations. He chooses to present his views vocally, in the midst of a performance, but such criticism is not without historical precedent. If his tastes run counter to those of the Critic, it is not because he is ignorant of the critic's views.

If he dislikes Beckettian, minimalist drama, he knows what he does like—Guignol movies. Observing the skyrocketing body count of contemporary movies, the critic Vincent Canby recalled the old Theatre du Grand Guignol of Paris, which presented short plays of violence, murder, rape, apparitions, and spectacle.[4] Such plays pandered to the "baser instincts" of the audience in just the way that specter-murders of scantily clad teenagers in the forest, or random Ramboesque violence does. Yet the *Oxford Companion to the Theatre* describes the Grand Guignol as appealing to an "oversophisticated and decadent" taste. Perhaps, in spite of the critic's alleged level of awareness, it is the custodian in Dallmeyer's play who is "oversophisticated" and jaded.

We strongly suspect that cannot be true. Why? Because the critic is a *man of taste*, not the youth. His approach to cultural objects is informed by a lifetime of superior aesthetic experiences. His comparative and historical sense enables him to see, to describe, and to evaluate things that the youth does not. Moreover, his opinion "counts" in a specific sense: his discourse plays an important role in mediating the relationship between artwork and audience. The custodian, on the other hand, simply howls at the moon.

THE PROBLEM

Why does the distinction between high and popular art persist in spite of postmodern predictions that it should vanish? This fundamental question forms the backdrop for the present work, which offers a solution as well as a group of conjectures backed by empirical evidence. It is a contemporary version of a much older problem, the problem of "quality," the distinction between good art and bad. Since Plato, the difference between artworks that merit sustained attention and those that merely offer ephemeral entertainment has been a preoccupation for students of culture.

In its classical form, this problem of quality no longer exists. The basis for such a formulation has come under devastating attack. Two strands of postmodernism, the "intellectual" and the "structural," lead to the expectation that aesthetic distinctions are in the process of collapse. Intellectual postmodernism is a version of postfoundationalism with relativistic implications. It denies the existence of absolute standards and aperspectival criticism, celebrating the diversity of form as expression without the assignment of evaluative labels. As a philosophical argument, it suggests there are no convincing reasons external to specific contexts of judgment for accepting aesthetic criteria that could justify distinctions between levels of quality. In consequence, the idea of universalistic standards of merit in artistic expression is groundless.

Apart from the intellectual attack on aesthetic foundationalism, there exist good reasons for expecting a vanishing difference between high and popular art as the supply of cultural objects increases and distribution becomes widespread. This "structural" view of high culture—dating at least to the time of Heraclitus—equates whatever is common or readily available with inferior aesthetic status and rarity with quality.[5] Institutions play the key role in maintaining or altering the hierarchy of objects, as well as the social inequalities with which they are associated. Corporate actors create and support culture through their allocation of resources, opening up opportunities for the diffusion of products. But the more a cultural object is available to the masses, the less it can be an indicator of status.

Judith Blau has recently argued for this type of cultural convergence (1988a). The rigidity of the cultural hierarchy is founded on the existence of cultural institutions that are differentially promoted by class interests and segregated cultural experiences. This state of affairs is reflected in the association of economic inequality with the flourishing of elite art and the concentration of high culture (Blau 1986a), as in the late nineteenth century when boundaries were finely drawn.

Today the institutionalized arts are located in the same social-economic matrix. There are "trivial differences between the social forces that govern elite and popular culture since they are both explained by virtually the same social conditions" (Blau 1988a, p. 8). The growth of the middle class, the spread of education, and the mass marketing of culture have led to the collapse of boundaries between high and low art. Whether one argues that as a cultural object becomes universal it is debased and erodes social distinctions or simply that wide dissemination of objects is the basis for social integration, cultural homogenization should be the result.

What is the evidence? First, there is very little concentration of high cultural suppliers. Opportunities to attend ballet, opera, theater are about the same in any large American city. Second, examined on a per capita basis across U.S. metropolitan areas, high culture is actually less concentrated. In this (tautological) sense, it has become "popular" as it has been widely distributed.[6] Third, social inequality impairs the development of both popular and high culture, such that cities with the greatest inequality have fewer cultural institutions of all sorts.

While there are various responses to these arguments, neither intellectual nor structural postmodernism is obviously or critically flawed. *Yet the boundaries between high and popular art do not seem to be disappearing.* We routinely employ this hierarchy in our cultural expressions. In the industrialized countries where it is most highly developed, there are few indicators that such differences are moribund. The postmodern watch for boundary-blurring and cross-genre experimentation is only successful when it takes place against a background of vastly more numerous traditional forms.

While the evidence on the widespread availability of culture is sound, it is only partly relevant. The distinction between high and low culture is not simply about opportunities to experience objects, but about who avails themselves of these opportunities and under what circumstances. In fact, persisting differences between high and low cultural forms *in spite of* this rampant availability makes it all the more pressing to determine the source of these differences. The "supply-side" argument does not show that the distinction between high and low culture is disappearing. It shows rather that the distributional view is inadequate to explain the obstinacy of the hierarchy in modern societies.

We need a new approach to the phenomenon of persistence. The differences between high and popular art are neither intrinsic to the art itself, nor simply an effect of the kinds of people that produce and consume cultural objects. Rather, they are a function of the *discursive practices that mediate the relationship between art and its public.*

Spectators and buyers confront cultural objects against a background of factors that predispose and shape their responses in particular ways. Some of these influences are the result of past socialization and education, based on exposure and experiences with art that produce various kinds of "cultural capital" (Bourdieu 1984). They are "first-order" influences—the lifetime accretion of a multitude of interactions with both people and cultural objects, often measured by educational attainment and family background. They are the factors that manifest themselves in what we commonly call a person's "taste."

Taste is the general predisposition to like and seek exposure to certain *kinds* of things. But other influences are apparent in the immediate context of exposure to art. I call these "second-order" influences because, though their effectiveness is also shaped by a multitude of past contingencies, they are immediate, situational, and local. Second-order influences are predisposing, like taste, but they predispose specifically rather than generally. Rather than causing one to like certain *kinds* of objects, they cause one to like *certain objects.*

These second-order influences are what I mean by mediation and they are the focus here. Opera may be attended by the upper classes, but the upper classes do not like all the opera they see and certainly do not attend all the opera they could. General background factors do not adequately explain the reception of particular artworks and they fail to account for important consumption patterns of the middle class.

The principal fact about modern consumership is that the most avid consumers appreciate *both* highbrow and popular forms.[7] Although social class and the taste for different kinds of cultural products are associated, these forms of appreciation may be radically different even *within* a class. Put differently, if it were simply true that the lower classes preferred certain kinds of art and the middle or upper classes fancied another—a strong association of "taste cultures" and "taste publics" (Gans 1974)—then there would be no need for a theory of mediation. But it is absurd to suggest that the middle and upper social classes do not participate in popular art forms—they often do so more frequently and with greater enthusiasm than the working classes.

In place of a "compositional" approach, which addresses the question of cultural hierarchy in terms of the *people* who constitute the audience for art, I take a "discursive" approach that focuses on the *practices* that mediate response to artworks. The compositional approach is largely silent with respect to particular reception issues, except to predict the characteristics of people that will be relevant. The discursive approach takes these background traits as given and concentrates on the analysis of patterns involving second-order, contextual influences.

The general solution to the persistence of cultural hierarchy in the contemporary world has more to do with patterns of discourse than the social composition of the audience. Broadly, the *response to evaluation* is the crucial factor distinguishing high and popular culture. Specifically, it is within the process of evaluation involving spectators, performers, and critics that the difference between high and popular art may be located.

To participate in high art forms is to acquire the potential for status enhancement through the process of building cultural capital. This much is well known. But it is also to commit oneself to a different kind of discourse, an alternative evaluative process, than that which characterizes low art forms. This process is foregrounded in the chapters to follow. To participate in high art is to forgo the direct and unmediated perception of the artwork itself. The principal consequence is the dependence of one's own judgment of artistic quality on the judgment of others. The process of symbolic exchange is neither conscious nor rational, but the language of rational choice theory may be employed simply to describe the bargain in its elementary form (Coleman 1990). Participation in high art forms involves a status bargain: giving up partial rights of control of one's own judgment to experts in exchange for the higher status that competent talk about these artworks provides. The status bargain, then, is *an exchange of prestige for opinion rights.*

This idea, combined with the notion that genre is the most important indicator of status, forms the nucleus of the book: for high cultural genres, opinions about particular works are more likely to be subject to the process of expert mediation than for popular genres. Because of this association, this difference in mediative capacity is in large part what we *mean* by high-status art forms. "Serious" works are those works about which critical talk is relevant.

The idea of *highbrow mediation* entails that the role of experts depends on the art form. "Experts," as the term is used here, are those who have some claim to knowledgeability by virtue of a distinctive professional activity. The art world, of course, employs a special name for experts who produce secondary discourse about cultural objects.

THE CRITIC AS MEDIATOR

> *Aesop*: Critick, Sir, pray what's that?
> *Fine Gent*: The Delight of the Ingenious, the Terror of
> Poets, the Scourge of Players, and the Aversion of the Vulgar.
> —*David Garrick,* Lethe; or, Aesop in the Shades *(1740)*

Matthew Arnold defined the enterprise of criticism with unconcealed self-interest: "simply to know the best that is known and thought in the world, and by in its turn making this known, to create a current of fresh and true ideas" (Arnold 1905, pp. 18–19). The idea that the critic should "know and make known" indicates Arnold's emphasis on mediation, which he saw as a filtering process—whether it is the "best" of anything is another question. Yet in the same essay he lends his own critical weight more than once to an important status denigration: "Everybody, too, would be willing to admit, as a general proposition, that the critical faculty is lower than the inventive" (p. 3).

For the "classical" critic, the act of mediation naturally entails a subordinate status in the art world and is the source of a great deal of ambivalence. The critic, Oscar Wilde notwithstanding, is not really a "creator" in the same sense as the artist.[8] Yet an examination of critics can tell us much of what is important about the difference between low and high art. Criticism is not extrinsic but instrinsic to the artistic process in the modern world. Critics are not objective referees of the best and worst, standing outside of the art world and judging its output, but participants in a stream of discourse that defines the cultural hierarchy.

The social role of the critic emerged over the past two centuries together with high and low art as identifiable categories of experience. It is not that critics have "caused" certain kinds of artwork to emerge as dominant. Rather, the categories of high and low are defined through a process of critical discussion that includes spectators, artists, and critics. Their activities are not the focus so much as their relationships in this "triangle of mediation." I will pay particular attention to the *patterns of judgment* that emerge from their interactions because it is here that the source of the difference between high and low art will be found.

GENRE AND JUDGMENT

Regardless of how a cultural object is created or received, knowing what kind of thing it is constitutes the first and most important thing to know about it. This precedes the evaluative question of "how good" it is. How good *compared with what?*

Throughout, I depend on the simple assumption that there is such a thing as cultural hierarchy, the idea that artworks have more or less prestige. Most people have no trouble ranking the Mona Lisa above a painting of Elvis on black velvet regardless of which one they love or hate. The source of this ability has less to do with the particular objects themselves than with our ability to recognize objects as *types* of objects. With respect to individual artworks, the term "genre" refers simply to the category of objects or events to which they belong. Genres in the modern art world are further distinguished as one of two main categories. Common terms for these categories are "high art" and "popular art" and they are hereby adopted for the present work.[9]

There are many works that bear characteristics of more than one genre, conscious attempts to manipulate the status of genres, and negotiations over the boundaries of high and low art. But the shiftiness of boundaries should not obscure the central importance of the distinction for judgments of quality as well as the cultural hierarchy. Competent consumers have no difficulty identifying the vast majority of works as highbrow or popular—given only that they know the *kind* of work it is: foreign film, stand-up comedy, opera, or heavy metal.

The position of genres is not permanently fixed. Considerable historical variation attends the class position of the audience, the kinds of patronage received, the prestige attached to appreciation of various art forms. Moreover, individual works acquire reputations within genres, assignments that are at least partly the responsibility of specialists. When works are *publicly* offered and experienced by more than just a few fellow artists and friends, they are subject to criticism, a judgmental process that is quite ubiquitous. It may be professional and public, or private and informal.

How good is a work? The answer to the question of whether something is good or bad, worthy or unworthy, is nothing more than the answer to a more fundamental question: *how are quality judgments made and expressed?* The idea of quality does not make sense in terms of general principles that apply to all fields. If social and cognitive processes operate to create a consensus within subfields of the art world, then quality is the expression of that consensus.

PERFORMING ARTS

> In five weeks what will be left of [my play]? A script,
> a press release, a couple of photos, and the reviews.
> —*Scottish director and playwright*

The performing arts are especially useful for an analysis of discursive mediation. Most of the analysis to follow relies on the use of a festival for the performing arts, the Edinburgh Festival Fringe. I focus on performances that involve a paying audience and one or more live performers, for the copresence of performers and audience leads to several important properties.[10]

Performances are fleeting, while the written word endures. Reviews outlive the longest performance runs and the most energetic publicists.

This fact—and not any inherent tendency of reviewers to castigate their subjects—leads many to think of the relationship between critics and creative artists as adversarial, which is untrue in a structural sense regardless of how performers might feel about it. It may be that Jason Robards's performance in *The Iceman Cometh* cannot be surpassed and Frank Zappa ingested feces on stage, but no one who missed the shows will ever know for sure. Of course, it is possible to record performances and replay them. But one cannot relive performances except in the imagination.

The presence of a live audience has obvious consequences for the critic.[11] As contrasted with books or recordings, the immediate, public reaction to the performance is impossible to ignore. The critic sits or stands with other human beings. Their copresence is continually felt and periodically intrudes—to mask the jokes, to cough, to cry, and sometimes even to leave in the middle (Elam 1980). A ticket is good for two performances: one for the show, and the other for the experience of being in a theater to see it (Ellis 1982). Such a difference seems especially obvious where the *staged* performance is not the only legitimate involvement of the audience[12] but it is equally relevant to high cultural genres.

Most performing arts critics prefer reviewing with a live audience.[13] Even previews have audiences—they are "exclusive" only in the sense that these audiences are unrepresentative of the general public. The critics who conscientiously and ceremoniously "ignore" the audience take a determinate position with respect to the rabble they sometimes pretend to scorn. Critics of *performance* drama and critics of the *literary* texts on which they are based do not experience the "same" objects, as noted by Charles Lamb, who preferred his Shakespeare from the book.

Live audiences characterize movies and museums as well as theater and cabaret, but with performance the *art* is live as well.[14] This ephemerality is what gives reviews their special power and significance. Emotional as well as artistic *responses* to critical reviews in the performing arts occur immediately, often before the end of the performance run. A "good notice" is occasion for rejoicing and provides motivation for the ensuing performances. A bad one elicits execrations, depression, and sometimes begins the search for new employment.

Thus, criticism, if it is timely, may conceivably *interact* with the art directly: either through the performers, by changing their orientation to their work; or through the audience, by promoting exposure and knowledge.[15] The mediation hypothesis suggests that it should do so for highbrow forms.

Today, criticism flourishes in centers for the performing arts such as New York and London. But so many factors affect the length of the run—most of them not under the control of company or promoters—that it is easy to attribute power to critics that they do not have. The use of critical quotations for publicity helped to create the sense that critics can make or break shows. Even if this were true on Broadway and the West End—and there is little hard evidence that it is—these remain distinctively different cases. Other sorts of artistic distribution systems exist. Some concentrate performances in time as well as space.

For an empirical handle with which to grasp highbrow and popular performing arts, arts festivals are ideal because of their diversity. Their organization, the social composition of audiences, and the internal characteristics of performances are all aspects of cultural hierarchy. For the idea of cultural mediation, however, the main features of interest are the relations between critics, performers, and spectators. The ways shows are selected, the diversity of genres, and the competition between performances are all aspects of the mediation process that must be considered.

THE EDINBURGH FESTIVAL FRINGE

Having a lot of things in one place also makes them easier to study. Edinburgh was an uncomplicated choice because it hosts the largest arts festival in the world and is beautiful besides. The two may be related. If you have to do a lot of tramping around, you may as well do it in a lovely place. The drawback is that you are frequently wet.

The empirical focus of the study is the Edinburgh Festival Fringe, described in Part Two. Each year, for three weeks in August, over a thousand shows spring up throughout the city, often in odd places. The Fringe is a great laboratory for the performing arts, encompassing all kinds of shows from theater and opera to comedy and cabaret, from student revues to political drama. Here we can observe the process of mediation at work, examining the ways in which highbrow and lowbrow forms are distinguished by the public, the performers, and the critics themselves.

The Fringe originated as a spontaneous buildup of performing groups appearing at the same time the official Edinburgh International Festival began in 1947. It is a rather special site owing to its sheer magnitude. One could argue that it is unrepresentative of other performing arts contexts. For an examination of the difference between high and popular art, since the Fringe offers more shows and more diverse performances than any other context, past or present, it is well worth studying. After years of fieldwork on the Fringe, my own feeling is that the number of shows is not what makes it unique, but the fragility of the boundary between life and performance art. When a researcher fails to pursue a subject with exuberance it is sad. But it is even sadder when the subject fails to pursue him, and the Fringe is nothing if not a predator.

The Fringe supports innovation and covets marginality, as suggested by its very name. Its ideology is markedly egalitarian. No central selection process determines the groups that appear. Anyone with the time and resources may come—anyone who can find space, that is. An administrative office circulates information and sells tickets but is guided by the overriding principle that no shows are promoted or recommended above others. No one—aside from the critics—makes judgments about quality. Audiences are left to their own devices.

This fact lends special importance to the myth of discovery considered in Chapter 5 and again in Chapter 9. The idea that hidden or unrecognized quality can be found amid the plethora of offerings is significant for critics, artists, and spectators. Spectators and critics comb through a program of over one hundred pages, looking for cues and remembering past performances. For the performing groups, an appearance on the Fringe is generally unprofitable in a financial sense. Many groups come simply for the experience, to make contacts with other actors and agents. There is keen anticipation of the reviews for a show. They are the concrete tokens of experience, to be clipped and stowed in scrapbooks and portfolios. Maybe, just maybe, someone—a critic?—will recognize the gem that could shine, oh so brightly, if only the polish were applied. Perhaps it is the talent for pretty dialogue, or a glimmer of brilliant acting in the midst of a sorry play.

The review process is journalistic in its details and the constraints placed on reviewers have a lot to do with the words that are eventually made public. This does not involve long, lone hours of scholarly preparation but a race to meet a deadline. The character of the evaluation itself can be affected by the space allocated and reallocated by someone other than a critic. A review of an artwork may not appear because the object is considered beneath an editor's notice. It may be written and rejected, or its form may be altered before its appearance in print. I examine these questions in the context of the *Scotsman*, the "review bible" of the festival, and the *List*.

Several methodological strategies are employed in what follows. Those that believe one variety of method is inherently superior to another may find some parts more convincing than others. Since I do not hold that view, I see no reason to engage in debates about method except in the context of particular research questions. To this end, I employ both qualitative and quantitative analyses.

The qualitative component of the study included an annual stint of participant observation as a critic for the *List* as well as interviews with critics and performers.[16] My rationale is to be found in Mark Twain's *Life on the Mississippi*. There is something remarkable about "firsts" and we should cherish them because of their perishability:

> When one makes his first voyage in a ship, it is an experience which multitudinously bristles with striking novelties . . . in such sharp contrast with all this person's former experiences that they take a seemingly deathless grip upon his imagination and memory. . . . If he make ten voyages in succession, what then? Why the thing has lost color, snap, surprise; and has become commonplace. The man would have nothing to tell that would quicken a landsman's pulse.[17]

Having reviewed for several years now, I find Twain's view convincing. Where it is relevant to the argument I include sketches of some first experiences as a critic. These should not be seen as "representative" but as an inventory of some of the issues one wrestles with from the viewpoint of one who is not an experienced wrestler.

To adopt a stance of methodological pluralism is not to claim all methods or methodological strategies are worthwhile. First, I am a great fan of storytelling, but this is a rhetorical method and not a research method. I use it simply to illustrate points that are supported through quantitative analysis, interviews, or participant observation. Second, some methods are simply failures. I attempted to conduct a large experiment to test the effects of critical notices before and after viewing two kinds of film. Owing to the fact that southern college students liked my "action" film so much and so thoroughly disliked my "serious" film, there was nothing else significant to report. The results are not worth mentioning. Another failure, illustrating a much different point, is reported in Chapter 9.

OUTLINE OF THE STUDY

The distinction between high and popular art is relatively new. An appreciation of this fact is important to the view that critical discourse is a mediator and determinant of value. I discuss these theoretical issues in Chapter 1 through the contrast with traditional perspectives on the high/low distinction.

The question of standards, embodied in a variety of discursive forms, emerges as crucial to the ideology of criticism and the notion of highbrow mediation because *reference to standards legitimates the transfer of judgment*. The status of experts is based on a special kind of knowledgeability, not simply their large volume of aesthetic experience. Their judgments, if they are to be followed, are putatively based on rationalized (justified) standards, whether explicit or implict. After all, there is no reason to grant anyone control over your opinions unless theirs are better than yours.

The idea of "standards" is addressed in many places throughout the book. It is inherently ambiguous between two uses. "Rule-based judgment" or evaluation in terms of aesthetic criteria is often taken to characterize true criticism. A second use is that of a threshold or cutoff, below which a work of art may not fall in order to be liked or appreciated. I have both kinds of standard in mind *but especially the important ambiguity between them* in arguing that the discourse of standards remains signal to the high/low distinction.

It is sometimes maintained that only with respect to the first kind of standard is the second relevant. That seems mistaken, since norms are rarely employed to justify a threshold judgment, but rather the particular features of the artwork in question. Standards cannot shift from one work to another so often that they lose all sense of stability. Even if such criteria are thought to exist, they must still be implemented through the concrete pronouncements of those who hold them.

This point is considered in one particularly revealing historical context in Chapter 2, while Chapter 7 discusses evaluation as an element of the modern critical review. An important implication of the threshold view is that some judgments are necessarily critical. Chapter 7 analyzes this use of standards empirically as a "bias" in judgment while Chapter 8 examines the correspondence between the views of performers and critics.

Since theater is an archetypal performance genre, it serves as my model of high art. Although theater is now a highbrow form, this was not so until the nineteenth century. Criticism as the formalized judgment of cultural products is more closely related to democratization than to elitism and inequality, which fostered the exegesis of classics. With the onset of the industrial revolution and the increase in wealth, greater numbers of artists and spectators created two markets. One was for the artworks themselves. Another was for information and judgments about these products. Experts who were once interpreters and guardians of orthodoxy took on new roles: educating the public, engaging in dialogue with artists, seeking to distinguish the good from the bad.

The great Age of Criticism in eighteenth-century London illustrates all of these patterns as well as the essentially social aspects of criticism (Chapter 2). With spectators shouting from the stage and occasionally even riots over playwrights and performers audacious enough to bring mediocre work before the public, criticism in the contemporary era is tame by comparison. Now journalists and editors are more likely to be critics than are professional wits or men of letters.

A detailed account of the Edinburgh Fringe constitutes Chapters 3 to 5. These qualitative results pertain to its history, organization, ideological features, and the interaction of criticism with performance. The more systematic results of the study follow in Chapters 6 through 8.

Are more favorable reviews associated with larger audiences? By most standards, that is the kind of question best regarded as empirical, warranting systematic data collection and analysis. Historians, ethnomethodologists, and literary scholars have distinctive methods to address cultural mediation and the role of critical discourse. Their accounts will be entered at the court of appeals, but the trial court will be needing findings of fact. What kinds of shows do people go to see? Do they read reviews before going? Do critics slant their views? Is there, in general, an association between the kinds of reviews shows get and the size of the audience that attends? Does the relationship between reviews and audiences depend on whether the performance is highbrow or popular? Having entertained these questions, anecdotes should be consigned to the attic of evidence. That answers are not to be found in the literature is not due to the absence of information on reviews—they are, after all, public—but to the absence of information on audiences.[18]

The idea of cultural mediation is just so much hot air if it has no empirical consequences. The cultural hierarchy is maintained and reflected by the different relationships of critics *to performers, to the public, and to high and popular art forms themselves.* Performers, spectators, and critics are mutually implicated in the triangle of mediation.

The main analyses address three sets of questions about the operation and effects of discourse practices. They are designed to show that critics matter more for highbrow genres and matter in different ways. First, do reviews influence spectators? Second, through what processes are the critical evaluations in published reviews generated? Third, how are critics regarded by performers? Chapters 6 through 8 contain answers based on a study of spectators, relating audience size to published reviews; comparison of the informal and published opinions of critics; and interviews with performers.

Chapter 6 begins with the distinction between specialists and aficionados. Those who are professionally involved with the arts and those who are avid consumers are not subject to the same process of critical mediation as the wider public. In the main body of the chapter I predict the size of the audience for shows at the 1988 Fringe and try to determine whether, independent of other factors, reviews made any difference. Larger audiences are associated with the reputation of the performing group and greater media coverage. More favorable reviews, particularly when they appear early in the run of the show, are conducive to larger audiences, but the *favorability of reviews is not as significant as the visibility* they provide. And whether a show gets reviewed is often a decision made by editors rather than critics.

For the idea of highbrow mediation the most important question is how the evaluation embedded in critical reviews affects the potential audience for highbrow and popular shows. The main finding, consistent with hypothesis, is that *reviews are more important for high art than popular art*.

All this suggests that any publicity, even negative, is good from the standpoint of attendance, though not for the performing ego. For highbrow shows, the evaluation makes a difference as well, but the largest impact of reviews for readers is as a source of information or a kind of "independent advertisement." Highly favorable reviews of shows about depressing issues can warn away potential spectators. Bad reviews of shows with sex, stars, or subjects with high cultural interest can promote attendance.

Chapter 7 considers the determinants of good reviews. I show that popular shows have an advantage in terms of the character of the reviews they get. Is it because they are, in general, better in the eyes of critics? If so, there is no evidence for highbrow mediation in the review process itself—such evidence would only be provided if it could be shown that high art is reviewed more critically. So I examine the question of whether reviewers say what they think.

This issue is difficult to address directly because asking critics whether they "slant" their reviews in a particular direction is like asking professors whether they speak the truth in their lectures. So it is approached indirectly, through a comparison of published reviews with the expressed opinions of the reviewers themselves. Although in each case published evaluations are more positive than informal ones, the difference is much larger for popular performance forms. The classical tradition of criticism, of not suffering fools lightly, rears its head.

I contend that critics themselves react to high and popular art in different ways. They display different "biases" or standards of reportage. This is not because "highbrow" critics are inherently different from "popular" reviewers—it is even true when the critic is the same person. The reason is not that there are unambiguous standards for quality in high cultural genres such that deviations are readily identified by people of trained capacity. And it is certainly not because critics are incapable of applying a "discriminating" aesthetic to popular forms. Rather, they apply distinctive patterns of discourse—different "sensibilities"—to different bodies of performance art.

Finally, Chapter 7 returns to the matter of standards by examining the consistency of reviews. If critics do not agree on the merits of what they see, it is hard to imagine that common standards are the cause of judgments. Consensus among critics is not high. Put very bluntly, *critics who review the same show are only slightly more likely than critics who go to different shows to produce similar evaluations.* Popular shows are not less consensual than highbrow. The only standard at issue is a threshold standard, a commitment to be more critical of high art.

The effects of this lack of agreement are profound and their discussion takes us through Chapter 7 and part of Chapter 8. It begins with a discussion of novelty. Brand new work is somewhat special. Reviews have a greater impact on the audience for new work. Performers, understandably, are extremely concerned with these notices. But reviews of new work, while not significantly more negative, exhibit less consensus than reviews of older works. That is, critics are *not* more likely to damn new productions, but they *are* more prone to disagree. This helps explain the intensity of the feelings surrounding critics.

Most performing artists are involved, at least occasionally, in the production of original work. Here it is quite difficult to generate an audience. But in just these same cases where groups are most vulnerable, critical reviews have a greater effect. Lack of critical consensus about new work may have a far greater impact on artists than simple negativity. In these cases, reviews—both good and bad—create high levels of uncertainty. It would not be surprising if, at least from the viewpoint of performers, great power and mystery were to attend the critical enterprise.

The relationship between artists and critics is explored further in Chapter 8, in particular the degree to which performers attend to reviews and the ways in which they attend. Even performing artists who seek to avoid their notices hear about them through the reports of others, and good reviews are more likely than bad ones to be transmitted informally. There is a mix of opinions on the value of reviews. Performers are not generally negative toward critics, but positive views were more often expressed by performers and directors in theater than in comedy or cabaret. Dramatic performers were also more likely to report having made changes based on critical recommendations.

The question of shared standards is addressed by using actual reviews to determine the degree of convergence between the views of performers and critics for the show during the course of the run. I argue that if there is any consistency in standards, then there should be similarity in performance judgments. Do critics and artists share beliefs about the merits and problems of specific performances?

I assess the extent to which performers' views mirror or diverge from reviewers, and whether this occurs before or after the appearance of reviews. If there are similarities between reviewers and artists when artists are interviewed before the occurrence of a review, such correspondences might be due to similar evaluative standards. If there are similarities when the interview occurs after the review, it could be due to shared standards or to the actual influence of the review itself.

But if judgments are *more similar after the reviews than before* the reviews, shared standards are not the cause. Comparisons between the actual reviews of shows and performers' views are used to show that directors and actors working in theater are more likely to take the substantive aspects of reviews into account in their thinking. For popular art forms this is not true.

The penultimate chapter offers a preliminary approach to two questions that require further research: how is it that the discovery myth persists? In Edinburgh, critics constitute an important presence owing to their numbers and the large opportunities for groups to get reviewed. Convictions among performers regarding their influence on spectators are very strong. Yet since reviews, even in the theater, are not the major influence on attendance, some explanation of this belief is called for. Owing to the functionality of the discovery myth and the tendency for people to remember confirmatory evidence, low levels of critical influence are generally unrecognized.

In Chapter 9 I also attempt to introduce a more realistic complexity to the process of spectatorship with the concept of "distributed evaluation." The explanation of review effects on spectators is not complete without considering the social uses of criticism. Reviews are not just written documents, but discussion points circulated within networks of friends. They are discussed, read and misread, and used to make decisions about attendance, which generally occurs in groups.

Evidence for this process is drawn from another festival, the Festival of Israel in Jerusalem. Truth be told, many spectators are not even involved in decisions to attend particular performances. Discussions about groups and shows are generated by social relationships as well as the media. In both cases the recommendation is often indirect—either by someone who has not seen the show, or through a review one has not read. Influence, that is, often takes the form of evaluations that are *distributed* among associates. To think that "word of mouth" simply involves the transmission of personal experience is to think too narrowly.

In the last chapter I discuss the main findings of the study and the concept of mediation as it augments the work of Herbert Gans and Pierre Bourdieu. The "society without critics" envisioned by George Steiner shows, quite contrary to the view he espouses, the importance of critics to the establishment of aesthetic value.

Finally, I offer suggestions for contemporary critics in the spirit of this enterprise. To celebrate critics by highlighting their role in the process of mediation is to pay far greater tribute than to carry on about their role in the shaping of values. To cherish routine reviewers by examining their impacts is to take them more seriously than to carp about their lack of training in the arts or their purveyance of the best that is known and thought. And to appreciate that the difference between high art and low depends on the status bargain provides a starting point for a finer understanding of a cultural hierarchy that is inevitable in the modern world.

PART ONE

THE CRITIC

Chapter One

CULTURAL MEDIATION AND THE

STATUS BARGAIN

I N THE WEE HOURS of the morning, the director of a small experimental theater company picked his way down the steps of Flesh-
market Close off the High Street in Edinburgh. He was anxious to
pick up the first edition of the *Scotsman* where he hoped to see a review
of his show. Before long, another man appeared, hesitated, then pro-
ceeded reluctantly down the steps: the director of the Royal Lyceum
Theatre, which had opened a show the same night. "Just taking the air,"
he smiled, "same as you."

The sociology of culture has little to say about critics because the mediation of the relationship between art and its public has only recently been
seen as problematic. Since the 1970s it has been recognized that debate
over the essence of art, over what "counts" as art, is unproductive.[1] Instead of the contentious and perplexing term "art," the concept of cultural object has been employed to cover the multitudinous variety of
particulars that may be considered art, or not, or borderline: a Rem-
brandt painting, a television episode of *The Young and the Restless,* a
poetry reading by a nude woman covered in chocolate. Since many of
the most interesting questions involve precisely the social sources of debates over such categorization, it is patently unacceptable to define a
field of study that excludes *in advance* many of the objects it would be
helpful to understand.

"Art" is the label attached to certain kinds of objects in certain ways
by networks of people who are involved in their production, distribution, and evaluation. Their claims are differentially accepted by a variety
of groups, including experts and potential consumers. "Art" labels are
an ideological resource used in debates about legitimation, power, and
status.[2] One way of symbolizing this point is rigorously to employ the
language of "cultural objects" rather than "art," but I prefer the older
term in most instances.

Even if we are consistent in making the substitution, doesn't this simply require one to distinguish between "high culture" and something
else, the No Play and the Guignol Movie or their incarnations in galleries, music videos, junk shops, and pet museums? Not unless we are willing to do so on our own, because the alternative is to accept the assis-

tance of experts. This maneuver, natural enough for some purposes, would completely undermine the attempt to understand the role of critics as mediators and maintainers of cultural hierarchy.

By accepting the views of experts, we fall headlong into the pit: the mistake of viewing critics as arbitrators or referees, operating outside the sphere of life they judge. The pit is an apt metaphor, for it was once literally the place where critics held forth.[3] For now, I will put such questions on hold in order to focus on the role of expertise in the processing of cultural objects.

The difference between high and popular art is not fundamentally a difference in the institutions that promote them or in the class background of their consumers. Rather, it is a difference in the process of *mediation*, a difference in the way that talk and text intervene in the relations between producers and consumers of art. To state it as a sociological hypothesis, the higher a work is in the cultural hierarchy, the more important is discourse about the object to its status. To state it in plain language, taste in high art is mediated, whereas taste in low art is not.

HIGHBROW AND POPULAR CULTURE

> Flatter yourself as much as you please, that your fine
> Stroaks of Wit, and Humour, and Morality, and all that, will
> receive Applause—But I'd lay five Guineas, if I had 'em, that
> I dress up a Pig or a Monkey, that shall give more Delight
> than the very best thing in your whole Play.
> —The Author's Triumph *(1737)*

The most significant form of cultural classification—the distinction between high culture and popular culture—has been with us since the seventeenth century (Bourdieu 1984, p. 2). Paul DiMaggio has argued the high/popular distinction is of particular interest because of its enduring use in aesthetic and policy debates, and because the distinction was "forged by the direct efforts of the status groups that employed it" (1987, p. 446; 1982a).

In this section I describe the analytical processes generating status differences between art objects. Next I discuss historical classifications and contrast class-based with discursive approaches to the high/popular division. The idea of critical mediation in high but not popular genres is implied by the view that the higher a work is in the cultural hierarchy, the more important is discourse to its reception.

The main analytical processes generating inequality in the prestige of art objects may be defined in relation to the processes that generate *social* stratification (Tumin 1985). First, audiences *differentiate*—that is, they identify—cultural objects that are intended for special notice from those that are not. The pictures in the museum, but not the fixtures, are reasonable subjects for admiration; the television programming but not the commercials; the street performer but not the drunk; drama in the church hall but not the liturgy. When we consider the drunk as performer, we have made explicit determination to do so, as a result of a hyperconscious extension of our aesthetic categories.

Second, spectators *perceive* (take the measure of) these objects as their personal histories and propensities interact with qualities of the objects themselves.[4] Are they similar to other objects? Are they comprehensible? Just what's going on in this painting, that graffito, this play, that comedy?

Third, they *assess* the relative importance of those qualities for the appreciation of the art form. Once objects have been differentiated and their essential characteristics defined, the *relative value* of these traits becomes important. Objects may be perceived as original, but the degree to which this is something worth rewarding varies greatly.

Assessment and perception are often inextricable in practice but mediation pertains mainly to the former. When a viewer is "led to perceive" a feature previously hidden, the description is rarely accompanied by neutrality as to the merit of that feature. Mediation in art implies influence on assessment by someone or something other than the beholder. For high art this is more likely to be an expert than for popular art, though when works have been canonized the views of experts do not need to be expressed directly.

Rewards, in terms of status or material values, are the ultimate outcome of the process. But here the analogy with social stratification should not be taken too seriously. Economic rewards do not bear a strong relationship with cultural significance: a great many poor patrons can equal a few wealthy ones. Both high and popular culture can be valuable or worthless. When we say something is legitimate or fine art, it is not because it has high economic value. Some say that the higher the aesthetic value, the less the economic worth of art, but this generally elaborates a statement of the meritorious nature (and unjustifiable neglect) of some favorite piece.

The importance of identification, the interdependence of perception and assessment, and the general process of stratification in art are crucial to understanding the distinction between high and popular culture. Just as the idea that some property of cultural objects themselves allows us to decide whether they are "art" or "nonart" is mistaken, there is nothing inherent in cultural objects that permits us to determine their status as "high culture" or "low culture." Cultural hierarchy is constructed, not discovered.

ORIGINS OF HIERARCHY

The hierarchy of the arts—indeed, the idea of "arts" themselves—is a modern fabrication. Poetry, music, and the visual arts were not grouped together in classical antiquity, the Middle Ages, or the Renaissance. While the ancient comparison between poetry and painting and the theory of "imitation" provided a basis for subsequent aesthetic theories, "art" referred to human activity in general as contrasted with nature. Except briefly in Periclean Athens, art was not distinct from craft (Hauser 1982).

Throughout the medieval period and the establishment of the great centers of learning, the social system of classification placed music with math and poetry with rhetoric and grammar, while the visual arts were taught in artisans' guilds. Musicians (*jongleurs*) were itinerant, performing an identical repertory for all classes of society and effecting a constant circulation between popular and court music (Attali 1985, pp. 14–15). From the fourteenth through the sixteenth centuries, court music took on a distinct identity owing to the spread of written music and the permanent employment of musicians by the nobility.

Not until seventeenth-century France, with the institutional separation of art and science and the debate between the "ancients and moderns," did the idea of "progressive" or scientific disciplines (based largely on math) and the "aesthetic" disciplines (based on creative effort) gain currency. In the mid-eighteenth century Abbé Batteux set forth a relatively complete system of the arts, designating as the *beaux arts* those that have pleasure as their end: music, poetry, painting, sculpture, and dance. Through Diderot's *Encyclopédie* and D'Alembert's *Discours preliminaire*, this system was disseminated throughout Europe.

Because those who developed the subject were secondary authors (excluding Kant), it has been argued that the modern idea of the fine arts originated in informal conversations among cultured gentlemen in Paris and London (Kristeller 1951). While artists themselves were more likely to focus on the specific techniques and principles of a single discipline, these "amateur critics" were interested in the appreciation of *multiple forms*—painting, music, poetry, and drama. From such comparisons, ideas of aesthetic beauty—as distinct from truth—began to develop, a thesis that helps explain why modern aesthetics tends to analyze art more from the standpoint of the spectator than from the standpoint of the artist (Kristeller 1952, p. 44).

In America, the distinction between high and pop culture emerged in the latter half of the nineteenth century as a result of institution building by urban elites that isolated and differentiated high culture. As Paul DiMaggio has shown, in Boston and other urban centers there were no sharp boundaries or general sentiments before midcentury about the kinds of arts that nourished the spirit. A "promiscuous combination of genres" characterized most arts establishments and there were no clear notions about the kinds of arts that were debasing and the kinds that were uplifting.[5] Yet within a few years the Boston theater would be criticized for mixing musical comedy with "legitimate" theater.

The important institutional innovation was the nonprofit corporation, governed by a self-perpetuating board that delegates artistic decisions to experts. Such institutions were managed by professionals, governed by trustees, and drew on the resources of wealthy donors. High-culture entrepreneurs developed an organizational form that allowed a well-defined status group to make universalistic, community claims even though the art they promoted was becoming continually less accessible to the lower classes. High culture emerged *in opposition to* popular culture (DiMaggio 1982a, 1982b).

By 1900 the programs of high-culture institutions such as the Boston Symphony and the Museum of Fine Arts had been purified by the exclusion of mere "entertainment." Barriers were successfully erected around certain kinds of cultural objects. Art had been sacralized and purified by removing certain objects from the temples of high art (e.g., reproductions and the work of living American artists from museums, popular music from symphony programs). The distance between performer and audience was increased by the hiring of professionals to implement changes in the conditions under which art would be produced and appreciated. The demand for critics and aestheticians was high, since classification into genres had become more important and the distinction between high and low culture required legitimation (DiMaggio 1982a). Culture had become an important means of class identification and participation in particular kinds of art could be a sign of good breeding. This was not only because people of low character did not appreciate high art, but because they did not know how to behave while doing so, with sober and reflective reverence.

Nothing is more revealing of the new dichotomy between high and popular culture than the nineteenth-century transformation of Shakespeare described by Lawrence Levine in *Highbrow/Lowbrow: The Emergence of Cultural Hierarchy in America* (1988). Levine shows that an acquaintance with the details of Shakespearean plays, characters, and language characterized a wide segment of the population for most of the period. Performed in a variety of settings and styles, from the church vestry to the tavern, the Bard *was* popular entertainment. Attempts to intellectualize his plays and appropriate them for the gentry were treated with contempt and sometimes violence.[6] Yet by the end of the century Shakespeare had been "converted from a popular playwright whose dramas were the property of those who flocked to see them, into a sacred author who had to be protected from ignorant audiences and overbearing actors threatening the integrity of his creations" (p. 72).

Of course, there is a difference between mixing the wrong people, mixing the wrong forms, and mixing the wrong behaviors. A simple, unidimensional distinction between high and popular culture is problematic owing to the fact that a number of important dimensions are often, but not always, associated with one another. In the main, two questions give rise to discussions about cultural hierarchy: who are the primary consumers of culture, and how do they approach it? Correspondingly, answers tend to emphasize either social class (the status of the social actors who patronize different art forms) or embeddedness in discourse practices (the forms of talk and writing that surround the reception and treatment of art). While a full account makes reference to both factors, a focus on discourse is preferable to a focus on class for studying the mediation process.

CLASS

> My audience is a real cross-section, except we don't give away any tickets to someone who looks really prim and proper. I've got doctors telling me afterwards they like the sigmoidoscope jokes.
> —*American comedian*

> I think it's nonsense [the saying] that "comedy is the new rock 'n' roll." It's still conservative. [In London] the audience is middle-class, well-educated, white people. I'm a radical socialist but our job is primarily entertainment. You have that duty first and foremost.
> —*South London comedian*

The phrenological origin of the terms "highbrow" and "lowbrow" reflects the preoccupation with social class and artistic preferences that characterizes so much of the sociology of art. In the late nineteenth century the interest in the measurement of cranial shapes often focused on the easily visible "brow" that could supposedly reflect intellectual and aesthetic capacity. "Lowbrowed" types such as apes, bushmen, and idiots were readily distinguished from "highbrowed" categories such as the civilized, the enlightened, and, highest of all, the Caucasian. Portraits of Shakespeare were set alongside drawings of the skulls of "primitives" to make the point in popular phrenological texts.

To be sure, there is an unfortunate tendency to conflate the idea that the preferences people express are determined by status differences with the idea that expressions of preference account for those very same status differences. Is it that the cultural objects favored by those with high status become highbrow? Or is it that a preference for certain kinds of things helps to bestow reputation and prestige?[7] In other words, is it the kind of art people consume that confers social status or is it the kind of status people have that determines the kind of art they consume?

To speak of "consumers" of art—that is, those who "appreciate," the "fans"—is to take a rigorously social approach to cultural objects: *those to whom the object appeals determine its "status" characteristics*. When Plato, in the *Laws*, said "pleasure of the right people is a good criterion of art," he had something like this in mind. In modern language, things that appeal to people of lower status are "lowbrow" or "popular," whereas things appreciated by those of higher status are "highbrow" or "elite."[8] In occupational studies, the proportion of women employed in an occupation can be correlated with the status of the occupation. So in art, the proportion of upper-class participants is linked to the status of the genre.

Pierre Bourdieu's theory of "distinction" (1984) is the most elegant treatment of this way of viewing the difference between "legitimate" and popular art, for it treats these concepts both as class markers and as varieties of taste, the very distinction drawn here. Taste preferences for cultural objects are determined by class position. Further, culture is a type of "capital" that can be employed in the generation and maintenance of status. This view can reduce to tautology, but need not. There are independent determinants of status of which cultural capital is only one—and probably not an important one unless it is broadened to include all forms of education and credentialing. In turn, one's network of associates (including one's past associates or "shadow network") is the key to understanding aesthetic choice.

Let us agree, then, that there is some kind of association between class and cultural preferences. But associations are not all of a kind. There is an important difficulty with the wholesale equation of—to use Herbert Gans's terms—"taste publics" and "taste cultures." A taste public is an aggregate of people who have the same tastes and aesthetic standards. This view is often implicit, but sometimes it is stated directly:

"appreciation of the fine arts is primarily associated with the taste of the upper classes, and appreciation of the mass media is primarily associated with the lower classes" (Walker 1982, p. 15).

Is it necessary to assume that only one set of standards—only one kind of "taste"—can be held at a given time? It is well known that high education and income, standard measures of status, are associated with, for instance, attendance at opera, symphony, and theater. This would justify speaking of these art forms as class markers—that is, having opera as an aesthetic preference indicates "upper status" or "highbrow" taste. The difficulty with going further with a "class" theory of cultural hierarchy is that *the converse is not true.*

First, going to the movies, watching television, and liking rock music are not confined to those with low education and income but are preferences diffused widely throughout the population. Highbrows, in a word, watch television and listen to popular music, and these are not "guilty pleasures." Professors of English literature whose lives are devoted to the critical analysis of "the best that is known and thought" spend hours luxuriating in science fiction and detective stories.

This observation, available to all who care to make it, is confirmed by studies of cultural consumption (DiMaggio, Useem, and Brown 1978; Andreason and Belk 1980). A 1975 national survey by the National Research Center for the Arts found that not only were those with higher education and income more likely to visit art museums, the theater, and classical music concerts; they were also more likely to go to movies and listen to popular music. A Ford Foundation study conducted at about the same time showed that college education was associated with an increased likelihood of experiencing musicals, jazz, rock, folk, and cinema as well as theater, symphony, opera, and ballet (1974, pp. 13–16).

Historically, the upper strata have never been averse to cultural products that we might now consider "popular" entertainment. In 1602, when recruits were needed for the English army, the playhouses of London were raided. These were thought to be a haven for idle and dissolute persons and, therefore, ideal recruiting grounds. Yet when the roundups were complete, "they did not only presse Gentlemen, and sarvingmen, but Lawyers, Clarkes, country men that had lawe cawses, aye the quens men, knightes, and as it was credibly reported one Earle."[9] The problem, as it remains today, is that entertainments widely thought to characterize the lower social orders are patronized by the upper orders as well.

In Italy, the Commedia dell'Arte with its simple staging, brilliant costumes, improvised dialogue, and stock devices appealed primarily to a mass Renaissance audience. Yet at the same time, it had a "curiously sophisticated and even brilliant side . . . capable of satisfying, with its spirited agility and wit, many of the most informed and educated minds" (Southern 1961, p. 210). This performance genre spread throughout Europe, applauded by all social classes.

By the nineteenth century, when participation in various forms of culture was employed in overt attempts to create or maintain status differences, conflict emerged in the major European capitols over which genres would be patronized by the higher social classes. William Weber links the development of the modern concert form from 1830 to 1848 to the rise of the middle class. He documents a high-status *popular*-music public as well as a high-status *classical*-music public.[10] The popular music public, dominated by business families but including members of the nobility, devalued musical erudition and reveled in the works of great virtuosi such as Franz Liszt. It was accused of mere novelty and showmanship by proponents of the German classical style, yet in terms of wealth and sponsorship of salon activity, members of the popular-music public were more prestigious than its classical counterpart.

These two high-status publics were distinct from the low-status concert world within which there was very little taste conflict. Artisans and the lower middle class who attended these inexpensive amateur concerts, choral societies, and promenade concerts enjoyed *both* popular and classical music (Weber 1975).[11]

In turn-of-the-century Munich, the Intimes Theater of Vallè (Josef Hunkele) helped to give the term "cabaret" its current connotation of "dubious theater" rather than the "legitimate" status it originally possessed. Vallè accommodated the public's desire for piquant entertainment by providing striptease scenes on the order of Mary Irber's "The Wedding Night." These skits were often prohibited by the police, whose very regular observers noted that the patrons of the theater were drawn from the "better classes" of society.[12] Following World War I, increased production costs led London theaters to favor long-running comedies, melodramas, and musicals at the same time that the social composition of the audience narrowed to the middle and upper-middle classes (Griswold 1986, pp. 148–55).

A second difficulty with confining the upper strata to legitimate taste in art is that social inequality no longer promotes the development of artistic institutions. With a relatively large and homogeneous middle class and a general expansion of leisure time, consumption of art *of all kinds* increases, including popular as well as fine art: "art can signify class differences so long as there are clear understandings of class membership, but fails to when class configurations are sufficiently complex" (Blau 1988a, p. 146).

34 CHAPTER ONE

DISCOURSE

In the play *Killer Joe* a father and son employ a hit man to bump off the mother only to discover they are not the beneficiaries of her life insurance policy. They have no way to pay the killer, who brutalizes the family and takes the daughter as payment in a harrowing finale.

> *Playwright*: The killer is a monster.
>
> *Critic*: But in a sense Joe is the moral character in the play. He requires this violent, incestuous family to fulfill their obligations and uses the necessary means to accomplish that.
>
> *Playwright*: Well, I hadn't thought of that but I suppose it's a fair point. You hire a monster and you've got to pay the monster's price.
>
> [*later*]
>
> *Playwright*: I don't understand how you review comedy. What's there to say about a comic? Either he's funny or he's not, right?

There is much difference between saying that education and income correlate with the appreciation of high art—which is undoubtedly correct—and saying that the *kind* of participation is likewise associated with social status. Since the middle and upper strata are more frequent consumers of many forms of art, it may be more fruitful to focus on the *nature of participation*, rather than the *characteristics of the people* who participate if we are to explain the persistence of cultural hierarchy.

Participation in art is inherently judgmental. Spectators prize or protest the objects they witness. But their assessment practices, in particular their *responses to the evaluations of others*, differ depending on the kind of thing it is, granting the cultural hierarchy significance and reinforcing its existence. In high art, evaluations are special because they involve a special kind of dependence on the part of the spectator, a dependence on the perceived standards of experts.[13]

A preexisting cultural hierarchy offers an opportunity to consumers that could not exist in a cultural democracy. I have called it a status bargain, because the process may be described as a symbolic exchange of prestige for opinion rights. One does not "give up" one's opinion, nor is it the case that one forms no opinion. But in high art, we are not all on an equal footing. High art consists of the cultural products for which the talk and texts of knowledgeable others are relevant. Association with high-status art forms provides prestige to the extent that one participates in legitimating discourse *about* those forms. In this kind of assessment practice the standards of knowledgeable others are *taken into account*.[14]

Discourse about quality often adopts a Kantian view of preferences. Yet post-Wittgensteinian philosophy and constructivist sociology have convincingly shown that goodness judgments are always and inherently comparative. There is no rebuttal to a shift in standards. Shifts expose their frailty. Artworks are not inherently "serious" or "entertaining." Quality is created through conversation and comparison with other products in terms of features and principles espoused by experts.

Goodness is ascribed to cultural objects by virtue of their comparative properties, in relation to other objects of the same type. The fact that a painting is "good" means it is a good painting, or good as a type of painting.[15] It is always possible to disagree with a judgment of quality by rejecting or questioning the standards by which it is made.

A critic is sometimes compared with an epicure. Because a connoisseur of whisky has acquired knowledge and developed sensitivities that are sharper and more acute than the rest of us, he sips a cask sample and ranks it according to criteria that are significant for lovers of single malt: color, nose, body, palate, and finish. But why these criteria? A much larger group of tasters gives precedence to price, grain content, and widespread availability. The response that their opinions are not relevant simply repeats the mistake of taking as relevant students of the malt only a particular group of students. But there is no *honor* in any affiliation outside that group. The status bargain dictates the terms of talk.[16]

Quality standards and quality judgments are ultimately created within contexts of discourse. This social construction of taste—and its imperturbable self-concealment—is exemplified in Angus Wilson's account of a Booker Prize committee. The members of the committee were reading many of the same novels being reviewed in the newspapers:

> As we saw the reviews appear of the books we were reading, we were constantly rubbing our eyes. Could this new weekly masterpiece really be the book that all four judges had agreed needed no discussion? There seemed behind this professional critical opinion some shadow world, some hierarchy that we knew nothing of. (Sutherland 1978, p. 93)

For those deeply involved in discussions about artworks just as for those who are unconnected with "legitimate" discourse surrounding an art form, a shadow world may indeed seem to exist. The committee's response should not be surprising, since "quality" is locally created. Informal networks of discussants provide judgments that may or may not be widely disseminated and can seem peculiar to other groups. The judges reflexively—through their own repeated evaluations—reconstitute the meaning of quality, inevitably disjunct with other, locally created meanings, but taking each other's expert judgment into account.

What is the status of judgments like these that seem inconsistent? How can they be the basis for the construction of art as high art? It is not the consistency of judgments (or their foundation) that matters, only the process of arriving at evaluations and the deference paid to some kinds of views over others. Most consumers and spectators are not privy to secret deliberations, but encounter only texts, the secondary discourse of criticism.

Bourdieu provides us with another way of describing the process. Cultural participation is framed in terms of two broad "aesthetics." The "popular aesthetic"[17] refuses to distance itself from the everyday world of experience. Cultural objects elicit responses in terms of their explicit contents. A photograph of a wrinkled old woman is not experienced as "beautiful" because its object is not beautiful—the treatment of form and shadow are of no inherent value. Wrinkles are wrinkles, and they are no good.

Bourdieu argues, of course, that this aesthetic is the possession of a particular class of individuals. The central cause of the popular aesthetic is that the less educated are "devoid of specific categories of perception [and] cannot apply to works of scholarly culture any other code than that which enables them to apprehend, as having a meaning, objects of their everyday environment" (Bourdieu 1968, p. 591). Like the novice ethnologist, those of "barbarous taste" are faced with a ritual to which they do not have the key.

Such a direct and *unmediated* mode of relating to realities and representations is distinct from the "cultivated disposition" or "pure aesthetic" that Bourdieu attributes to those of higher socioeconomic status. It is detached from the natural world and experiences art in terms of form. This "pure gaze" of artistic perception associates the elements of representation with each other and with other elements in artistic traditions rather than the everyday world. This aesthetic depends on "distance from necessity" in economic terms:

> The aesthetic disposition, a generalized capacity to neutralize ordinary urgencies and to bracket off practical ends, a durable inclination and aptitude for practice without a practical function, can only be constituted within an experience of the world freed from urgency and through the practice of activities which are an end in themselves, such as scholastic exercises or the contemplation of works of art. (Bourdieu 1984, p. 54)

Since this "pure aesthetic" is dispositional, it quickly becomes invisible to its possessors, deriving actively from the insensible familiarity with culture as an "enchanted experience" learned in the context of family and school. The illusion of immediate comprehension gives rise to the sense that the appreciation of cultural objects is a matter of "natural" taste, to the view that, in the words of one of Bourdieu's informants, "Education, Sir, is inborn" (1968, p. 609).

Even if class is not associated with "taste" in any simple and direct fashion, the idea of distinguishable "aesthetics" is sometimes useful as a device for characterizing contemporary discourse practice. However, Bourdieu's "sociology of distinction" is based on first-order, generalized dispositions and ignores the local production of quality. The aesthetic disposition may alternatively be viewed as a propensity to engage in particular discursive practices. Through the practices in which cultural objects are embedded, the production of valuative judgments about art maintains and reinforces the cultural hierarchy on which the status bargain depends.

Cultural capital, as expressed in pragmatically knowledgeable talk about art, is useful in interaction as a "status" dimension, a kind of conduct that conveys voluntary compliance or deference (Kemper and Collins 1990). By displaying cultural preferences, one communicates information about the self and implies affiliations with various kinds of groups. Talk about art is an important signal of position in social networks. It is often and conveniently assumed that high-status groups are the only groups with which people wish to affiliate, but this is patently untrue. First, some groups are not open to general membership. They are closed symbolically as well as socially, and their boundaries often constitute reasons for scorn as well as honor.

Second, there are often reasons why people wish to display diverse and popular affiliations rather than restricted highbrow tastes. Relational work involves the establishment of common bonds that "distinguish" parties to a relationship from the larger groups to which both members belong. In exchanging attitudes, agreements, and support, it is often useful to appreciate similar cultural objects, *regardless* of their position in the cultural hierarchy. But it is crucial to display, at the same time, appropriate *attitudes* toward the object. These attitudes may be seen as Bourdieu's "aesthetics," or, more rigorously, as "discourse practices."

The appreciation of lowbrow culture is a significant phase in the development of many groups. Self-depreciation often follows the differentiation of a group into higher and lower statuses as a means of promoting or reestablishing solidarity. As Peter Blau noticed, the first person in a group with intellectual pretensions who admits he prefers watching television to the symphony acknowledges a weakness (1986 [1964], p. 49). This admission encourages others to do the same, conceding their lowbrow tastes as well. Self-depreciating modesty, promoting social ties, is another interactional reason that popular culture gains a foothold in the same groups where highbrow tastes might be expected to hold.[18]

Discursive practices may also be observed in the development of texts. They are rooted in the Kantian position that the judgment of taste, the aesthetic intuition, actually precedes the pleasure gained from the aesthetic object. In philosophical terms, aesthetic judgments, as distinct from both moral and scientific judgments, rest on feeling but also claim universal validity. That is, the ascription of beauty follows the immediate, direct delight that comes from the contemplation of an object's form. The feeling induced is special—not to be confused with lust or desire—and it is universal because it is disinterested. Kant argued that delight is not based on deliberate interests, for one feels completely free in regard to the liking accorded an object. Since it not based on any conditions of the object or the self, one has reason for demanding a similar delight from everyone (1978 [1794]).

This conception is akin to that employed for highbrow forms. Indeed, the notion that aesthetic judgments are somehow subjective *and* universal—that is, available to all under the right conditions—is at the root of "high" discursive practices where categorization in terms of quality, legitimacy, or seriousness is paramount. It may be discourse about internal qualities of the object—or it may be about the object's relationship with its social context. "Popular" discursive practices, on the other hand, assign objects to categories in which the "universal" validity of judgment is of no account. No transfer of judgment is involved, but neither is there any status enhancement.

"Quality" in art, then, is the kind of property that can only be applied to high art, to certain cultural objects. A painting or a play is said to be good or bad or mediocre, and it is not simply in the way we perceive those objects but based on some standards that are said to have been applied. It would make sense to say, "it's a very high-quality composition" or, perhaps with hesitation, "it seems to me a very high quality composition," proceeding to give reasons for that appreciation, an interpretation, and so forth. Although one can say, in English, "I viewed it as a high-quality composition," this seems to call for some additional explanation, or suggest a qualifier before reasons are adduced. (It might mean something like, "I was determined to take it seriously" or "Although most people wouldn't have given it a second thought, I did.")[19]

SERIOUS ART AND ENTERTAINMENT

Can all this be reduced to the issue of "serious art" and entertainment?[20] If serious art is simply art about which discourse matters, then according to the idea of highbrow mediation it can. But it is difficult to offer a clear sense for "entertainment" and it is better to beware the term. Entertainments are of diverse kinds and do not consist simply in belly-splitting laughter, but also in emotional experience. High art is sometimes thought to be the source of sublime motivation, as expressed by the nineteenth-century writer who recommended that the emotions produced by a concert should be put to good use: "never to suffer oneself to have an emotion at a concert without expressing it afterward in some active way . . . speaking genially to one's aunt, or giving up one's seat in the horsecar if nothing more heroic offers."[21]

What about "seriousness"? The claim that a work "is serious" or "is to be taken seriously" may simply say that "further discourse is warranted," generally in print and by a relatively small number of critics.[22] High-status literature, for example, is often equated with "serious" literature, as opposed to "formulaic" fiction with conventional plots and characters, oriented toward escapism. For high art, criticism may bring about adjustments within the cultural hierarchy, highlighting those properties that would justify continued discussion, debate, and interpretation.

But the claim that "there are things that are beyond criticism and things that are beneath criticism"[23] implies that certain characteristics of an artwork invalidate or discourage discursive analysis. Are popular objects really *beyond* discourse? Of course not, as the field of popular culture studies demonstrates. The simple presence or absence of discourse does not distinguish high and popular art. In principle, a limitless set of observations can be made about any cultural product. The views that works of popular art do not "bear up" to critical scrutiny or that popular shows contain less to analyze and interpret, are false. The things that are said by the *audience* after a popular show do not exhaust the kinds of things that are said by experts.

So the main difference between high and popular art is not that the latter functions for escape, relaxation, or entertainment, whereas highbrow products offer a different "kind" of aesthetic experience (moral education, spiritual fulfillment, or something else).[24] That view implies the peculiar position that highbrow art is somehow *not* entertaining and neglects the social fact that the consumption of cultural goods has social and not simply personal consequences (i.e., it affects the way one is viewed by others).

So what is popular art? There is an important sense in which, like pornography, you know it when you see it.[25] Chris Lynam, the English comedian, ends each show with a variant of the following routine: "Do you know how Sir Laurence Olivier became famous. What? [*cups ear toward audience*] . . . you think it was by doing Shakespeare? Nonsense. It was the same with all of them—by sticking a firecracker up his arse and lighting it." At which point, Mr. Lynam strips naked, inserts a large firework between his buttocks, and lights it.[26]

No mystery that we should be able to render such identifications quickly and painlessly. We have been socialized in a culture within which this knowledge is widespread and primary. It is not an awareness that "others" would like certain objects. We do not render judgments by asking ourselves whether artworks will appeal primarily to the masses or the elite.

With works that have been positioned in the cultural hierarchy we know *how* to speak about them, and this *how* has to do with the kinds of arguments one will accept for or against their goodness. This does not mean that popular objects are of uniform quality, but that matters of quality are discussed in different terms and the opinions of experts are irrelevant. Assessment practices need not take account of special knowledge, relations, or comparisons. Judgment is unmediated in the sense that an "expert's" opinion is no better than anyone elses—not in the sense that people do not care about the opinions of significant others.

CULTURAL MEDIATION

I have argued that the difference between high and popular art is not fundamentally a difference in the institutions that promulgate their products or in the class background of consumers but a difference in the process of *mediation*. The relation between producers and consumers of art is not constant. It entails different levels of expert involvement. The higher a work is in the cultural hierarchy, the more important is discourse about the object to its status. Taste in high art is mediated by experts, whereas taste in low art is not.[27]

The hypothesis of high cultural mediation implies that judgments about this class of cultural objects are not individualistic, direct, or unaided. Rather, it consists of an influence process deriving not merely from general subcultural values and preferences but from experienced characterizations by authorities. Specifically, it holds that reviewers are taste makers and gatekeepers, structuring the experience of audiences, cultural consumers, and even artists themselves.

For objects lower in the cultural hierarchy, this process is essentially different. According to this concept of mediation, the purview of cultural arbiters is limited. Since the Roman satirist Juvenal, the image of the masses, with their gladiatorial contests and circuses, has been associated with the belief that popular entertainments and "mass cultural" objects pacify, exploit, and desensitize people to "higher" pursuits and appreciations, leading them to a kind of "slavery of taste." Whether or not they foster such degradations, it would be more accurate to say that the masses simply pay no attention to the discourse of experts—a most reasonable objection if one is an expert.

All critics are consumers but not all consumers are critics. There is a difference between those who have the time, interest, and privilege to write or broadcast their views about art and those who simply talk about it "off the record." Throughout this book, I will not consider the critic as merely a consumer whose views are public, but rather as a mediator who can potentially influence the behavior of others, both artists and spectators.

The empirical chapters that follow address the question of the extent to which critics do perform this mediating function and how it is related to cultural hierarchy. That critics are cultural mediators implies considerably more than that people read or listen to them. It implies more than the attunement of critics to trends and their popularization of movements. Specifically, it implies that the judgmental content of their discourse has an impact on the art world and its public. Critics, in short, should have an effect on some cultural objects but not others. This may be called a "highbrow effect" but the relationship between high art and cultural mediation is interactive. High art is subject to a mediative process, but the very existence of the process affirms the position of genres in the cultural hierarchy.

Students of culture have tended to assume that the primary roles in the art world are those of the artist and public. Because critical discourse is derivative, it has been largely ignored (Foster and Blau 1989, p. 19). Yet critics are fundamental players in the culture game. Their position needs to be treated as more than a matter for speculation—and certainly more than a matter for speculation by critics themselves.

Chapter Two

CRITICS IN THE PERFORMING ARTS

> How strangely some words lose their primitive sense! By a
> Critick, was originally understood a good judge; with us
> nowadays it signifies no more than a Fault finder.
> —The English Theophrastus; or, the Manner of the Age *(1702)*

C RITICISM HAS a special significance for the performing arts.
Scholars are quick to insist on the importance of the higher
forms of criticism—an endorsement of their own profession—
but the ubiquity of reviewing and its seemingly "derivative" nature have
rendered the "common" review nearly invisible. Though the roots of
criticism extend back to antiquity, the modern practice is best viewed as
having Enlightenment origins. In this chapter I discuss the distinction
between "criticism" and the related practices of commentary and theorizing, reviewing and critique. The Age of Criticism in the English theater is examined as a prelude to the argument for the importance of
"standards" to evaluation. Finally, the modern practice of criticism is
introduced.

CRITICISM AND COMMENTARY

Criticism as we know it is a modern activity. Its predecessor is commentary, the exegesis of classics. Prior to the seventeenth century, commen-
taries—from a simple running gloss on a classical text to voluminous
works devoted to interpretation—governed the intellectual life of both
Eastern and Western civilizations. Originating in divinatory reading of
signs and omens, the main task of the exegete was to explain and clarify
works that were generally agreed to be foundational, such as the Ho-
meric, Confucian, Vedic, or Biblical canons (Henderson 1991).

Both modern criticism and classical commentary produce written
texts concerned with the interpretation of antecedent cultural objects.
Differences in assumptions about the nature of those objects highlight
the novel features of the modern enterprise. Classical canons and scrip-
tures, even where they comprise portions of commentary, are held to be
profound, comprehensive, coherent, and moral. They contain no superfluous or trivial elements. Their inconsistencies are only apparent.[1] This
framework imposed a very different set of constraints on the commenta-

tor, whose responsibilities were the elucidation of obscurities, the resolution of apparent contradictions, and the explication of meaning. Evaluation of the classics was not an issue, since their greatness and centrality to social and moral behavior were paradigmatic assumptions of the exegetical enterprise. Hence, there was no issue of standards.

Criticism takes these issues as problematic. The critic's task is not only to determine how but *whether* a work is profound, coherent, or moral. Are the details of its design consistent with its theme? Do its internal contradictions function evocatively as ambiguities or are they just evidence of sloppiness? Indeed, in a postmodern context, are consistency and unity even desiderata? Although it is possible to discern the workings of commentarial thought in modern treatments of the aesthetic canon, this critical approach is associated with the Enlightenment.

A variety of connotations now surrounds the term "critic." One is the relatively neutral sense of "one who pronounces judgment" from the Greek word *kritikos*. The others are judgmental themselves, with reflexive features that have never been lost on those with an interest in art and culture. A critic may be one skilled in judging the qualities of artistic works or, more specifically, one who passes severe or unfavorable judgment, a censurer, faultfinder—a "caviller."

These two meanings of "critic" are important for the argument of the book. They express the difference between "criteria" and "thresholds." On the one hand, the critic assesses the merits of work with reference to explicit or implicit standards. On the other, a critic is someone who is not easy to please.

In reference to the activity the critic performs, the French word "critique" was adopted by many in the early eighteenth century, but "critick" persisted in use through Johnson and the dictionaries. Sir William D'Avenant introduced the principles of French criticism in *Preface to Gondibert* (1651), but the French influence on the English Restoration was as much in terms of the behavior of spectators as in the art form itself. English gentry admired the society of Louis XIV, but particularly the wit and conversational agility that would make the speaker a *critic*: someone with a keen intellect, striking fear in the hearts of those who dared depart from accepted standards (Smith 1953, pp. 182–83).

AESTHETICIANS, CRITICS, AND REVIEWERS

> *Performer*: This paper still doesn't have a real critic.
> *Editor*: You're damned lucky we don't.

Different kinds of people produce various kinds of secondary texts about cultural objects. The distinction between reviewers and critics is a crude and commonsensical typology. Often the terms are used interchangeably.[2] In a general sense, a review is a brief composition, reacting to a specific work, whereas a piece of criticism tends to be longer and more reflective, on a variety of themes, even departing from artworks themselves. A review summarizes and evaluates to a readership that may not be familiar with or have made judgments about a work. In common parlance, however, it is critics who write reviews.

These ways of drawing the distinction have some merit, from assumptions about their potential audience to the presence of copy deadlines. In terms of readership, criticism analyzes and explicates for a more specialized audience, many of whom are familiar with the work or artist, whereas reviewing is addressed to the general public.

Wide visibility may be provided by several kinds of gatekeepers who control access to the public—critics, dealers, brokers, promoters. The critical role is less market-oriented than any of these. In this respect there is a sharp line between a critic and other kinds of mediating roles, for instance, a museum director who *directly* selects works for display.[3] Who so acts ceases to be a critic. A critic *qua* critic is a judge of merit. Discourse, not decisions, is produced.

The use of criteria for evaluation has often been viewed as of primary importance in institutional theories of aesthetics. Becker distinguishes "aestheticians" who develop the premises and arguments used to justify and evaluate works as "art" from "critics" who *apply* aesthetic systems to the evaluation of specific works and artists (1982, pp. 131–64). Such a constrast is highly idealized. Aesthetics disdains discussion of specific works, save as examples of system. Yet Becker admits that when an established aesthetic theory does not provide legitimation for cultural objects as art, institutional activities such as criticism simply proceed in its absence. No systems or principles are necessary to endorse or condemn specific works, and aesthetic theory is sometimes developed after the fact (e.g., for the "readymades" of Duchamp). Even if they are available, principles are not applied unproblematically, as we will see shortly.

The most extreme version of this view holds that critics not only *use* principles, but are the *guardians* of principles. DeLaurot held that the function of criticism is to maintain the vigor of moral and cultural values in society (1955). This weighty responsibility of critics endows them with a role akin to priesthood and their influence should be correspondingly vast. A critic may even be a censor, determining what can and cannot be viewed (Manfredi 1982, p. 91).

But this view bloats the capacity of critics to affect taste and is exorbitantly optimistic about the potential or anticipated effects of criticism. The emergence of many "expert" roles characterizes industrializing societies, but the jurisdictional claims of professionals are not typically made by critics. To the extent that attempts have been made, associations of professional critics have not demanded or succeeded in obtaining a monopoly on secondary discourse. The issue of "who may criticize what" in public has never been resolved or even widely debated. "Apostles of culture" such as Matthew Arnold and Alan Bloom, "critical theorists" such as Herbert Marcuse, Jürgen Habermas, and Terry Eagleton, "specialists" in the history of medieval architecture, and journalists who write weekly pieces on television are all characterized as "critics." There is little reason to wield the cold chisel of scholarship in narrowing the domain of the term.

Brooks Atkinson distinguished the reviewer, who attends a performance as a member of the public in order to provide news for people interested in the theater, and the critic, who reads scripts, attends rehearsals, writes something more "profound, judicial, and long-term" (Greenberger 1971, pp. 168–69). Atkinson thought of himself as a simple reviewer but to Broadway he was the archetypal critic, influential in making and shaping careers. What Atkinson wrote was *news* in an important sense. The review that appears in the contemporary mass media must be timely. Criticism in specialized monthly or quarterly publications, besides addressing the specialized audience, ranges far into the past for its subject matter, and afield to philosophy, literature, and social thought for its themes.

That the reviewer is primarily a reporter whose product is "merely descriptive" is a notion whose falsity is apparent in the evaluative content of nearly all reviews. It confuses the "feature" article that contains background information and often interview materials with critical reviews of art. "Journalistic" reviewers are, if anything, *more* inclined to include brief, summary judgments of quality than "academic" reviewers.

Ignoring the ways that individuals define themselves and restricting interest to matters of structure, the underlying dimensions conflated by the distinction between "critic" and "reviewer" are generated by the following questions:

1. *What is the scope of treatment?* Is the focus one work/artist, or many?

2. *What are the assumptions about audience exposure?* Is the readership assumed to be familiar with the content of the material in question (which reduces description and emphasizes interpretation)?

3. *How timely is the report?* What is its temporal relationship to the first performance or appearance of the work? Is there a deadline involved for its composition?

4. *What is the primary occupation of the author?* Is the writer a scholar, artist, or journalist? To what degree does the writer specialize in this particular genre?

To the extent that the text is wide in scope, spatiotemporally distant, assumes prior audience exposure, and is written by a specialist, it is an "aesthetic treatise." To the extent it is narrow, proximate in time and space, assumes inexperience, and is written by a generalist, it approximates the "notice." This implies that the eighteenth-century "critic" might be best viewed as the forerunner of the modern "reviewer," while the modern "critic" occupies a specialized, academic niche with little access to the general public.[4]

THEATRICAL CRITICISM

> But, when the curtain's down, we peep and see
> A jury of wits, who still stay late
> And in their club decree the poor play's fate;
> Their verdict back is to the boxes brought
> Thence all the town pronounces it their thought.
> —*John Dryden,* Sir Martin Mar-all *(1667)*

As the industrial era began, artists achieved a measure of independence from noble patrons. A wider segment of the public acquired the time and resources for an interest in leisure activities. With the increase in wealth and opportunities for aesthetic pursuits came the fear of being cheated or simply lacking taste. Experts were sought to interpret canvases, texts, and other works, helping the potential buyer to form an educated opinion or, put cynically, just telling him what to think. Experts who were initially interpreters and guardians of orthodoxy became mediators: educating the public, engaging in a dialogue with artists, and seeking to distinguish the meritorious from the meretricious—in short, assessing quality. In this sense we may speak of the creation of a market for judgments about the performing arts.

The neoclassical phase of English theater from 1660 to the end of the eighteenth century has been described as the Age of Criticism in the English theater. It could as well be called the Age of the Spectator or the Critical Spectator because at first there was no clear distinction between critic and spectator. The London audience of the time was "more compact and unified in opinion, standards, and behavior than ever before or since" (Smith 1953, p. 179) and the theater occupied a more important place than at any other period of English history (Gray 1931, p. 3).

Since a small number of playhouses dominated the period, choosing plays was not particularly troublesome—spectators could see everything if they so desired. But whether to *like* a play was a different matter. And the expression of one's likes and dislikes was a matter of reputational significance. Informal, conspicuous opinionating was a means of obtaining prestige in networks of upper-class and upwardly mobile gentlemen.[5]

Although theatrical periodicals had begun to appear, until late in the century the mainstays of criticism were the "tyrants of the pit" (Arthur Murphy, *Zenobia*, 1768), in Dr. Johnson's words, a race of "dull, judicious rogues." The self-proclaimed, "volunteer" critic was a desirable if often despised social role. The term "critic" was used almost interchangeably with "beau" and "wit" to denote a familiar social status. One's personal reputation could be established through judicious vocalization. The public abuse and denunciation of plays, books, and morals was a kind of "gentlemanly accomplishment" (Smith 1953, pp. 15, 32).[6] Within the elite social stratum, criticism was seen as the enactment of a democracy of opinion. But since actors were lower in social status than the critics themselves, this democracy, like those in the political sphere, favored one class above another.

The social contexts of this criticism were drawing rooms, taverns, coffee houses, and the theaters themselves. These gatherings could became a "town meeting of the pit." Early arrivals were common in order to discuss the play beforehand. During the play, critical comments, often audible and distracting, would fill the air.[7] Praise and vituperation would continue at the coffee houses afterward. By contrast, Shakespeare's audience may have been noisy before the play began, but was generally silent—apart from prodigious feats of nut cracking—during the performance (Harbage 1941, pp. 11–12).

No special qualifications were required, or thought to be required, for the exercise of the critical faculty.[8] The classical ideal that glorified the exercise of individual judgment in accordance with accepted moral and aesthetic principles was considered prescriptive for the behavior of spectators. The "critic" was merely exercising this judgment, and indeed, playwrights were literally "on trial" for presuming to bring their work before the public jury.

Neoclassical principles by virtue of which drama was to be judged dealt with such matters as (1) the unities of time, place, and action, (2) the distinction between tragedy and comedy, (3) the rule of "decorum" by which speech and action should be appropriate to character, and (4) the just distribution of rewards and punishments. But while a consensus reigned that there *were* rules for playwrights, their specification and application were subject to little or no agreement at all. The discursive practice of the period depended on the *existence* of principles, but the *principles themselves* were not the most important focus. Shakespeare, to use the clearest example, was generally considered a paragon, but his work contained many clear violations of the rules.

The conflict between deductive criticism based on rules laid down by the ancients and the idea of taste in which adequacy of a work was judged by a discriminating public did not always go unnoticed. But this intellectual and philosophical question was not particularly bothersome.

Critics were free to assume that good taste was an agreement between the rules and individual preference. Johann Christoph Gottsched, a literary theorist of the German Enlightenment, argued that one can correctly judge the beauty of a work when one has perceived it, even without directly consulting the principles (Hohendahl 1982, p. 47). Taste is fallible, since it depends on correspondence with the rules.

But no rule contains within itself all the conditions for its application. Every critic had his own priorities as regards the most important of these rules, and the means by which drama could be said to conform or deviate therefrom. So debates about what actually constituted good work as well as what counted as examples were endless:

> The man who would become a critic . . . had to take his stand on one side or the other of each of these [controversies]. He had to be ready to give a complete, reasoned theory of drama, its aims and the most effective means by which these aims could be reached. He had to find his way about in the controversy over the ethical basis of all drama. . . . Once past [this] danger . . . the new critic must make his definition of tragedy and comedy clear; he must decide whether to emphasize the ethical or the aesthetic theory, pleasing instruction or instructive pleasure. He must decide whether a play should hold the mirror up to nature or should arrange the facts of life in a way conducive to more righteous living. The unities he would perforce accept in theory, but he must decide whether to interpret them loosely or strictly; for there was authority for either interpretation. (Gray 1931, pp. 13–14)

To criticize was to hold firmly to some set of standards and to apply them rigorously. This court of opinion in the eighteenth century was stocked with men of character who felt that "literary stupidity is a crime against the intelligence of the human race and were determined that in their presence it should never pass unchallenged" (Smith 1953, p. 45). In effect, the fearless and eloquent slandering of a play—especially one in progress—could be seen, at bottom, as the love of justice.[9] Passive watching was not only rare, but undesirable. In the words of a Charles Macklin character: "The Town has always a right to interrupt, and disturb a Performance—It is their prerogative, and shows their Taste and their good Breeding."[10] The "Town" denoted the refined and critical spectators, thinkers, and men of Taste.

Still, it is more likely that criticism was not always so taken, and certainly not by the dramatists:

> Is all this crowd barely to see the play.
> Or is't the poet's execution-day—[11]

As a means of status seeking, the evaluation of drama was often undertaken in accordance with membership in the playwright's social network and often centered around particular drawing rooms and coffee-houses. The army of critics could "on opening night launch an attack on a new play so fatal as at once to destroy all present or future chance of its success, and to leave the unfortunate author with his reputation in ruins" (Smith 1953, p. 16). The audience often divided into vocal factions supporting and opposing the playwright. Although some might be won over, opinions were often established in advance through preexisting allegiances. The opening night of Sheridan's *Rivals*, appropriately enough, was attended by antagonistic claques, and the opponents succeeded in the closing the show after the second performance.[12]

Throughout the period, descriptions of critics in the audience are prominent in the dramas themselves.[13] Special attention to critics is merited in prologues or epilogues calculated to intimidate or win them over, as indicated in this prologue from Arthur Murphy:

When first the haughty critic's dreadful rage,
With Gothic fury, over-ran the stage,
Then prologues rose, and strove with varied art
To gain the soft accesses of the heart.[14]

Historically accurate though this might have been, it was Dryden whose sociological sense of the prologue was keener:

For who can show me, since they first were writ;
They e'er converted one hard-hearted wit?[15]

The Rehearsal by George Villiers, Second Duke of Buckingham, was the most notorious and widely imitated instance of a type of drama that passed judgment on this significant portion of the audience. The Duke himself had initiated a theater riot not ten years before the premier of the play in 1671 and was a critic of renown. The play has been described as "an arsenal of offensive weapons" for critics as well as an attack on Dryden's own critical views.

Plays of this nature were written by actors such as David Garrick and Charles Macklin, as well as the gentlemen critics, often as a means of attacking rivals. With names such as Miss Brilliant, Sir Conjecture Positive, Sneer, Lady Critic, Lord Dapper, Catcall, Honestus, Mr. Sneerwell, Sourwit, Miss Bashful, and Solomon Common Sense, playwrights indicated the *kinds* and *temperaments* of critical judgment, which was sometimes well considered but often rendered after the first speech of a play, or in the midst of conversations with actresses and ladies of quality.[16]

Though English newspapers existed by the 1620s, it was another century and a half before pamphlet criticism of single plays and actors was replaced by regular news space devoted to "performance reports."[17] By the 1770s, new plays were reviewed in a dozen daily or weekly papers.[18] By the end of the century the profession of theater critic was fully developed (Gray 1931).

Newspaper critics ("puffs") were considered the worst when they engaged in unrestrained flattery.[19] There was no element of discrimination—no standards—involved. Many were simply advertisements for the work of friends or even one's own.[20]

> Honest John Bull—before a sturdy elf—
> Now claims no right of judging for himself;
> To PUFFS from Theatres gives up his vote,
> And kindly thinks all *true*—because 'tis wrote.

These words from the epilogue of Richard Cumberland's *The Natural Son* (1784) perfectly express both scorn for puffs and those whose opinions were influenced by them. Individual judgment was not only a right but an obligation. In the contemporary art world, independence of judgment is now the main characteristic of popular art. As theater became a highbrow art form, critics became more influential.

Throughout the Age of Criticism, criticism (both written and oral) tended to be disapproving rather than constructive. The threshold, or tolerance for perceived faults, was low. This example from *The Devil's Copybook* (1786, quoted in Rigg, 1982, p. 19) surpasses in scurrility anything by George Bernard Shaw, Kenneth Tynan, Bernard Levin, or John Simon:

> Mr. Bensley's Glanville only operates to awaken those sentiments in the mind which will occur when we are confined to the mortification of seeing and hearing him performing, namely sentiments of amazement that a man so weakly gifted and repulsive in almost every faculty that is necessary to the completion of an actor should have interest and effrontery sufficient to appear before a rational audience. It may be a compliment to the charity of the nation that such a man is permitted to perform, but it likewise conveys the awkward implication that a British audience can be insulted with impunity.[21]

Or consider Hazlitt's opinion of Stephen Kemble (brother of the renowned John Philip Kemble): "We see no more reason why Mr. Stephen Kemble should play Falstaff, than why Louis XVIII is qualified to fill a throne, because he is fat, and belongs to a particular family."[22]

Beyond the negative tone of the critic, the early tendency was to focus on qualities of the play itself rather than its performance. Gradually, over the course of the eighteenth century, attention turned to the importance of acting and the interpretation of roles. Garrick himself was criticized for showing too much of his own personality rather than submerging it in the fictional character.[23] The contrast between "old" and "new" styles of acting provided a matter of debate for critics. Readers delighted in comparisons and evaluations of alternative interpretations of roles. Moral standards were seldom of critical concern and technical aspects of production increased in importance.

The critic became less and less identified with the pit, and by the early nineteenth century the profession was well established.[24] Performances received notices in the dailies, monthlies, and the more than 160 theater periodicals begun between 1800 and 1830 (Donohue 1975, pp. 143–44).[25] Since the middle and upper classes tended to avoid the theater during this period, it is likely that the readership wanted to remain informed about the actors, who were often famous.

With the emergence of the repertory system and the increasing familiarity of the audience with the plays, critics no longer emphasized the drama as a whole but the relative merits of players in particular roles, or with other roles by the same player. William Hazlitt, writing for several theater periodicals, reserved most of his space for acting and interpretation. Such criticism "was by necessity descriptive, yet unmistakably judicial" (Donohue 1975, pp. 144–45). The "pontifical" tone, suggesting a superior knowledge of the work and objective standards for evaluation, had come to replace the vituperative and adulatory accents of earlier writing.[26]

The review format was now familiar: (1) a detailed plot summary for new pieces; (2) the analysis of action, language, and sentiment; (3) the evaluation of performances. The behavior and responses of the audience were frequently discussed—unsurprisingly, since journalistic critics had themselves emerged from the ranks of the critical spectator and the theater was not darkened as it is today. But the evaluation was, and remains today, the most significant feature of the review.

EVALUATION

> Fear not to lie—'twill seem a sharper hit;
> Shrink not from blasphemy—'twill pass for wit;
> Care not for feeling—pass your proper jest,
> And stand a critic, hated yet caress'd.
> —*Byron*, English Bards and Scotch Reviewers

> It's all bad, especially in parts.
> —*Roger McGough*, "Critic's Poem"

Evaluative elements in a review are expressions of judgment. They may be distinguishable statements, rating the work as a whole. They may characterize artists, performers, or qualities of the object. They may be distributed as modifiers or implied throughout descriptive and analytical writing. A "good review" is one that is *read as* a recommendation of the event. Evaluative statements have the status of performative speech acts and are significant in two ways: (1) they do the work of warning off potential spectators or encouraging them to attend; (2) by telling what is good and what is bad, they direct the reader to like or dislike certain things.

The view that recommendations must be explicit to function as such is inconsistent with the use of reviews in everyday situations. The degree of explicitness varies according to both the subject and review genre. When critics were vocal spectators at the theater, vegetables were often expressions of evaluation, but in the modern world an iconography of judgment has developed involving stars, thumbs, letter grades, and yes/no tags.[27] Popular genres and reviews are more likely to be explicit about evaluations than highbrow genres and "critical essays." The more elaborate and differentiated discourse that defines highbrow art is thought to be undermined by unjustified, summary judgments.[28]

If evaluation is the most important function of the review, then the *construction* of quality judgments is crucial. The comparison of sport with performance art is instructive. To an interplanetary observer it might seem strange that for live performances involving a high degree of improvisation (athletics), there are never disagreements about quality, whereas for performances that involve comparatively little variation (art), dissensus abounds. Put another way, where variability in action is high we have no trouble agreeing about outcomes, whereas in highly standardized, repetitive performances, there is a notable *lack* of agreement.[29]

The reason is that athletics is organized competitively such that the rules for the performance are *embedded in the game itself*, codified and enforced by referees and umpires. In the sports world, a clear and consistent definition of quality is institutionalized in a "final score," in view of which any unique or commendable individual performances must be justified. The "whole" is clearly evaluable, apart from the individual performances of the actors, managers, conditions of performance, and the genre.[30] With two teams it is only a matter of whose performance was "better." That is what is measured by the final score, and, besides, there is never an attempt to play the same game again. In sports, writers are not called critics but rather journalists or commentators. The discursive possibilities are limited to analysis and interpretation because the evaluation is shared by all.

Both high and low art share the features that only one team plays and performance standards do not reside in the art itself. Regardless of status in the cultural hierarchy, any observed conformities must be enforced by the external power of the state or the financial power of patrons and spectators. Absent these controls, performance that is "different," which deviates from established practice, is often viewed as innovative and desirable. Comedians such as Gerry Sadowitz in Scotland or Andrew Dice Clay in the United States gained notoriety through vulgarity and insult that went beyond prior levels of vulgarity and insult. Tom Stoppard's *The Real Inspector Hound* collapsed the boundary between mediator and artwork by incorporating two critics into the action of the play.

We have seen in the Age of Criticism that standards were not *of* work but external to art, reinvented, reflected, and reified in the public arena through the discursive practices of performers, spectators, and critics. The importance of standards to evaluation increases with position in the cultural hierarchy. For high art, "standards talk" is required to maintain the status bargain in which opinions are not completely one's own. Whether Sadowitz's vulgarities are acceptable depends on the size of the audience for his shows. But the scribblings of Jackson Pollock depend on the engagement of experts and a public that grants critics influence over their opinions.

Standards are not simply rules for judgment, and in the contemporary period there is much dissensus. Eighteenth-century critics made much ado about rules and canons. Surely they could more readily be characterized as possessing some agreement about performance criteria. If a rule states, for instance, that "all action should take place within twenty-four hours, in one place, or in places readily reached within the time of representation," then a more-or-less confident judgment can be rendered based on whether this has been achieved, with appropriate inferences about the worth of the performance. Yet critics differed so much in which rules had priority and stringency with which they were to be enforced that they are best seen as providing a framework for argument without dictating judgment.[31]

For high art, effective judgment is offered *with respect to* rules, principles, or standards rather than as a (purely) subjective response to the artwork. Evaluation must be justified and, to that end, it is "reasoned." In high art, one likes something because it is good. In popular art, something is good because one likes it. Kantian aesthetics is an attempt to resolve the dilemma that surrounds this bald statement of the problem.

A contemporary example of the principled rationale may be found in the People's Republic of China. It is particularly interesting because realist principles for the interpretation of art are themselves unchallenged.[32] Rather than providing criteria for evaluation, they function as criteria for justification, as this review of *Uncle Dog's Nirvana* by Guo Xiang illustrates:

[The directors] did not rely on old methods, but incorporated modern techniques such as psychoanalysis, stream of consciousness, symbolism, metaphor, and inner soliloquy . . . in order to explore different levels of the characters. . . . In a fit of madness, Uncle Dog speaks with the landlord Qu Yongnian, who represents his illusions and recollections. . . . Did all these forms and methods deviate from realism? No, we should know that realism is neither a lifeless model nor a photographic reflection of life. It will be continuously innovated, enriched, replenished. The aim of using new forms and methods . . . was to reflect practical life and illustrate the characters' dispositions, not simply for the sake of eccentricity and stream of consciousness. So the play does not diverge from the realist aesthetic category. (*People's Daily* [24 November 1986])

"Principled" judgment is crucial to the ideology of quality in highbrow art worlds. Postmodern influences have undermined the classical view of standards and rendered principled judgment less visible through new vocabularies and conceits. But justificatory criticism is not merely an elective feature of high aesthetic status, for the mediative process is central to the cultural hierarchy.[33] The warrant for "standards" in the context of quality judgments resides in the fact that reference to them facilitates the conversion of the "subjective" or merely personal into an "objective" or justified claim.

As I have intimated, rules that guide judgment are only one kind of standard. A standard may also be a level, a "cutoff value" or "threshold," as expressed by the phrase "up to standard."[34] This notion of the critical recourse to standards hinges on the idea of variability—it makes no sense to evaluate a work of art as superior unless others are judged as inferior. If every review is positive, a critic has "no standards." When a critic says she is maintaining standards, she means she will not give a good review to just *any* work of art: "The most important thing a critic needs is a standard and it really doesn't matter what its specifics are."[35] Credibility is low when the existence of a standard cannot be inferred because of sameness in evaluation. Variation in judgments is taken as *evidence for* underlying standards, even if it says nothing about what they are.

A critic is no critic who likes everything. Where evaluation is not possible in any meaningful sense (i.e., where it is not free to vary from positive to negative), interpretive discourse is especially relevant. Clear examples are the production of catalogs and invitations to openings issued by art dealers, and "jacket" criticism found on record albums. The popular music industry publishes periodicals that contain reviews and the evaluations are necessarily positive. They are paid for by the distributors themselves.

Should the "same standard" apply to all works? Many critics say the source of the work should not and does not affect their judgment. In Scotland, such critics are often viewed unfavorably.[36] This issue is prominent in the minds of both critics and performers, since the use of a different yardstick might indeed convert an unfavorable notice into a favorable one. Other reviewers speak as if the type of performer constituted the crucial aspect of the quality threshold that should be applied: the true professionals; the meticulous, commercial craftsmen; the amateurs; the rough-and-ready experimenters. All are capable of presenting good or bad work *of their kind*. A large minority of critics say they use a kind of sliding scale that takes account of the budget, the support, and the working conditions when evaluating dramatic work.

MODERN CRITICS

> If the producers wish to lift something from this
> review for advertising purposes, they may quote us
> as saying, "It lacks everything."
> —*Wilella Waldorf*

The palate of cultural fare increased dramatically in the twentieth century. Playgoers in Restoration London had relatively limited options. In the contemporary period the sheer number of cultural opportunities in any one genre presents not only the problem of *what to like* but also the problem of *what to see*. This question is the focus of Chapter 6 and allows a direct test of the idea that critics have an impact on the audiences for theatrical performances.

Nineteenth-century criticism was practiced by the man of letters who laid claim to superior knowledge of the play, the performance, and the aesthetic context of the production.[37] Twentieth-century criticism is more often the business of journalist and editor, who must provide basic information about work as well as an evaluation. It is characterized by great diversity in the backgrounds and interests of writers, ranging from the journalistic to the professional.[38] Still, most conventional stereotypes about critics—their power, or brilliance, their arrogant omiscience, or reptilian meanness—were in place long ago.

Notwithstanding the rise of the audiovisual media, most criticism is still a published affair. Many newspapers have four or five critics on their editorial staffs, while most magazines, television, and radio stations employ no full-time critics at all.[39] Of the total editorial pool of the American news media in the 1970s, 2.2 percent covered cultural news (including critics)—about one-fifth of those who covered sports but still a relatively large number. English's survey of American critics revealed that only 40 percent were full-time reviewers and 40 percent spent less than half of their time reviewing (1979, p. 24). Most critics also write arts stories, announcements, fillers, profiles of stars, and background features.

With the exception of those who work for large daily papers in major urban areas, most critics cover more than one artistic field. Common assignments combine art and architecture, film and theater, or music and dance (sometimes including opera). The degree of specialization varies by location. In larger metropolitan areas a critic is more likely to cover a single art form, but about 40 percent of reviewers cover three or more art forms (Brown 1978, p. 35). Performing and visual arts critics often serve as book reviewers for items in their fields. Full-time critics covering only one field of the arts are a rarity, though this occurs in the most important urban markets and the national newspapers. With the emergence of periodicals that specialize in reviews such as *Entertainment Weekly*, the number of professional and full-time critics is increasing.

The typical performing arts critic, according to these surveys, may have worked briefly in at least one of the art forms he reviews, but is not a performer or practitioner, given a primary occupational role as journalist. This contrasts with the literary critic, or book reviewer, who is often a writer or academician. Writers are much more likely to be reviewers than performers.[40] By the nineteenth century, some individuals were identified *as* "critics" but most are still involved in other aspects of the literary world.[41]

In the large and influential theater worlds of New York and London, a great variety of beliefs have been developed about critics. American critics are generally believed to be more powerful than English critics, but whether the public genuinely follows their advice or producers simply respond to it is not known with any confidence. On the West End and Broadway, audience support is generally taken to be the principal determinant of the length of a run, but this is true only after the initial contract, which can be terminated by the producer of a show (or sometimes the company) if it fails to reach the break-even figure for two to three successive weeks. A profitable run depends on the costs of a show, but in London can require a play to linger four to six months (about 125 to 200 performances at 8 per week).

The length of a run is affected by many factors: special publicity, the presence of well-known stars, the practice of "nursing" a play (even at a loss) to fill a gap in the schedule or employ actors. Just as the presence of one or more stars may increase a run, the length of their contracts may diminish it, along with the receipt of subsidies, hot weather, the day on which a play opens, and the time of year (Goodlad 1971, p. 150).

That the factors promoting popularity are complex does not constrain but *encourages* the growth of ideologies about the critic. I will examine these beliefs and their sources in Chapter 8. For now it is sufficient to note that if a show has good reviews and large audiences, this might be an "effect" of the criticism, an "agreement" of the views of critics and audiences, or a simple "alignment" based on fortuitous features of the case. On the other hand, one may observe that there are a large number of plays with recognized artistic merit that have small audiences, and take this as evidence that the success of plays is independent of reviewing. The views of critics and audiences do not always correspond.

In New York it is frequently assumed that the power of critics is overwhelming (Engel 1976; Booth 1991). But does this mean that negative reviews will reduce audience size? It could just as easily be that the expectation of such a reduction is a self-fulfilling prophecy, causing management to curtail the run for fear of incurring losses.

Certainly, the daily and weekly critics are perceived as powerful, particularly those at the *New York Times*. One conventional explanation for this is the high cost of tickets. Viewers want assurances of value for money and critics are investment counselors. A second idea focuses on the economics of play production, which shifted from the repertory system in the 1920s to the production of complete plays that could pay for themselves only by long runs. In a repertory system, plays that flopped could be quickly replaced and not undermine the finances of the company as a whole, whereas in the modern system all of the financial eggs are in one basket. Since *any* factor affecting audience size is magnified under these conditions, critics began to receive associated deference (Wilson 1973, pp. 384–85).

Frank Rich, deemed the most influential Broadway critic until recently, proposed that the practice of lengthy previewing, common since the mid-1960s, may have further distorted any straightforward relation between critic and audience. He described a Broadway musical that previewed seventy-one times at full price. The critics, who knew as well as anyone else what judgment the Town had rendered, attended the press performances after almost 90,000 spectators had already seen it: "When the negative reviews finally did arrive, they were merely autopsies confirming the corpse's death by natural causes" (1991, p. 32).

Lehmann Engel proposes a historical explanation for the perception of the power of the critic: the shift in the occupational origins of producers (1967). While producers once came from within the theater world itself, modern producers now possess largely business backgrounds, enhancing the influence of theater critics: "a bad press means no run for a new show, a mixed reception usually means a short run, and a favorable set of notices generally produces a long run."

In the 1920s producers began to use favorable quotations culled from reviews to promote shows. In the beginning these were blurbs in small ads. The practice extended to full-page blowups in the *New York Times*, ads consisting of nothing but favorable excerpts, brief phrases in lights on the marquee, and complete reviews on billboards. Promoters understandably viewed reviews as useful for publicity. For this purpose, positive evaluations and phrases are the only relevant parts of a review. These legitimate the critic—often no more than a journalist or layperson—as an authority, as someone whose opinions should be taken seriously. While dissenting aspects of the text were considered nothing worse than useless description, it was generally believed that readers relied on reviews for guidance and entertainment. This ad-usage provided visibility for critics. The producers, then, popularized the critics, *advertising the critics as well as the show* and creating, in Engel's words, "the Golem that threatens them" (1967, p. 178).

Critics themselves were not slow to realize the possibilities of quotation. Edouard DeLaurot called this a subtle form of duplicity: "the review which, mordantly unfavorable as its general tone may be, manifests an observance of fealty by the calculated inclusion of a few mitigating lines . . . that ask to be 'lifted' by the publicity agents" (1955, p. 5). Few reviewers would admit to doing so, but many *write* as if they do, for the simple reason that quotability is a generalized motivation for writing, namely, to be reproduced and discussed by others in the art world. A general indicator of success as a critic is the *degree to which one is quoted* not by publicists but by other writers. Mel Gussow, in a front-page obituary of Mary Martin, reveals the depth of the tendency: "In reviewing her performance in 'South Pacific,' Kenneth Tynan said that she reminded him of something Aldous Huxley wrote about the minor Caroline poets: 'They spoke in their natural voices and it was poetry'" (*New York Times*, December 1990, p. 1). The "subject," Mary Martin, is characterized by a certain quality (natural poetry), but only via a collation of four additional actants and four linkages—the *Times* critic ("Mel Gussow") quotes a London critic ("Kenneth Tynan"), quoting the legendary "Aldous Huxley" on "minor Caroline poets."[42]

While it may well be true that promoters increased the visibility of critics, this does not in itself provide any reason to think that quotations have any impact on audiences. In contemporary society high levels of exposure create skepticism and reduce the extent to which consumers rely on advertising claims. There is something peculiar about believing critical excerpts when they are selected by persons directly interested in your ticket purchase.[43]

In the major markets, the "classical" concept of the critic, standing as a powerful but often pernicious guardian of the arts, is still widely held. But *most* performance art does not take place in New York and London. Their position at the apex of the cultural world subjects shows to special dynamics. There are major difficulties involved in separating the influence of reviews on *actual* attendance from their effects on *opportunities* for attendance—via their effects on profit-conscious producers and backers. This is one reason why the major markets are not the best place to study the process of mediation.

I have considered the changing nature of modern criticism from its origins in commentary through the development of a specialized critical role. This role has itself evolved from the active spectator of the eighteenth century who primarily sought to enhance his reputation, to the publicist who mainly hoped to improve attendance, to the independent judge who sought to guide audience perceptions, and finally to journalists with differing audiences and degrees of expertise.

No more reigns the critical cult of Juvenal, of the Hypercritic, of the violent denunciation of performances that fall short of established standards and are perceived as boundlessly offensive. But that is not to say that most of us do not enjoy the occasional aim for the jugular. The idea that critics must criticize—that there are standards that must be upheld—still legitimates and maintains the cultural hierarchy.

Experts are central to the discursive view of mediation and the critical review—a public discussion that evaluates an artwork—is the most consequential kind of discourse. Mediation implies that the higher the status of a work, the more important is criticism. It is not the mere quantity of discourse or the presence of evaluations that distinguishes high and low art but the principled construction of those judgments and the response to these judgments by audiences and performers. Standards involve criteria or cutoffs below which a work of art may not fall. Reference to standards legitimates the transfer of judgment on which high art depends.

PART TWO

THE FRINGE

Chapter Three

DEVELOPMENT OF THE FESTIVAL FRINGE

> Vague shapes are seen in the mist, or rather you imagine
> them from a hint here and there of far-off shadows. You
> realize that something tremendous is hiding there in
> the immense impenetrability.
> —*H. V. Morton,* In Search of Scotland *(1929)*

THE NEXT THREE chapters examine the Edinburgh Festival
Fringe. This is not intended as a comprehensive history, but as
an overview of a concentration of artistic energy, the likes of
which the world has never known. In this chapter I focus on the development of the Fringe and the importance of space to innovation and
participation in the performing arts. A discussion of genre as a classifica-
tory device introduces the peculiar problem of quality that arises under
conditions of large size, extreme diversity, and an egalitarian ethos. In
the next chapter I examine the modern Fringe as an artistic distribution
system and the contemporary shift toward comedy. Chapter 5 focuses
on the central myth of the Fringe, the ideology of discovery that em-
powers critics, motivates artists, and captivates spectators.

ORIGINS

The Fringe begins in Edinburgh, "the heart of Scotland, Britaine's other
eye."[1] Where the Firth of Forth narrows off the North Sea, the Old
Town slopes down the crest of a volcanic ridge. This medieval town of
turrets and tenements up to twelve stories high was crowded, dirty, and
smelly—from whence its nickname, Auld Reekie. The main street, a
long Scots mile, descends gradually from the massive Castle to Holyrood Palace, a royal residence long before Mary, Queen of Scots, arrived
from France in 1561. Beneath the castle rock and across the gardens to
the north, the eighteenth-century "New Town" is a precise opposite, a
planned masterpiece of wide streets, elegant urban squares, symmetrical
classical buildings. And climbing rapidly from Holyrood Park is yet another contrast, a mountain in the midst of the city. "Old Arthur's Seat,"
wrote Charles Dickens, "towering, surly, and dark, like some gruff genius." Felix Mendelssohn thought it was a panorama painted by God.

Even daily trips have their fascination. You turn a corner and there it is, a sudden and unexpected *discovery*—a slice of the Salisbury Crags, a glimpse of the Grassmarket, a new angle of the castle.[2] Robert Louis Stevenson, who died five decades before the first festival, dimly felt what the city would one day offer:

> These are bright and temperate days with soft air coming from the inland hills, military music sounding bravely from the hollows of the gardens, the flags all waving on the palaces of Princes Street—when I have seen the town through an air of glory. On such a day the valley wears a surprising air of festival. It seems as if it were a trifle too good to be true. It is what Paris ought to be. It has the scenic quality that would best set off a life of open-air diversion. It was meant by nature for the realisation of the society of comic opera.[3]

But the society that welcomed Bonnie Prince Charlie and Queen Victoria lived near the filthy slums of the Cowgate, and the fascination of the city is to be found in this duality. Edinburgh is "respectable and God-fearing, rebellious and scornful in its debauchery. It was not just that the city was physically divided between its two antithetical quarters, the duality was more subtle, being contained within the breath of every individual" (Massie 1994, p. 177).

These physical and social contrasts provide a more convincing reason why the world's largest and most diverse arts festival hatched in Edinburgh than the quality of its performance traditions. Until recently Scottish drama was "undistinguished and derivative" (Hutchison 1977). Only the Traverse Theatre, much younger than the Fringe, might be considered a company of international repute, specializing in original works (Macmillan 1988).[4]

The Fringe, which now dominates the festival it fringes,[5] is better suited to the twisting passages and secret closes of Edinburgh's Old Town than the planned Georgian magnificence of the new. Its name and concept reflect spontaneous growth, inconsistency, and a stoic response to the most excruciating artistic circumstances. Like the Scottish weather, there are no guarantees. You expect clouds, but when the weather breaks, the view takes your breath away.

The first glory of the Fringe is the name. The multiplicity of implications reflects the diversity of the affair itself. Even the earliest groups of performers were welcomed and assisted by the city of Edinburgh, praised (on occasion) by the official festival, and reviewed by the critics. "Fringe" has never meant outcast or pariah. As a modifier, it is wonderfully evocative, connoting creativity, scruffiness, oddity, scandal, frivolity, youthfulness, frothiness, and frippery. It can be attached to all sorts of activities, from theater to sociology, making them marginal and secondary. But it is also a frontier, a limit, a periphery. A fringe is a border, but an ornamental one. Its threads may be straight or twisted. It is an area in which reception is weak or distorted. Finally, it is a benefit granted, over and above your wage. The Edinburgh Fringe is a postmodern phantasm.

"So what is the Fringe, anyway?" In Edinburgh, I have never heard anyone ask more than once. Neophytes seem immediately to grasp the meaning of "It's a fringe kind of thing." They know it will be mildly deviant. It makes perfect sense to say that some Fringe productions are fringe, but some are not. A group of Edinburgh go-go dancers puts on a show called The Big Tease. A rapping rabbi fuses Jewish humor with dance music to create Kosher House. The Edinburgh Fringe also hosts many of the most conservative, mainstream acts in Britain. Princess Grace reads poetry at St. Cecilia's Hall to commemorate the American bicentenary. Anthony Hopkins directs Bob Kingdom's one man show on Dylan Thomas.

The term "fringe" was first used by a critic who bemoaned the location of *Everyman* at Dunfermline Cathedral, so far out on the "fringe of the Festival."[6] But Alistair Moffat, former administrator and Fringe historian,[7] attributes its proper coinage to Robert Kemp, writing in the *Edinburgh Evening News*: "Round the fringe of official Festival drama there seems to be more private enterprise than before" (14 August 1948). Edinburgh was thus spared the ear-scrunching label of "Festival Adjunct." The new term was quickly adopted by the media and used by performers by the end of the 1950s. "Additional Entertainments" had become the Fringe. No festival was without one.

The first official Edinburgh Festival in 1947 took two years to organize and was a response to the loss of the great continental festivals during the war. In the words of Owen Dudley Edwards: "The very sense of the wound in the war-torn Earth forcing its lacerated edges together characterizes the makers, the city, the artists, the press, the public: artists came to affirm that the wound had to close" (Edwards 1990, p. 17). With Rudolf Bing as founder, an enthusiastic Lord Provost in John Falconer, and Queen Elizabeth as Patron, this first festival generated more interest than anyone had a right to expect. But eight groups, uninvited and unannounced by the official program, performed during the festival period in small, sometimes converted theaters.[8] In virtually any American city so many offerings would constitute a reasonably large festival in the 1990s.[9] Together with such highbrow works as T. S. Eliot's *Murder in the Cathedral* (performed by the Mercury Theatre of London), *Macbeth* (by an amateur group from Edinburgh), and Strindberg's *Easter* (at the YMCA), the Manchester Marionette Theatre performed a series of puppet plays in the restaurant of a movie theater. From the outset, variety was the only truly consistent feature of the Fringe.

The "official" International Festival is upscale compared with its poor relation. Jonathan Miller, chairman of the Fringe Society, recollects that the Fringe was "condescended to, looked down upon, and even rather hated by the organisers [of the official festival], something which polluted the main event."[10] Some have seen the symbiotic relationship between the official festival and the Fringe as something like the difference between high and low art. But although there are organizational and financial differences, that association is quite wrong.

The Edinburgh International Festival boasts generous sponsorship and features a program of acts, often quite extravagant, selected by its director. The program is completed well in advance (unlike the Fringe), the marketing is international, and many tickets are distributed through advance sales to tourists. Many Fringe artists view it as elitist, traditionalist, and stodgy, though invitations to perform are still coveted. By the late fifties, the contrast between the theatrical conservatism of the Festival and innovativeness on the Fringe was common wisdom. One playwright claimed that "Nobody in their senses would go to the official Festival." An actor griped that only at the Fringe could one find anything "virile and youthful.[11] Kenneth Tynan wrote that the "Festival Society gives an impression of disinteresting itself in the theatre."[12] Such views are now voiced in reference to the Fringe itself, owing to the development of the supervenues and the growth of comedy discussed in the next chapter.

Declining numbers of professionals at the Fringe made it easier for the International Festival to view its gypsy multitudes as creative amateurs who did not produce "quality" shows. Relations between the two organizations suffered. In the late 1940s information about "other events" was available in the official program, but in 1952 a proposal for formal inclusion of the Fringe was rejected. Nor were other kinds of relationship—cash subsidies, an annual award, or even, ten years later, program listings—considered seriously (Moffat 1978, pp. 26, 51).

The idea that the existence of the Fringe posed a threat to attendance at the official festival is difficult to take seriously, since current official Festival shows are sellouts even with hundreds of competing productions. In the 1950s, however, the Festival Council, chaired by the Lord Provost of Edinburgh, took this view. In 1964 licensing laws were tightened for temporary performance spaces, a move intended to restrict the Fringe. Oddly, one of the most famous shows ever to premier in Edinburgh and popularize the term "fringe" through its very title was *Beyond the Fringe*, an invited revue that appeared at the official Festival in 1960.[13] The Festival, worried about the growing success of the Fringe, commissioned four Oxford and Cambridge talents for a series of sketches that would go "beyond the fringe" style of humor.

A change of Festival directors in 1966 was associated with the rapid growth of the Fringe and the improvement of relations. Peter Diamond began to invite Fringe groups, the Traverse Theatre in particular, to the official festival. Even performers who view the festival as restrictive and elitist are enormously flattered by an invitation to appear, and the "move up" is considered a public recognition of excellence. In 1969, a mention of the Fringe was allowed in the festival *Programme Brochure*. With the success of the Fringe in the 1970s and the formation of an efficient administrative organization, relations were normalized as amicable partners, each profiting from the existence of the other. Ever larger crowds of spectators and critics arrived each August.

It is difficult to say when "fringe" began to mean something more—a "style" of performance or an "approach" to drama rather than simply a performance that was not sponsored by the "official" festival. The meaning of fringe theater has thus expanded to include a nationwide and even international style of theater that is innovative and sometimes ingenious, often by new playwrights and companies, performed in any kind of space. The Fringe incorporates all styles, genres, and subgenres: the one-person show, the ten-minute play, the subversive, the decadent, the staid, and the slick.

Not unexpectedly, responses to this unsupervised variety have ranged from invective by Church of Scotland deacons to accusations that the success of the Fringe has rendered the organization rigid and its art traditional. Particularly revealing was the organization in 1987 of the Fringe Fringe Society, a self-consciously political, creative spur to Fringe bureaucratization and sobriety. A venue called the Edge was established for the production of musical acts and late night comedy as well as short plays in a club setting. By the second year, the need for advance scheduling resulted in a program of alternative comedy not dissimilar to that found throughout the city and the alternative Fringe disappeared soon after. It was impossible to "outfringe" the Fringe.

But the dissolution of the Edge demonstrated the limits of performance innovation in the highly competitive setting of Edinburgh. Organizational constraints are imposed largely by local regulations rather than the umbrella Festival Fringe Society, which operates primarily as a ticket service and information source for both performers and audience. The Fringe itself is a competitive performance market. There are no institutional biases toward aesthetic conservatism or avant garde innovation.

SPACE: INNOVATION, INTIMACY, PARTICIPATION

In 1570 the Dutch mapmaker Abraham Ortelius called his compendium of seventy maps a *Theatrum*, the Latin word meaning a place for viewing. He meant to denote both the act of seeing or spectating and the places where things would be seen. Spectating in odd places is the second noteworthy feature of the Fringe. It brings us closer to a world in which art is integral to life, invading our space and our awareness.

The performance spaces, or "venues," are in some ways the key to understanding the phenomenon of the Fringe. The use of nonstandard staging and setup areas was always required by the sheer number of performances and the limited number of traditional theater spaces. There are more than two parents of invention, but necessity is surely one of them. If you come to the Fringe, you should not expect a proscenium. The staging area, according to one Fringe director, "has no clear wings. It meant a last minute rethink—how to place the flats. Changing costumes has been a nightmare. They have one so-called changing room but we find it easier to put makeup on in the flat. You perform just about anywhere; just grit your teeth and get on with it."

The need to use available and often eccentric performance spaces has been converted from a presentational constraint into an integral part of many productions. Shows have been held in buses that tour the city. An actor held individualized performances in a closet. One show was offered by reservation in the privacy of one's own home. Another, advertised as "by invitation only," required the audience to call a special number to find out the location. Year-round theaters like the Traverse with dressing rooms and permanent staff are a blessing and a rarity for performers who come to Edinburgh expecting confusion and unpredictability. The rule has always been to anticipate chaotic hardship. Woe to those who have not booked venue and lodgings in advance.

High levels of tolerance are required, along with stoic responsiveness and adaptability. The dress rehearsal of Michael Green's *Coarse Acting Show* in 1977 was stopped by the police when the neighbors complained of noise, so the rehearsal was continued in mime. The same year Rowan Atkinson, now one of the best known British comics, performed a one-man show for the Oxford Revue. Recognizing a clear failure after opening night, the show was canceled for three days while a new revue was written. Rupert Gavin's National Revue Company arrived in Edinburgh only to discover their lodgings were in a dilapidated tenement so tiny that sleeping space on the floor was taken by turns (Dale 1988).

Early Fringe venues were, of necessity, converted halls because the official festival occupied most of the fully equipped theaters. Even today, a minority of Fringe venues have permanent theater or public entertainment licenses.[14] As the city sought to cope with the demand in the 1960s, the proliferation of companies required more and more spaces. Church halls were used from the outset and school halls were permitted in 1969. After more than twenty years of following a "one hall per group" policy, many groups began to share spaces. By the early 1980s up to seven groups would share a venue, opening at ten in the morning and closing long after midnight. For the 1976 festival alone, nineteen new spaces were opened, an unparalleled growth.

By 1994, the program listed 188 distinct venues, many with more than one space, exhibiting an improbable variety.[15] They range from the back bar of Holyrood Tavern just up from the queen's palace to Greyfriar's Kirk House, near the graves of Covenanter's executed for their religious beliefs. They incorporate state-of-the-art performance centers like the University of Edinburgh's George Square Theatre and Edinburgh's new home for opera, the Festival Theatre, as well as the sanctuary of the fifteenth-century Rosslyn Chapel where the Holy Grail is said to rest. Do you prefer the opulent Cafe Royal in the Georgian New Town or the cozy squalor of the Celtic Lodge near the Edinburgh Castle?

The basement of the Netherbow Arts Centre next to John Knox's House on the Royal Mile or the Theatre Workshop near the Water of Leith might be considered "traditional" performance art sites. But the Hermitage of Braid is used for open-air performances of Shakespeare's *The Tempest* and the audience might be spirited off to Inchcolm Island in the Firth of Forth for *Macbeth*. The Royal Botanic Gardens serves just as well for a play about Linnaeus as Calton Hill, the unfinished eighteenth-century "acropolis," does for the freakish Jim Rose Circus Sideshow. The bottling room of the Caledonian Brewery hosts a ceilidh dance—which will be in progress as the audience leaves the gospel concert at the Seventh Day Adventist Church.

However appropriate or inappropriate the space, Fringe style is in large part an ecological adaptation that implies innovation, intimacy, and often participation.[16] Since performing artists have been forced to meet the requirements of spaces designed for other purposes, innovative staging practices have been fostered in Edinburgh and sometimes they have become an end in themselves. A Fringe director notes that "our play needs a smaller, intimate house—it won't work in a big hall. The style of acting dictates the intimacy you need for the play—mumbled lines, eye movements." The understated, naturalistic, "small movement" style is only possible in relatively close spaces, with the staging area in close proximity with the audience.[17]

The corollary of closeness is that player-spectator involvements have become characteristic of the Fringe. They are sometimes written into innovative scripts for the stage, or planned into the routines of comics and cabaret artists. In this sense Fringe theater may be closest in spirit to Tudor theater, where the stage was not clearly demarcated from the audience—often it had just been cleared of tables for the evening's entertainment—and was devoid of all but the simplest props. The audience in the Tudor interlude, as in today's Fringe, would often be included in active, participatory ways and enjoyed a special intimacy with the players (Johnson 1970).

Participatory theater involves breaking the fourth wall separating spectator and performer. In works such as *A Grand Scam*, characters in Fringe plays speak directly to (or from) the audience, step off the stage, reflect on their own roles, and generally disrupt theatrical conventions in ways that can no longer be considered radical. Participatory methods have come to characterize popular art even more, in interactions between comedians and hecklers, and cabaret acts such as *The Doug Anthony Allstars*. These three Australians, whose instrumentation consists of a lone guitar, began to appear on the Fringe in 1987. Angelic voices contrast starkly to onstage routines that are more readily described as incitement than participation: throwing themselves bodily into the audience, climbing the balcony in pursuit of beer-throwing spectators, French-kissing heterosexual men in the audience.[18]

Adaptivity and flexibility in using the available spatial and physical resources provides performers with the opportunity to realize high levels of originality. Far from scaring off audiences, this diversity has become a positive attraction. Growth in the context of "participatory democracy" is more than just an organizational problem.[19] The reduction of uncertainty is equally a question of cognition, for people do not choose shows randomly. This feature is critical to testing the argument of the book, for the practical difficulty of selecting a show is an opportunity to observe the process of cultural mediation in action. Until now, I have treated the issue of "genre" only tangentially, but it is a concept of theoretical and operational significance, underpinning the notion of cultural hierarchy.

THE QUESTION OF GENRE

> *Sociologist*: What made you decide to classify the show as "cabaret"?
>
> *Performer*: [*distressed*] What do you mean? It's not "cabaret"—it's "theatre." How could it be anything else?
>
> *Sociologist*: [*pointing to the program*] But right here it says: "performed to acclaim in cabarets all over Europe."
>
> *Performer*: That's "*in* cabarets." That doesn't mean it *is* a cabaret. I don't think it's "cabaret" just because it's got a few laughs it in. Actually it's a very tragic piece.

Participation in the cultural hierarchy is expressed through performance choices. The character of the audience and the variety of tastes expressed through spectatorship and conversation are important to the mediation process. In the absence of diversity to provide a basis for comparisons, no investigation of highbrow and popular taste is possible. Located in relatively stable positions in the cultural hierarchy, genre differences have consequences for the likelihood of critical impact. For the Edinburgh Festival Fringe, the evolution of this diversity is the story of the development of a multitude of genres together with various forms of audience involvement.

Artworks are never, except in highly unusual or purposive cases, experienced without expectations. The most important kind of expectation is based on knowledge of genre, the category to which a cultural object belongs.[20] Works receive an initial ranking in the cultural hierarchy simply by being classified. The ensuing association of a work with similar artworks is status-defining, for genres themselves possess cultural status. Evaluative processes occur both within and between categories of cultural objects, but particular works rarely "transcend" their genre. This is the reason it is important to consider the meaning of "kind" terms and classification systems.

The experience and appreciation of works of art may be analytically prior to their evaluation,[21] but in practice this is not the case. Much of the evaluative work done on an object and, according to the idea of cultural mediation, *the way in which the process itself will operate* depend on the kind of work an object is perceived to be. These expectations are difficult and in most cases even impossible to overcome. The knowledge that you have been invited to witness a "modern dance" or a "circus" so overwhelms all other features of these performances that they cannot be evaluated at the same levels in the cultural stratification system.[22]

"Kind" terms are those that can take the indefinite article. In logic, they are subject to the "no overlap" condition: no kind terms may overlap unless they are related as species to genus. But in everyday language, it is not only possible for boundaries to overlap and blur—this is one of the most powerful and illuminating situations. Because all are "kind" terms, genre is closely related to the ideas of "medium" and "style." Movies, we might want to say, are simply a medium, within which highbrow and popular genres may be distinguished—horror films, Westerns, art films. Styles are more specific still.[23] The similarity is that all are meaningful generators of social expectations and all are subject to stratification and ranking processes. The problem of the conditions under which media are coextensive with genres is less important than the existence of expectations and reputational hierarchies.[24]

Genre is sometimes used narrowly to indicate certain kinds of "formulas" in the production of cultural objects, such as stories with highly predictable structures that guarantee the fulfillment of conventional expectations: the detective story, the Western, the romance, the spy story. These "formulas" may be conveyed through any number of media (film, television, books, periodicals). Genre may also be used quite broadly: in literature, for example, to designate the very broad types of drama, prose fiction, or lyric poetry, or even the categories of tragedy, comedy, romance, or satire (Cawelti 1976, pp. 1–8; Frye 1953).

"Genre," as the term is employed here, means nothing more than a set of cultural objects that are generally recognized as having significant similarities. Such classification is a social construction, a device that, on the one hand, offers clues as to a producer's intended meaning, and on the other, facilitates criticism through a pragmatic, comparative routine (Griswold 1988). By knowing what kinds of cultural products are generally grouped together, the critic works with known baseline contrasts. By knowing the kind of entity on display, a consumer invokes general expectations for the nature of the cultural experience to be obtained.

DiMaggio's discussion of artistic classfication systems provides the central distinctions. (1987). In one sense genre is a socially defined, ritual classification system that is generated by the social order. In this view, such society-wide characteristics as status diversity, access to higher education, inequality, and intergroup interaction affect the differentiation, degree of hierarchy, universality, and ritual strength of the artistic classification system. By stipulating that a classification is a social construction, based on significant and recognized similarities, one grants, as Griswold puts it, that genre is "neither an assertion of what is actually out there nor a desperate direction of works into convenient categories" (1990, p. 1582).

Genre is used to measure status in the empirical chapters to follow. This is possible because ritual classification systems are related to the "institutional" classifications generated by characteristics of the specific systems that produce and distribute art. Where classifications are widely held within a society, any attempt by commercial or artistic interests to modify or introduce new genres must contend with the cultural authority of preexisting ones and is likely to fail. In the postmodern world, such attempts are likely to be heralded as innovative rather than blasphemous, but ritual and institutional classifications correspond more often than not.

DiMaggio specifies three "industry-specific principles" each influenced by the network of individuals and organizations involved in the production, funding, and regulation of cultural objects (1987, pp. 449–52). *Commercial* classifications are proposed and propagated by profit-seeking agents in modern societies. Since they attempt to enlarge markets for products, their boundaries tend to erode ritual classifications. *Professional* classifications are generated through struggles among artists themselves. Since competition between artists produces a need to innovate and differentiate new genres, these boundaries tend to be narrower and less universal than socially generated ones. *Administrative* classifications are distinctions created by organizations for management purposes. They are not systematically narrower or broader than the ritual classification system. I use them, therefore, as the main indicator of status, dividing genres into "high" and "low" positions on the cultural hierarchy.

Attempts at innovating new genres should be least successful as we ascend the cultural hierarchy because more is at stake. "Theater" has existed since agrarian times, with origins in archaic religious festivals and costumed performers (Southern 1961). But performance types have undergone massive change. In nineteenth-century America, the most popular varieties of theater were pantomimes, imported from France and originally derived from the Italian *commedia dell'arte*, extravaganzas consisting of female dancers with lavish scenery and costuming, variety shows with both stage acts and "waiter-girls,"[25] and minstrel shows based on images of southern Negro folklore (Engel 1967, pp. 3–5). By the turn of the century, these forms had virtually disappeared, replaced by the revue (a series of songs, sketches, and routines) and gradually evolving into musicals and musical comedies.

The distinction between high and popular art does not make sense except with reference to genres. The discussion of high and popular culture does not suppose that individuals possess knowledge of particular cultural objects, but only some knowledge of a *hierarchy of genres*.[26] I have argued that one of the most widely shared elements of modern culture consists in the awareness of which *kinds* of cultural objects are highbrow and which are popular. Therefore, the most important questions of cultural mediation center around *differences* between highbrow and popular genres.

CLAIMS TO DIVERSITY

> True theatre cannot be institutionalized. It is rough, outlaw,
> dangerous, rabid, and might just bite. Like the Fringe. It
> sprawls uncontrollably. It needs a trim.
> —*Andrew Dallmeyer*

As the Fringe grew, it was not just the number of performances that increased but the number of genres as well. A detailed account of Fringe administrative genres is provided in the following chapter. Here I outline the broad features of the development of forms, emphasizing the *importance of diversity claims rather than quality claims*. Diversity is a product of egalitarianism at the Fringe.

The dramatic spectrum is fully represented from classical Greek theater through Shakespeare, Restoration comedy, and the moderns to a profusion of experimental work and political theater including socialist, gay and lesbian, feminist, and Scottish nationalist varieties. Just as the Fringe always provided a forum for smaller and more unusual works in drama, so in music the large concerts by international orchestras at the official festival came to be supplemented by smaller-scale pieces. Poetry readings by the Saltire Society, folk operas in Scots, concerts by local musicians, folk music, miracle plays, puppet shows,[27] and comedy became standard by the early 1960s. In 1965 the Theatre Workshop was formed to promote children's theater, though their shows would not appear in the Fringe program for five more years. The Scottish American Ballet Company was formed for the 1969 Fringe. By the end of the 1960s, the Festival Fringe included examples of all modern Western performance genres.

Though most of its shows were straight-backed, distinguished theater, early Fringe performances heralded genres that persist today. Political theater, broadly conceived, has long been an important part of the high-art world. Its archetype might well be the 1973 publicity photo for Birkenhead Dada: a man sits on toilet with the sign "Art is the diarrhoea of the bourgeoisie." The production of these cultural objects in connection with agitprop theater was viewed as a "tactic" by groups that conceived of their art in instrumental terms, with themes that range from socialism, through Scottish nationalism, to Third World and environmental issues.

Glasgow Unity Theatre, one self-consciously proletarian group, was formed in 1941 by amateurs from various Glasgow clubs who sought a more socially involved theater and aimed for working-class audiences. Unity viewed the first Edinburgh festival as essentially a bourgeois activity and two productions for "the masses" were developed. Though this company lasted only a decade, an Edinburgh Peoples' Festival linked to the Labour Movement ran for two years in the early 1950s (Hutchison 1977, p. 103). These early shows were generally ignored by the critics, probably owing to a dislike of politically tainted theater. To ignore is not to damn but to bewitch—critical silence implies that such art is beneath notice.

Their invisibility did not persist. By the early 1970s, political drama was alive, well, and recognized as a creative force. The most prominent groups were John McGrath's "7:84" company and its offshoot, Wildcat Theatre. Their theater for the working classes was often based on Fringe techniques, ignoring the conventions of traditional drama, even asking the audience to sign petitions after the show (McGrath 1981). Subjects such as the Highland Clearances, the Scottish National Party, the labor movement, and the presence of U.S. interests in Scotland were treated in performances laced with music and cabaret. Such pieces were topical and often extremely professional. Political theater was now part of the world of serious art and regular reviews were guaranteed.

Leftist and avant garde groups attempt to disrupt capitalist or aesthetic performance forms. They seek to undermine the social hierarchy but they reinforce the cultural hierarchy through the earnestness and obscurity of their work. Class consciousness may or may not be involved, but if so, it is only raised through talk about the meaning of the production. The very practices that explicitly seek the destruction of high art solemnify it by participating in subculturally specific discursive moments.

In the 1990s political theater no longer has the socialist cast it once did. A staple of this earlier type of Scottish drama was often working-class, "hard man" characters with subservient women. Now other social justice issues have been brought to the fore by feminist and gay theater companies. Just as the socialist and radical theater of earlier decades attempted to break down the barriers of high art by bringing a kind of "instructional" theater to the working class, the new companies solicit a broad audience. Glasgow Unity Theatre sought to create Scottish plays about ordinary people. Four decades later Clyde Unity Theatre adopted a closely related name, inspired by their ideals to perform plays about another kind of "ordinary people," often lesbian or gay. Shows are typically taken from the Fringe to venues such as a center for unemployed workers or an AIDS hospice. Like many of his socialist predecessors, director John Binnie expresses some antagonism for the idea of "high art":

> I hate plays like [Tom Stoppard's] *Travesties.* You have to know quantum physics and politics in Switzerland in the 1920s. Recently I got into an argument with an American who said that theater should be about Frank Wedekind's *Lulu* kinds of plays—sit for three hours in a heavy, dreech trance. No. A better paradigm is *42nd Street.* It has an essential truth to it.

But it is the importance of talk, the discussion of themes and meaning, that locates political theater *with* and not *against* classical drama.

> Our shows have got to work in two kinds of places. Our last play was a tender lesbian romance. In the housing schemes lots of people have never seen two women kissing. It provokes a reaction. They smoke and burp and talk during the play. We have a workshop afterwards to talk about issues. You get people through the disgust.

Gay and lesbian issues have been raised by popular artists, but theirs is camp humor without any overt political message. Prominent lesbian comediennes attack men no more or less scathingly than other women comics. One of the most controversial artists in recent years is a disabled comic billing himself as Steady Eddie, whose humor depends largely on spastic jokes.

In addition to political theater, Scots theater has two wings, one with its primary support among Edinburghers themselves, middle class and traditional, the other emphasizing original work. Such groups as the Edinburgh People's Theatre secured a niche by presenting works in the Scots language both for ideological reasons and in an attempt to insure a committed local audience. Sponsored by a whiskey firm, they provide an "interval dram" for reviewers. Onstage66 supports its "serious" work during the rest of the year with a drawing-room comedy during the Fringe, while established professional groups such as Communicado and Borderline are invited to perform at the International Festival as well as the Fringe.[28]

The level of "professionalism" at the Fringe has always provoked intense discussion. While professionals were present at the first Fringe, Scottish amateur theater flourished after the war in an atmosphere of enterprise and ardor. A once common perception, now false, is that the Fringe consists mainly of lowbrow material produced by students and amateurs.[29] The Fringe rapidly became a showcase for student and university groups, many of whom specialized in new and innovative productions, or cabaret and revue.

These popular genres received a fair share of press coverage. Since critics were assigned to cover the official festival first, their spare time consisted of "off hours" shows that were more likely to include light entertainment. *After the Show*, first presented by the New Drama Group in 1952, indicates the original function of revue: a series of sketches at the end of the evening's entertainment. For the few London reviewers, this was the main opportunity to view the Fringe in its early years, a fact that helps to explain the visibility and growth of revues, comedy, and cabarets that now occupy all hours of the day. The long-term success of the Cambridge Footlights and the Oxford University Revue began in 1964 when their shows included several of those who would form Monty Python's Flying Circus.

Student groups such as the Oxford and Cambridge University Players developed the practice of living and working together, partly out of financial necessity. This spirit of comradeship and creativity in the use of performance space was quickly associated with the Fringe "style" of drama and remains common practice today for groups of all kinds. According to a London-based Scottish director, "There are twelve of us in one flat. It's boosted the morale being together like that. We'll be happy just to cover our costs. . . . When we audition we try to get people to the pub afterwards to find out whether we can live with them."

Up to two dozen university groups still appear each year, performing not only straight theater but competing in terms of slickness, wit, and cabaret artistry in the "revue" format. The audience knows what to expect when they go to see medical students performing shows such as "The Enema Within," "Satanic Nurses," "The Cunning Linctus." They offer scatological humor, mad doctor jokes, prostate exams, and buffoonery to an audience of *both* students and medical professionals. The humor is bitingly satirical and sometimes interest-group oriented (e.g., opposing government policy toward the National Health Service). Student papers review these productions, but national papers and the *Scotsman*, publicly committed to the review of all first performances, often ignore them.

The perceived association of student groups with lowbrow genres[30] does not hold in practice. They are just as likely to produce experimental or classical theater as comedy. In 1961, an attack by a director on "intellectual" plays was aimed at student groups. Oxford and Cambridge[31] produce both revues and drama, and many other young actors and actresses look to the Fringe to obtain their first dramatic reviews. The National Student Theatre Company, founded in 1977, and the National Youth Music Theatre are based on a national competition and cast from talent at the National Student Drama Festival. The shows are generously supported and highly professional in staging and production. Local authorities send groups such as the Leicestershire Youth Theatre and Nottinghamshire Education that serve as umbrellas for large numbers of performances, many of which have difficulty getting reviewed. They are sometimes seen as "studenty" or "amateurish" productions put on for the benefit of parents and friends.[32]

The relation between professional and amateur performing groups (only some of which are organized by students) has shifted over the decades.[33] Increasing numbers of amateur groups in the late 1950s were associated with a declining presence of professional companies that had performed at the Fringe since the outset. By the mid-1960s the Fringe was mostly an amateur affair, a fact that has had lasting reputational consequences.[34] But during these same years, the Traverse Theatre began to make its reputation at Kelly's Paradise, once a famous brothel in the Lawnmarket. Professional participation began to increase and by 1977 over sixty professional groups were performing at the Fringe.

The assumption that professional groups provide a higher standard of quality and attract larger audiences may not be true. Many groups are specifically formed for productions at the Fringe and die immediately afterward, or after a brief tour. Many young professionals are recent university graduates. With the growth of the Fringe in the early 1970s, the number of professionals had increased to such an extent that they were accused of misusing the Fringe as a place to call on tour rather than a forum for new material: "They just come here to be loved and to play safe."[35]

To what extent are the shows themselves *new*? The question is important because the reputation of an artist, group, or playwright is distinct from the reputation of a work itself. In the case of a new work, little is known in advance about its subject, themes, style—and nothing is known, in principle, about its appeal.[36] This leads to the liability of newness examined in Chapter 7. Even in the earliest days of the festival, as we have seen, there was ample fare to sample. Edinburgh and Oxford, then the dominant university groups, as well as professionals like the London Club Theatre group, were committed to British and world premieres. Since the 1960s there have been large numbers of familiar names and standard dramatic works but the number of original performances grew with the Fringe.

In 1971 nearly fifty new plays presented had, by and large, done poorly at the box office. John Milligan and Allen Wright, arts editor of the *Scotsman*, organized an award for the best original works of theater in 1973. Owing to the size of the Fringe the number of awards, called Fringe Firsts, was not fixed,[37] but the competition was limited to works that had not been performed more than six times in the United Kingdom. This highly visible marker of excellence was an attempt to recognize and promote original work. The number of eligible productions grew to 138 within five years. By 1991, 210 British and world premieres could be seen, while in 1994 there were 296 new theater performances.[38] With an average of four or five awards per week, the chances of winning such recognition are small but not miniscule.

One final aspect of performance variation is often quite mistakenly associated with cultural hierarchy. I have in mind differences in the perceived acceptability of manipulations involving various types of performance, usually associated with sex, violence, sacrilege, profanity, and so forth. More than thirty years ago, International Festival director Ian Hunter was generally appreciative of the Fringe but publicly objected to its "sexy sketches": "while I have anything to do with the Festival we will keep to the articles of association to present the very highest art."[39] As far as the official festival was concerned, the Fringe tended to promote such tastelessness as part of a dangerously lowbrow brand of entertainment. Permissiveness is a familiar avenue for debates over quality and cultural hierarchy, since sex and violence "stretch the margins."

Outrage, both public and private, over performance manipulations involving sex, violence, and blasphemy is an annual feature of the Fringe.

However, these particular moral boundaries are generally unrelated to questions of high and popular art because they are *breached at both ends of the cultural hierarchy*. They shade into pornography, the "lowest" of brows, as well as the sensationalism of highbrow performance art involving irreverence, violence, and nudity. At the Fringe, the limits of permissiveness have been trespassed so often that they can hardly be observed. It is not an exaggeration to say that there are annual controversies because artists, both highbrow and popular, actively court them for the purpose of attracting spectators. Do the breachings constitute the necessary freedom for aesthetic creativity or simply enable objectors to equate serious theater to vulgar entertainment?

In 1962, at the Edinburgh International Drama Conference a naked lady was wheeled into view as part of the first Happening in Britain. This was consistent with the philosophy that "performances" were to be found everywhere and barely heralded the kinds of disrobements, impieties, and oddities that were to follow. A few years later the New York company La Mama presented *Futz*. The bestiality and nudity in this performance mightily stirred the press, though few would admit to having seen it. *Satan's Ball* in 1977 depicted Christ crucified naked. In 1994 a production of *Passion* by Synaesthesia was moved from Greyfriar's Kirk House to another venue because of its erotic depiction of Jesus and Mary Magdalene. Lesbian trapeze artists in *Appetite* (1995) attracted the media with a publicity photo involving nudity for a show that contained none.[40]

A salacious or violent reputation is generally thought desirable in the competition for audiences. A Fringe publicity guide for performing groups explicitly states that "Sex sells." As one actor said, apparently without irony: "We had big debates and finally decided not to use the nudity and violence of the show to sell it. So we just warned people on our posters that it contained this kind of material." Sensationalism does not differentiate highbrow and popular shows. A new American comic was disturbed when spectators walked out of his show owing to its vulgarity. Other artists in his venue congratulated him: "you should be selling out before long." In the late 1980s one student production (entitled *Damage Your Children*) featured a game-show format with a twist: the children of the participants were progressively mutilated. The *Scotsman* reviewer, sharing the horror felt by most spectators, rewrote her review twice[41] trying to make sure she had achieved a consistent and unambiguous text for the readership. Within a day, the review had been magnified and posted as publicity by the group.

Scandal, secured from performances featuring sex, violence, blasphemy, and other audience manipulations designed to shock, is well within the boundaries of the Fringe. In 1995, after years of acerbic commentary on immorality and distastefulness by conservative councillor Moira Knox, an eponymous award was initiated to celebrate the most offensive show on the Fringe. The boundaries of low and high art involve the process of discourse that surrounds such performance manipulations, and have little to do with the character or content of the manipulations themselves.

EGALITARIANISM

Attribution of "festival standard" to Fringe shows (by which one means the International Festival), pays compliment to the official festival without impugning the Fringe. One would *expect* huge variation within such a colossal performance agency. Not just size, but an inclusionary selection process is responsible. The Fringe ethos of aesthetic egalitarianism is, more than anything else, its hallmark. Owing to growth by accretion and the absence of any official administration for more than twenty years of its existence, no means existed to apply criteria to filter the kind of performances that would be offered. This historical contingency has become a bureaucratic principle, the One Commandment.

The right of *any artist* to perform any kind of work, to solicit an audience, and to succeed or fail is important to the ideology of the Fringe. As a principle, the One Commandment of scrupulous fairness was established by the first Fringe Society administrator, John Milligan: "Thou shalt not promote one group above another."[42] As articulated in the 1976 Fringe program: "Artists come . . . at their own risk. . . . Any form of quality control is either by the artists themselves or their public, in a direct, immediate one-to-one relationship, with no middlemen. The essential quality of the Fringe is its spontaneity and complete artistic freedom." But Fringe policy is of no use to the tourist or Edinburgher who has climbed the many steps through Lady Stair's Close and on up the Royal Mile to the Fringe office. Confronted with a thousand shows, the perplexed punter[43] is often advised to "look at the reviews." Bound by policy and ideology but knowing the uneven characteristics of the shows, the staff often demures to the critics. "Read the reviews," they say, "we don't recommend anyone."

With youth groups, amateurs, and a large proportion of new works, variability in every aspect of production is neither surprising nor moot. The Edinburgh Festival Fringe is the largest, but there are other arts festivals that eschew selection mechanisms. This leads to a quandary. From automobile manufacturers to university research institutes, claims about the "quality" of the product are important for promotional purposes. The modern Fringe administration, described in the next chapter, seeks to maximize ticket sales but cannot champion groups or shows. With over a thousand offerings it literally does not know, in any specific sense, what its product *is*. Therefore, it is not an option to promote the quality of Fringe shows, or even to promote the quality of Fringe art as a whole, say, in competition with the International Festival.

In consequence, diversity claims become much more significant.[44] What can be promoted is variety and contrast, the richness of choice. What can be sold to the spectator is a chance, the chance to experience something rare, something funny, something unusual, something bawdy, something pure, something classical. For spectators and critics, a ticket to a Fringe show is a ticket to something *discoverable*. For performers it is different kind of chance. Former administrator Michael Dale stated boldly that it is "wrong to think of groups . . . as being in pursuit of excellence" (1988, p. 61). The act of participation alone is important. But the myth of discovery is important as well, as we will see in Chapter 5.

Mirroring debates over aesthetic merit in the wider society, the discourse of quality often centers on "trends." What's the likelihood that you'll see something good this year? Is it a good year or a bad one? Is artistic excellence increasing or decreasing? One account holds that "quality," that mysterious but still crucial property of aesthetic objects, has decreased with larger numbers of performances—as if "bad art drives out good" or quality were a zero-sum resource. The idea is that the vast increase in quantity has somehow reduced the number of high-quality performances or simply made them impossibly difficult to find. Correspondingly, there have been calls for a limitation on the number of plays offered, appeals for quality control, and more diffuse complaints that the Fringe is simply too large.

But no such policy has ever been brought to the board of directors or seriously considered. The reason is that the alternative account, based on the myth of discovery, is simply too powerful. Quality can be discovered, given the discerning eye, in almost any *kind* of production. Its presence is relatively unpredictable. It may be found in the oddest of places and most peculiar of circumstances. The sheer availability of performances, performers, and types of performances at the Fringe—indeed, in the contemporary art world—has not undermined the idea of merit. Its identification has become a process of "sifting through" the dross for the gems. From the myriad of performance offerings, one searches for the powerful, the delightful, the profound. Whether a student *Hamlet* by Derek Jacobi, the first play by the next Sam Shepard, or side-splitting sketches by Monty Python's successors, spectators and critics hope for a "find."

In this chapter, the origin and development of diversity at the Fringe has been outlined as an introduction to its contemporary organization and administration. There are many who say the Fringe represents the True Spirit of Art, which is, unintendedly I think, to identify that spirit with entrepreneurial capitalism rather than elite patronage. But what they have in mind is the innovative effervescence, the sensation of limitless artistic freedom, the fact that performance is substructure and not merely superstructure. For a month each year, on a craggy firth in central Scotland, Art is King.

Chapter Four

FESTIVALS AND THE MODERN FRINGE

> The Fringe is a loud and blinding firework. You light
> a fuse and stand close.
> —*Richard Crane*

> This is mind-boggling. It's one of the best kept secrets in the
> world. Nothing compares to it. I mean, people had told me
> about it, but even that didn't prepare me.
> —*American actor*

S O DIFFICULT is it to describe the modern festival that journalists and writers who are not natural quantifiers suddenly become
enamored of numbers. They know they cannot see everything.
Their readers know that. Any pose of familiarity with the whole of the
Fringe is transparently fraudulent.

> DID YOU KNOW? If every Fringe performer were to arrive in Edinburgh at the
> same time, they would fill 177 buses! If you went to every single performance
> on the Fringe it would take 3 years, 5 months, and 25 days non-stop! If you
> bought a ticket to every show it would cost £5,851.33! The most enthusiastic
> Fringe goer in 1992 bought 168 tickets for 84 shows! There are 12 Fringe
> performers for every one of Edinburgh's 714 pubs. There are twenty-four
> productions of Shakespeare! (Press release composite)

The tourist is often introduced to Edinburgh's Fringe by a trip to the
main office not far from Waverley Station. Making one's way up the
High Street on a clear August day is as near to performance heaven as
one gets in this world. Arriving at the Fringe office, a hundred meters
below the castle, I collect a dozen leaflets for shows before making it
through the front door. I greet the folks I know and climb the stairs to
collect my press accreditation card, number 544, from the new press
officer. The old one has had a well-deserved nervous breakdown and no
one is a bit surprised. The metaphors that crop up most frequently in
conversations with Fringe staff involve madness: "we're about half-sane
here"; "oh, just the normal craziness."

A new staff member enters the backroom with a shiner. He has removed some illegally posted flyers and been punched in the eye by an
overzealous publicity agent. A tall man prances about, dressed as Hitler
from the waist up, in stockings and garters. He has arrived unannounced

from London without a venue for his one-man Nazi cabaret. There are Kung Fu rappers outside and singing acrobats on a collapsable bed next to the ticket queue. The din is ruthless, phones ringing on all sides. I answer a persistent ring since none of the other ten people in the room notice. Someone wants to know when "The Brass Band" is on: "it's been left out of the program," he informs me. Maybe they're at the "official" festival, I suggest. No? I ask someone. Not the wrong festival, but a year too late. Such confusion is anything but rare.

HOW TO SEE THE FRINGE

Every spectator faces the problem of deciding what to see, but in Edinburgh one is faced with a problem not found at other arts festivals. The program itself is so large that substantial commitment is required simply to familiarize oneself with the choices. Of course, some spectators are more systematic about it than others. Many make no more than a desultory effort. But if you revel in opportunity and are thorough, the task is formidable indeed.[1]

The earliest festival programs by John Menzies simply listed all Fringe shows as "Other Events." By 1954 a special program was produced by Edinburgh printer C. J. Cousland and by the end of the decade even performers with prior reputations could ill afford to trust their own publicity efforts without a listing. During the 1960s, programs ranged from twenty-four to thirty-two pages. When a full-time administrator took charge in the early 1970s, preliminary handbills appeared in March with a circulation of 20,000 nationwide. But the size of the Fringe made this a poor guide, since many groups failed to appear and others came too late. The "official" program appeared in late June, a four-page newspaper with a circulation of 78,000.[2] This practice of issuing the final program barely six weeks before the start of the festival continues through the present. In the mid 1990s, 300,000 programs were distributed annually, consisting of fifty-word descriptions of each show with main listings of over 100 pages (Figure 4.1).

With 1,200 shows and less than a month to see them, efficient organization is imperative. It's not unusual to see people making schedules. When I first met Trisha Emblem, assistant administrator from the Fringe office, she inquired how I had decided what shows to see at my first Fringe. Quite confident of my method, I described the priorities, colorations, circlings, underlinings, schemata, notations, glosses, and annotations required for the most effective allocation of one's precious time. Bemused, she responded with a half dozen alternatives: "I like to collect

BOADICEA THEATRE COMPANY   o |•²•³

Venue 55 - Randolph Studio, Institut Francais d'Ecosse, 13 Randolph Cres. Tickets 225 5366   G4

SAVAGE / LOVE Sam Shepard and Joseph Chaikin's hauntingly familiar journey through the human experience of love. A dynamic, dangerous, raw-edged production by a group of internationally acclaimed performers. Love can be savage and dangerous, no wonder we're afraid to leap into the void to achieve its tender moments.
Aug 15-Sept 3 (not Sun 21, Tue 30) 3.00pm (3.55) £3.50 (£3.00)
Special Offer: Savage/Love with TRANSLUCENT THEATRE's 'Tounges' £5.50

BOB DOWNE AND THE HOLLYWOOD HORNS   °•|•²•³

Venue 33 - Pleasance, 60 The Pleasance. Tickets 556 6550   L11

■ **BOB DOWNE AND THE HOLYWOOD HORNS** The beige sensation is back! From daytime television to bigtime superstar; Australia's king of kitsch has binned his backing tapes and returns to Edinburgh with his own big band for an all-singin', all-dancin', all-polyester 'hysterical homage to the worst showbusiness excesses' *Guardian*
Aug 10-17,21-25,29-31,Sept 2-3 10.20pm (11.35) £7.00 (£6.00)
Aug 19-20,26-28 10.20pm (11.35) £8.00 (£7.00)

BOILERHOUSE   °•|•²•³

Venue 15 - Traverse Theatre, Cambridge Street. Tickets 228 1404.   J5

★ **BOW TO THE BEAST** by Barry Graham. Multiple award-winners Boilerhouse (The Dorm, Infernol, Play, Boy) return with this exhilarating solo performance. Homo Sapiens has proven itself to be the most ungrateful species on earth, killing anyone who offered a message of compassion. Enter the Psychopathic Christ...ADULTS ONLY.
Aug 14,19 12.30pm (1.40) £7.00 (£4.00)
Aug 11,16,20 3.00pm (4.10)
Aug 12,17,21 5.30pm (6.40)
Aug 13,18 8.00pm (9.10)

JANE BOM-BANE   o |•²•³

Venue 42 - Beneath the Spider's Web, 260 Morrison Street. Info 556 4836   J3

■ **JANE BOM-BANE's** in town again ... with her 'eccentric songs' (*Folk Roots*), bellowing pump-organ and round-a-way wrong rhythms and rhymes. Keep your stop-light green and let the 'Queen of the funky harmonium' (*Exploding Cinema*) with her 'majesty and wit' (*Time Out*) send you spinning way beyond the reaches of the Fringe...
Aug 15-27 (not 21) 8.00pm (9.15) £4.50 (£2.50)

BORDERLINE THEATRE COMPANY   o |•²•³

Venue 3 - Assembly Rooms, 54 George Street. Tickets 226 2428   G7

THE ODD COUPLE By Neil Simon. Gerard Kelly and Craig Ferguson star as the infamous duo in this hilarious up-dated comedy classic. Take one anarchic slob and one neurotic hypochondriac. Separate them from wives. Mix together in the same Glasgow flat. Result - a recipe for one seriously funny play.
Aug 15-18, 22-25 3.00pm (5.00) £8.00 (£6.50)
Aug 19,20,26,27 3.00pm (5.00) £9.00 (£7.50)

LORRAINE BOWEN EXPERIENCE   °•|•²•³

Venue 98 - Marco's, 51 Grove Street. Tickets 228 9116   K3

■ **LORRAINE BOWEN EXPERIENCE** Billy Bragg's singing tutor, the Doris Day of 90's Glam, Lorraine takes you by the hand through tales of love, lust and shopping. 'The loveliest, silliest, kindest, kinkiest of British humour' *Vancouver Courier*. 'Thank God somebody knows what the Fringe is supposed to be about' *The List.*
Aug 12-Sept 3 10.00pm (11.15) £5.50 (£4.50)

BOYS OF THE LOUGH   o | 2 •³•

Venue 72 - Queen's Hall, Clerk Street. Tickets 668 2019. Credit Card Hotline 667 7776   M10

■ **BOYS OF THE LOUGH** Shetland fiddle TV star ALY BAIN leads energetic internationally famous, ever-popular, globe-trotting Grammy-nominated Edinburgh favourites! A spirited annual celebration of Scottish and Irish traditional music! With Kerry accordion virtuoso Brendan Begley! Their 15th year of Fringe success. Standing-room-only!
Aug 26-28 7.30pm (9.30) £8.00 (£7.00)

BRADFORD PLAYHOUSE STUDIO GROUP   o |•²•³

Venue 36 - Festival Club, 9-15 Chambers Street. Tickets 650 2395   K9

★ **ENTHUSIASTIC MEN** by the author of 1993's Festival success 'Nativity'. 'The fortunes of five men who spend their holiday working on a steam railway - an excellent mixture of comedy and pathos spiced with keen observations of the frailty deep inside each of us'. *Yorkshire Post* Winner of 1992's Tetley Trophy.
Aug 14-27 3.50pm (5.15) £5.00 (£4.00)

THE BRADSHAWS   °•|•²•³•

Venue 50 - The Music Box, 9c Victoria Street. Tickets 220 4847   J8

THE BRADSHAWS. Buzz Hawkins is the creator of radio's favourite family. He will introduce you to Alf, Audrey and little Billy Bradshaw. An ordinary family living an ordinary life in an ordinary two up two down terraced house. The Bradshaws are real people, anyone who thinks otherwise is fictitious.
Aug 12-Sept 3 6.00pm (7.00) £6.00 (£4.00)

BRAHMA KUMARIS   o |•² ³

Venue 11 - Diverse Attractions, Riddles Court, off Lawnmarket Tickets 225 8961   J8

■ **RETURN TO WONDERLAND** Alice returns to Wonderland to find everything has changed. White Rabbit has gone freelance, Humpty Dumpty is in bits and the Mad Hatter has become sane! A lively family show for children from 3-103 including song, dance, mime, magic and extravagant costumes. Great fun, meaningful message.
Aug 15-20 6.00pm (7.00) £2.00 (£1.00)

THE DREAM OF A RIDICULOUS MAN Streetwise adaptation of Dostoevsky plus Australian Aboriginal Dreamtime equals fantastic journey to a better world.
Aug 8-13 7.30pm (8.45) £2.00 (£1.00)

Venue 115 - Brahma Kumaris Centre, 20 Polwarth Crescent Info 229 7220   L2

RAJA YOGA MEDITATION The antidote to festival fatigue. Regain Peace and Energy with the ultimate medicine - Meditation. Introductions daytime/evenings.
Aug 15-Sept 3 (not 21,28) 10.30am (12.00) Free
Aug 15-Sept 3 (not 21,28) 2.30pm (4.00) Free
Aug 18,18,23,25,30,Sept 1 7.00pm (8.30) Free

JO BRAND & SPECIAL GUESTS   o 1 2 ³•

Venue 59 - Edinburgh Playhouse, 18-22 Greenside Pl. Tickets 557 2590.   G11

BEST OF THE FEST 3 Jo Brand - star of her own highly successful Channel 4 series 'Jo Brand Through The Cakehole' and winner of the 'Club Act of The Year' at the British Comedy Awards returns to Edinburgh for one night only.
Aug 29 11.00pm (1.30) £10.00

BRAVE NEW WORLD THEATRE COMPANY   o |•²•³•

Venue 99 - Hermitage of Braid, 69a Braid Road Info 447 7145   P2 Outer

■ **THE TEMPEST** OPEN-AIR PERFORMANCE! Upon entering the world of 'The Tempest', you will be alone with the elements and Shakespeare's most magical of creations. Witty and entertaining, intelligent and powerful, BRAVE NEW WORLD return to Edinburgh on their most extensive national tour. Come and 'experience' us out in Morningside for 'a breath of fresh air'
Aug 14-Sept 3 2.30pm (4.30) £4.00 (£3.00)

PETER BREAM - PIANO RECITALS   o 1 2 ³•

Venue 31 - St. Cecilia's Hall, cnr Niddry Street & Cowgate.   J10

■ **PETER BREAM - PIANO RECITALS** Three appearances only by the British Pianist. Haydn: Sonata in E Flat Major Hob. XVI/52; Brahms: 6 Klavierstucke Op. 118. Tickets from Fringe Office or at venue 30 minutes before recital.
Aug 30, Sept 1,2 6.05pm (6.55) £5.00 (£3.50)

THE BRIAN COLLECTIVE   °•|•² ³

Venue 19 - C, Over-Seas House, 100 Princes Street. Tickets 225 5105   G7

★ ■ **DUDES WITH DICKS** Physical theatre. A multi-perspective study of masculinity in the Nineties. An all male theatre group confront personal issues of universal importance. A performance that is powerful and visually provocative. By men, about men, for everyone.
Aug 10-20 11.30am (12.15pm) £4.00 (£3.00)

SARAH BRIGNALL   °•|•²•³•

Venue 38 - The Gilded Balloon Theatre, 233 Cowgate. Tickets 226 2151   J9

★ **NIGHTSHIFT** A scary and hilarious new black comedy. There's dirty doings down at the minicab control office where Maisie is all alone. The phone starts to ring but it's not just a taxi the caller's after. Written and directed by the creators of the West End smash hit 'Anorak of Fire'.
Aug 13-Sept 3 2.30pm (3.45) £5.50 (£4.50)

BRI NYLON FIVE   °•|•²•³•

Venue 36 - Festival Club, 9-15 Chambers Street. Tickets 650 2395   K9

AN EVENING OF UNPROTECTED SEX The Double-Act for 94! Resident comperes of Edinburgh's favourite comedy club, Gordon Dempster and Jem Parker now give it to you their way. Teaming up with keyboard maestro and allround smoothster 'Richard', the Nylons have landed! 'Very, very funny' *BBC Radio Scotland*
Aug 13-20,28-31, Sept 1-3 11.45pm (12.40am) £5.00 (£4.00)
Aug 21-27 7.00pm (7.55)

BRISTOL EXPRESS THEATRE COMPANY   °•|•²•³•

Venue 33 - Pleasance, 60 The Pleasance. Tickets 556 6550   L11

A MEETING IN ROME In March 1884, the enfant terrible of Swedish drama, August Strindberg, left for Rome to meet Henrik Ibsen, the revolutionary Norwegian playwright. Michael Meyer, the internationally acclaimed translator / biographer of Ibsen and Strindberg, imagines how the conversation might have gone... Michael Meyer's perfectly proportioned drama' *What's On.*
Aug 12-16,18,21-25,29 4.00pm (5.00) £6.50 (£5.50)
Aug 19,20,26-28 4.00pm (5.00) £7.50 (£6.50)

THE PLAY'S THE THING! (PT 9) The award-winning Bristol Express Festival of New Writing presents rehearsed readings of 4 new plays. 'Distinguished by it's almost unique ability to find writers of genuine interest' *Independent.*
Aug 17 12.15pm (2.45) £3.50 (£2.50)
Aug 20,27 11.00am (12.25pm)
Aug 22 5.30pm (8.00) **See Daily Diary for titles**

27

Figure 4.1 Fringe program page, 1994.

these Fringe systems. Of course, we don't get time to see many shows ourselves."

Fortified with this knowledge and several more years of experimentation I offer a short version of the system. Some practical guidance is never amiss.

First, go through the Fringe program—134 pages in 1995—and tick off everything that looks interesting. Briefly scan the blurbs as you go. That should narrow it down some. Don't be greedy. Limit yourself to, say, no more than 200 shows. Anyone who can't narrow it down to 200 shows is a performance addict and there is no known cure except for participation in the occasional Fringe Marathon.

Next, go back through the shows you've ticked and reread all the descriptions again closely. This time reduce it to 100 possibilities. You can see 100 shows in three weeks, but you will not enjoy it.

Next, make a list and divide it into three or four periods of the day. My personal preference is (1) before six, (2) between six and ten, and (3) after ten. Without much trying, you will find that before ten o'clock your list will be dominated by theater and music, afterward by comedy and cabaret. In the morning, you will get a number of children's shows if you care to start early.

So how many shows can you really see, assuming you've got the full three weeks and a few days of previews?[3] One cabaret reviewer saw over 100 each year except the year her mother died midway through, when she only managed 80. If you go early, stay late, and eat on the run, you can indeed see 4 or 5 shows each day. But it requires a flagon of masochism, and you will find yourself prisoner at your own aesthetic orgy, sulking and miserable. A walk in the Cairngorms or the Pentland Hills is highly recommended on Sundays. Arthur's Seat is high enough, but not far enough away.

The next trick is to schedule your shows, noting the start date on your calendar and the time. Go ahead and schedule four or five per day—figuring you will really see only about three—happily accumulating your well-earned cultural merit points. Since you'll note the *last* date on each entry, you can readily review, each day, your backlog of unseen shows. Should you experience excruciating anguish at the prospect of missing some show approaching its last performance, a longing and anticipated regret at the passing of something never to be witnessed again, why then you cancel your day plan and hasten forth. If Dario Fo or Joe Orton by a youth group from the East Midlands was on your list, you can stay at the pub. There are always a few seemingly unmissable shows around which the remainder can be slotted, but the trick is discovering what they are in advance.

Do you read the reviews? Do you talk to other Fringegoers about what they have seen? Do you attend the hot tip? The rest I leave to your own devices.

FESTIVALS AS DISTRIBUTION SYSTEMS

Festivals are essential distribution systems for the arts, just as a concert season, or a set of record companies, radio stations, and record outlets.[4] The festival setting differs from other kinds of distribution such as Broadway or local programs arranged by entrepreneurs, repertory theaters, and arts councils. Like the theater or concert season, festivals are concentrations of performances in time, often with an explicit aesthetic rationale, whose organization creates both scarcity and abundance through clustering. A festival is a retail outlet on which consumers have converged, an audience actively seeking exposure to a variety of cultural products.

As features of the performing arts world, festivals are increasingly important. The temporal concentration of resources in a local setting enables the recruitment of nationally and internationally known performers and promotes increased interest in the types of art represented (e.g., the recent proliferation of jazz and folk festivals).[5] In 1991, according to a survey by the Policy Studies Institute, there were 527 arts festivals in Great Britain, but most of these are relatively new. Only six festivals were established before the turn of the century, while over half (56 percent) had been established since 1980. Most festivals are held on an annual basis, generally between May and August, and typically last eight to fourteen days (Policy Studies Institute 1992).

Festival settings—whether theater, dance, comedy, music, or a mixture of these—imply concentration. Concentration heightens competition among shows and increases the extent of public awareness by creating a preoccupation for the print and audiovisual media and an increase in informal talk. Festivals formed before 1945 tend to be music festivals, while general arts festivals, constituting 40 percent of all festivals, are a modern phenomenon. Presentation of a multiplicity of genres is typical. Excluding festivals that concentrate on a single art form, the median number of art forms covered by general arts festivals is ten.

Festivals are the laboratories of performance art. In normal settings, including Paris, London, and New York, the art world is "segmented." Cultural density is low owing to temporal and spatial separation. Openings occur at different times and places. The daily routines of rehearsals, work, writing, and marketing take place in different spaces. Temporal concentration at a festival creates a momentary art world bounded by time and place, serving as the focus for interaction among performers, promoters, directors, producers, talent spotters, and playwrights as well as spectators and critics. Moreover, it increases the direct competition between shows for spectators and attention.

GROWTH, COMPETITION, AND CENTRALIZATION

A more or less standardized set of complaints about the Fringe arises every year: "the Fringe is too big"; "there's too much junk"; "the big venues are taking over"; "it's not like it used to be." Such complaints represent more than simply views of the Fringe. They are competing versions of what art should be. A complete account of festivals would consider the social composition and physical arrangement of audiences, the economic and organizational context of decision making, and the internal characteristics of the artworks. But for examining questions of cultural mediation, the main properties of interest are close to the issues raised by the annual litany of grievances at the Fringe: nonselectivity, size, concentration, centralization, and diversity.

Nonselectivity

A Fringe is not planned, as Jonathan Miller once said: it simply accumulates. Not size, but the way that performances reach the public is the central issue. The defining characteristic of a "fringe" is nonselectivity, the use of a "nonjuried" method of accepting performers. Different means are available for implementation, so long as there is no decision-making process based on aesthetic criteria.[6] Selective systems differ in important ways from nonselective systems. The former are designed to incorporate systematic influences on the process of recruitment, insuring that either performers or performances have certain desirable features. Selective systems attempt to reduce risk by filtering out "low-quality" art, or just art that is likely to lose money. The reason complaints about quality are often heard on the Fringe is the absence of such selectivity.

The Edinburgh Fringe is nonselective in that it incorporates all performing groups that apply. It has no preestablished limit, and does not manage performance spaces.[7] Canadian fringes often operate as venue managers and there are limits on the number of shows that are accepted.[8] Generally, a first-come, first-served priority system is used, with percentage quotas for local groups, nonlocal groups, and international groups. In Toronto, local groups are selected using a lottery. Owing to its large and active theater community, so many local groups vied for the limited number of places that suspicions of *covert* selectivity led to the adoption of this dramatically random method in which about one in seven applicants succeed. Each of these nonjuried methods is implemented on an egalitarian principle: no groups are promoted by the administrative organization.[9]

Still, to say that there is no artistic selection or censorship in Edinburgh does not mean there are no constraints. Any individual or group is free to perform, but it must still be able to afford the listing, the travel, the lodging, and contract for a venue.[10] And to say that any group may perform on the Fringe is not to say that any group may perform in any *venue* on the Fringe, as will be discussed. The level of competition between shows is extremely high, but because of the small scale of production the economic consequences of failure are less severe than they might be. You can lose your shirt, but not your house.

Size

The sheer size of the Edinburgh Fringe—whether a gleeful opportunity or a terrifying monstrosity for the spectator—is ideal for a systematic assessment of the cultural mediation hypothesis. The volume of performances on the Fringe reflects the "massification" of culture but more in the sense of cultural supply than the search for profit. Most groups do not go expecting financial gain. The fact that most shows do well to break even is widely known and not a deterrent.[11] The total number of shows is some unknown function of the amount of aesthetic energy available and the attractiveness of Edinburgh as a performing site. One London-based director owned that all she had to do was place an advertisement in *Stage and Television Today*: "I had 200 phone calls and auditioned 40. Going to the Fringe is the draw. Later people called up saying 'I'm desperate to go to Edinburgh.'"

Given the size of the festival as a whole, the concentration of performances in Edinburgh each record-setting August is the most intense in all of human history. The growth characteristics of the Fringe depend on whether we take the number of groups or the number of shows as our criterion. A graph of the number of performing groups (Figure 4.2) takes the logistic form that characterizes many growth phenomenon.[12] From small beginnings in the 1950s there is gradual but relatively smooth development in the 1960s, followed by rapid growth in the 1970s and a leveling off in the 1980s. In recent years the number of groups increases again, though slightly. Although there is no precise "takeoff" point, by the early 1980s the present size had largely been

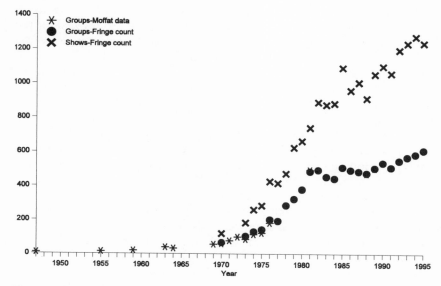

Figure 4.2 Growth of the Fringe, 1947–1995.

reached. Nearly 500 groups appeared on the Fringe in 1982. Subsequently, the number of performing groups has fluctuated at around 500 until the recent growth period.

Growth in the number of shows was more rapid in the 1980s than the 1990s but has been relatively continuous since 1970, as Figure 4.2 illustrates.[13] To put this in perspective, few arts festivals in the world today can boast as many as 100 distinct shows. The average festival in Great Britain hosts two dozen performances or events (Policy Studies Institute 1992). Yet in the past quarter century the number of shows at the Fringe has *increased a full order of magnitude*, from 120 in 1970 to 1,237 in 1995. In the decade since 1985 it has only twice failed to reach 1,000. Both fascination and anxiety have always accompanied the presentation of statistics on the size of the Fringe. By 1988 the central office sought to allay the fears of performing groups—as well as Edinburghers themselves—by claiming that the Fringe was getting smaller: "the idea that the Fringe gets bigger and bigger every year is an urban legend." Yet that claim relied on the extraordinarily large 1985 festival. By the late 1980s the number of shows began to increase once more and since 1990 set new records nearly every year. One hesitates to make predictions about the future size of the festival.

Behind the anxiety is a question: how can the Fringe keep getting bigger without an adverse impact on the size of the audience? Competition for audiences is extremely intense and the fear is that the growth of

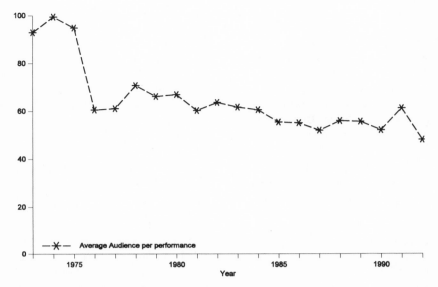

Figure 4.3 Average audience size, 1973–1992.

the festival is outpacing the growth of its public. Since 1970 the number of individual performances (not shows) has increased from 700 to over 13,000. Average audience size may be calculated by dividing estimated total ticket sales by the number of performances. Figure 4.3 indicates that the audience for a typical performance has indeed declined over the years. Even if we discount the exceptionally high counts for the early 1970s, there is a gradual decline in the number of paying customers from the late 1970s through the early 1990s. Average audience size is lower in the 1990s than at any other period. Performers look out over audiences that are half the size they were twenty years ago.

But the average number of performances for a given show has not remained constant: companies have tended to play longer runs in order to recoup costs. The mean number of performances per show increased from 5.83 in 1970 to 10.52 in 1994. So while the average number of spectators per show is only half as many as two decades ago, the average number of performances has nearly doubled. That is, *the average number of tickets sold per show has remained relatively constant since the mid-1970s.* Indeed, the two least successful years occurred in the late 1970s. Ticket sales in 1991, with well over 1,000 shows, were better than in 1979, with only 426 shows on offer. The average Fringe show does not have smaller audiences than in the past, but with longer runs there are fewer spectators for each performance. It is easy to see why competition among groups is serious and reviews seem more important.

Concentration

The fascination of critics, tourists, performers, and even Edinburghers with the Fringe has as much to do with the experience of *compression* in time and space as sheer size. Apart from the major urban centers of art and cultural accomplishment, large gatherings for performance purposes are generally limited and sporadic. The festival experience shifts cultural objects to the foreground. Culture is unavoidable—or avoidable only by intentional concentration on daily routine. You trip over it if you do not watch your footsteps.

In Edinburgh, shows are concentrated within a three-week period in August.[14] Groups commit to a specific number of performances in advance. Though extended runs are possible, they rarely occur even for successful shows because audiences rely on the preprinted program. Competition for audiences is further intensified by the clustering of two dozen or more performances on certain days and times. Each day, a listing called the *Daily Diary* is produced in broadsheet format (front and back) and distributed free at many venues throughout the city (Figure 4.4). This provides an overview of all Fringe shows at each time period. At peak periods over a dozen performances may have simultaneous start times—and, of course, these shows also compete with the International Festival as well as several other festivals.

Concentration of performances also involves a spatial dimension. Although early Fringes utilized spaces as far away as Dunfermline, the geographical boundaries of the Fringe did not expand much until 1966 with performances in Portobello and on Morningside Drive south of the city center. Although the local audience grew as venues on the outskirts came into use,[15] transportation difficulties and the surfeit of choice in the downtown area reduce the potential audience of tourists and visitors.[16]

Figure 4.5 provides a schematic map that designates each venue by number. Such maps are stapled into the Fringe program and used by audiences as their main guide in finding shows. Code numbers are keyed to locations. The pattern of venues is determined by the architectural history of the city, itself shaped by the topography of the landscape and urban development dating to the eighteenth century. Venues may be divided into three concentric circles.

As indicated by the directional arrows pointing off the map, a small number of venues would be considered outlying. Here, actual and psychological "distances" coincide.[17] Taxis to these areas are expensive and buses to these areas run less frequently. Sometimes—I speak from experience—they stop running before the end of a late performance. The tourist located in the city center thinks hard before venturing forth.

8.00 p.m.

MURDER IN THE CATHEDRAL   (9.30 p.m.)
Aethelflaed
45—Old St. Paul's Church & Hall   H10

PIETER DIRK UYS   (9.30 p.m.)
Assembly At The Meadows
116—Assembly At The Meadows   M8

NICK REVELL   (9.30 p.m.)
Assembly Rooms
3—Assembly Rooms   G7

MUSIC SESSIONS   (Midnight)
Ceilidh House
9—The Ceilidh House & Tron Jazz Cellar   J10

RABBIE BURNS YER TEA'S OOT!—THE MSFITS
THEARE CO   (9.30 p.m.)
Diverse Attractions
11—Diverse Attractions   J8

OBSCURITY KNOCKS   (10.00 p.m.)
The Festival Club / Adam House
36—Festival Club   K9

MASQUE OF ROSSLYN 1398-1993   (10.00 p.m.)
Glen Theatre
118—Rosslyn Chapel   P1 Outer

RED HOT DUTCH WITH DOMINIC   (9.00 p.m.)
Dominic Holland
33—Pleasance   L11

* A STRANGE BIT OF HISTORY   (9.00 p.m.)
In-Theatre Bratislava Csfr
41—Hill Street Theatre   G7

KIT & THE WIDOW—STUFFED AND MOUNTED
(9.10 p.m.)
Kit & The Widow
47—The Cafe Royal   G9

* STILL CRAZY AFTER ALL THESE YEARS
(9.00 p.m.)
Helen Lederer
3—Assembly Rooms   G7

* THE TENDER MERCIES   (9.30 p.m.)
Mania Productions
21—Roman Eagle Lodge   J7

* MY BOOZE HELL BY LITTLE JOHNNY
CARTILAGE   (9.00 p.m.)
Johnny Meres
51—Stepping Stones Theatre   J7

WHISKY GALORE   (9.45 p.m.)
Prime Productions
13—Harry Younger Hall   H12

THE THIRD POLICEMAN   (9.45 p.m.)
Ridiculusmus
119—Calton Centre   G13

THE ORANGE PENGUIN   (9.15 p.m.)
Risk Theatre
98—Marco's   K3

DAVE SILK'S SHINY STOCKINGS   (9.45 p.m.)
Dave Silk Jazz
39—Anderson's   K5

MARK THOMAS   (9.00 p.m.)
Mark Thomas
3—Assembly Rooms   G7

* BLOODSTREAM—ANDREW BUCKLAND
(9.45 p.m.)
Traverse Theatre
15—Traverse Theatre   J5

* CLEVER BOY   (9.00 p.m.)
The Vaults
18—The Vaults   J10

TONIGHT: LOLA BLAU   (9.50 p.m.)
Studio Thy '81—Theatre Miriam
73—Edinburgh College Of Art   K7

8.10 p.m.

THE SAME OLD STORY   (9.45 p.m.)
Downtrodden Theatre Company
82—Southside '93   L10

8.15 p.m.

* SEMI-PRECIOUS   (9.30 p.m.)
Dinosaur
70—Caledonian Club   F8

* LYSISTRATA   (9.45 p.m.)

* ALAN PARKER—URBAN WARRIOR—LIVING ON
THE EDGE   (10.00 p.m.)
Alan Parker—Urban Warrior
33—Pleasance   L11

* PARSONS AND NAYLOR'S RICH GREEN PAGEANT
(10.10 p.m.)
Parsons And Naylor
51—Stepping Stones Theatre   J7

TESTING   (10.00 p.m.)
Ricochet Dance Company
62—St Bride's Centre   K1

* GREEN ARE MY PASTURES   (10.15 p.m.)
Spokesong Theatre Company
98—Marco's   K3

* A NEWER WILDERNESS   (10.30 p.m.)
Tartan Rose Theatre Company
43—Royal Museum Of Scotland   K9

BLOOD AND GUTS—THE DOUG ANTHONY
ALLSTARS   (10.30 p.m.)
Doug Anthony Allstars
2—Fringe Club   L8

FRINGE CLUB DISCO   (2.30 a.m.)
The Fringe Club
2—Fringe Club   L8

LES EPIS NOIRS   (10.30 p.m.)
F.E.A.S.T. At The Fringe
73—Edinburgh College Of Art   K7

* THE CITY IN THE SEA—LA PINGUICOLA SULLE
VIGNE (ITALY)   (10.30 p.m.)
Theatre Workshop
20—Theatre Workshop   D6

9.10 p.m.

EDMOND   (10.40 p.m.)
Ardour
101—Rifle Lodge   F10

9.15 p.m.

ATTILA THE STOCKBROKER AND JOHN OTWAY
(10.30 p.m.)
Attila The Stockbroker And John Otway
46—Church Hill Theatre   N3

* IN HIGH GERMANY   (10.00 p.m.)
C
19—C Theatre   G7

JENNY ECLAIR—PEROXIDE COMEDY
(10.15 p.m.)
Jenny Eclair
33—Pleasance   L11

* THE ANGEL AND THE BOUNCER   (10.30 p.m.)
Glitteris
33—Pleasance   L11

SICK AS A PARROT   (10.15 p.m.)
Parrot
51—Stepping Stones Theatre   J7

* LYON RAMPANT   (10.45 p.m.)
The Vaults
18—The Vaults   J10

JULIAN COPE   (11.00 p.m.)
Julian Cope
2—Fringe Club   L8

9.20 p.m.

AS IS   (10.50 p.m.)
Frantic Theatre Company
4—Theatre Zoo   J7

KIT & THE WIDOW —STUFFED AND MOUNTED
(10.30 p.m.)
Kit & The Widow
47—The Cafe Royal   G9

9.30 p.m.

ASIAN MUSIC CONCERTS   (11.00 p.m.)
Acoustic Music Centre
36—Festival Club   K9

I'LL TELL YOU WHAT HAPPENED...
(10.45 p.m.)
Milton Keynes Madness
66—Scottish Health Service Centre   C2

GODS OF GLAM   (11.30 p.m.)
Platform One—Live!
96—Platform 1   H5

Figure 4.4 Portion of *Daily Diary* page, 1994.

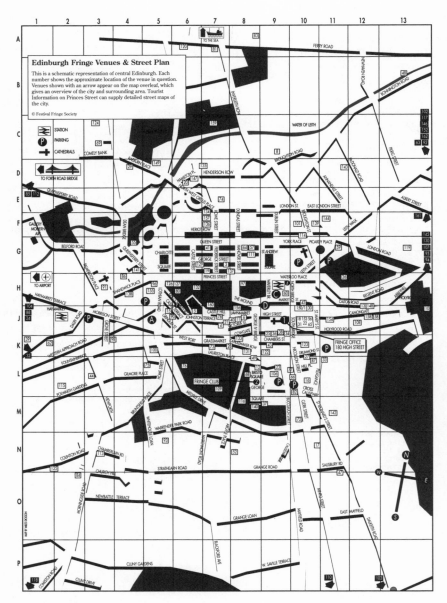

Figure 4.5 Map of Fringe venues, 1994.

A second, narrower circle is based primarily on physical distance from the center but barriers of transportation, geography, or familiarity are still important. These may be distinguished from the "inner circle" venues coveted by groups and preferred by audiences. Rental costs for performance space reflect this circumstance. The city center is roughly located at an eighteenth-century garbage dump called the Mound, where now stand the National Gallery of Scotland and the Royal Scottish Academy. The central venues are located within a ring from the outskirts of the Georgian New Town in the north (the Theatre Workshop, St. Stephen's Hall), around the unfinished "parthenon" of Calton Hill and Holyrood Palace at the bottom of the Royal Mile, to the south at the Queen's Hall and the Bruntsfield Links, where King James teed off the earliest games of golf. Marco's Leisure Center marks a kind of boundary to the west, beyond which one must be adventuresome.

Concentration in time and space has artistic consequences, as we saw in the preceding chapter. In addition to stylistic consequences, the premium on central spaces has tended to reduce the duration of performances. One-hour performances, which are not unusual for comedy outside the festival setting, have also become common for theater.[18] Longer performance slots are often simply unavailable and one adaptation is simply a reduction in the running time of shows. A second is that much new writing is timed for this constraint. Performances of "reduced Shakespeare" in which all of the Bard's plays are performed in under an hour, or medleys of plays, are a related result. Finally, this reduction in the time of performances has coincided with the increase in comedy (to be discussed) and effected a kind of short comedic play for one or two actors, often written by a stand-up comic who wants to expand his or her range. Such a genre will not stand on its own as an evening's entertainment, but on the Fringe, where shows are not expected to last much longer than an hour, they are a useful adaptation.

Centralization

The Fringe had its origins in spontaneous accretion around the official festival. From the chaotic press launch through the crush of performers at the Fringe Club to the virtual Renaissance Fair of Fringe Sunday, there is a sense of wild, aesthetic release and disorderly creativity. But the organizational structure that operates the Fringe must be seen in relation to its environment, in terms of both the acquisition of resources and the functions it performs for performing groups, public, and press. It facilitates and promotes art, but not specific instances of art. An arrangement for enabling and maximizing the number of performances, facilitating the flow of information about those performances, and organizing the purchase of admission, the Festival Fringe Society has developed structures that expand and contract according to the annual cycle.

The operational goal of the society is the provision of a framework for the distribution of performance art on the principle of self-selection. The cost of membership in the society is trivially small. It is run by an elected board, but the most significant structure is the permanent administrative office. While formally bureaucratic, with a continuously employed staff bound by regulations set by the board of directors, the office is shaped by the constraints posed by the production technology it organizes.

Because the "units" involved are performances, no sequential or functional dependence of activities constrains the behavior of individual companies.[19] Even the temporal formation of groups is variable. Each company or venue operates with relative autonomy. The notion that the Fringe is "unorganized" is a misnomer. Rather, it is organized to ensure a high level of decentralization. The society does not match groups with venues, or regulate the relationships between them. The setup of performance spaces, licensing, box office, and conversion of vacant spaces to theatres is left to the groups themselves and the venue managers they contract. Though the activities of the administrative organization have expanded significantly with the growth of the Fringe, it does not "control" the artistic offerings: "That's the great and frightening thing about this organization. If this whole building were zapped away by a UFO, something would still happen in the summer. We organize and harness it, but we're powerless to stop it."

The evolution of specific forms of organization occurred in fits and starts, but the more sophisticated systems of information management have developed during the past ten years. In 1951, Edinburgh University students set up a reception center for student performers, providing meals and accommodation. The first attempt to organize an "official unofficial" festival in 1954 was unsuccessful owing to reluctance by groups who held "higher" aspirations—namely, an invitation to the International Festival. In 1955 a central box office and a performers' restaurant was opened in the Old College building of the university, but lost money because of disuse by professionals who apparently saw it as a "student" arrangement. A Fringe Club, box office, and information bureau were opened in the YMCA in 1959.

The Festival Fringe Society first formed in 1958 at the initiative of Michael Imison, director of the Oxford Theatre Group. Only eight groups appeared at the organizational meeting, partly due to the "curious slip-up" that no professional groups were invited (Moffat 1978, p. 43). Another meeting was held, representing less than 40 percent of the groups on the Fringe. A management committee was supplemented by representatives from "established" performing groups. Such groups benefited from the informal organization of the Fringe and were unlikely to propose any fundamental changes. The Fringe could remain open to the needs of the groups, avoid moves toward greater selectivity, and remain focused on the objective of providing access to audiences during the festival period. In 1969 this society was incorporated as a company with charitable status, governed by a board with seven directors, in which groups could be members.

Most of the present functions of the society were established at the outset and performed on a volunteer basis. No professional administrator was appointed until 1970 and then only part time. The society provided for the publication of a complete program, an information bureau and club, and a central box office. These basic services are still provided and constitute the core functions of the administrative office.

John Milligan, the first administrator, took a full-time position in 1972. He organized a Fringe Club on the Royal Mile, providing food and drink for performers who held their own cabaret each night.[20] A permanent staff of five now operates the Festival Fringe Society on the High Street below Edinburgh Castle. The most significant constraint for this organization is the annual cycle that culminates in a thousand August performances. Performers and directors commit only to produce a show sometime during the next festival, a decision that can simply be revoked through cancellation.

Since one of the main problems in organizing for the arts is the conflict between the demands for planned activities and organizational certainty and the alleged indifference of the creative muse (Blau 1988b, p. 275), the solution invoked by the Fringe organization is both flexible and adaptive. Staff size reflects this annual cycle, from the addition of temporary help in April to the peak of some sixty-five workers hired during the festival for administration, box office, press office, and Fringe club. Revenue is generated by grants, sponsorship, and the groups themselves. A participation fee is charged to performing groups, plus a fee for each program listing and 7.5 percent commission on tickets sold through the Fringe box office.[21] Direct marketing of souvenirs and other merchandise has become increasingly important in recent years.

The modernization of the Fringe office began in early 1986 under the administration of Mhairi Mackenzie-Robinson and Trisha Emblem. A large fund-raising campaign allowed the Festival Fringe Society to lease and renovate a building on the High Street below St. Giles Cathedral. These permanent premises opened in 1988 and a new array of information services followed.

To assist spectators in selecting shows, a Fringe Find service was developed, consisting of a terminal-based search system located at several points throughout the city that allowed spectators to search for shows by genre, time of day, group, and recently by theme. This local facility was a precursor to the development in 1995 of a World Wide Web site, an internet facility allowing those with a computer, modem, and graphics capability to scan Fringe events from anywhere in the world.[22] The entire Fringe program is available electronically at the same time as the publication of the printed version, with the advantage that each late entry, program change, and cancellation is immediately reflected in the searchable database. After a show or group is selected, a link is available to the city map to facilitate its location. Remote users are allowed to enter their own reviews of shows and make comments about groups.[23]

In 1992, ticket sales were computerized. The box office now had accurate information on ticket availability for all shows as well as immediate counts of sales afterward, a process that formerly took weeks. Tickets could be distributed from the Fringe Office by post and phone as well as through several remote locations. The permanent staff grew to undertake expanded marketing functions and in-house merchandizing of Fringe paraphernalia.

Performers at the Fringe are geographically diverse, as shown in Table 4.1 in Appendix D. Although 86 percent are from England and Scotland, for most foreign performers it will be their first appearance in Edinburgh. In light of this diversity, attempts were made to improve conditions for international groups with the addition of an invited foreign member of the board. Work permit rules were changed, exempting foreign players from the need for permits to appear at the Fringe.

From the end of one year's ticket count until the appearance of the next year's program, the primary function of the office is the provision of information to performing groups rather than to the public. Groups are conscientiously "educated" in the mechanics of a Fringe appearance, a service that is viewed as an attempt to level the playing field for newcomers. A series of monthly bulletins is produced, explaining the nature of the festival, alternatives of time, space, and scheduling, how to rent a venue, information on public entertainment licenses, typical forms of publicity and press listings, and the printing of tickets and posters.[24] In the late 1970s, because of the large number of English performers, annual meetings were initiated in London to advise and train groups in the process of appearing on the Fringe. Since U.S. performers are the next largest group, these meetings were expanded to U.S. locations in 1993.

Equally significant changes are related to the expansion of media functions. As the number of performances grew, media coverage increased. The mid-1980s saw more space devoted to the Fringe by London-based papers, some of which set up special Edinburgh offices for the duration of the festival. Interest by foreign journalists increased as well. Television and radio coverage mushroomed and was regularized in a number of feature programs. As media demands on Fringe staff increased, a full-time press officer was designated. Although companies had sent clippings, recordings, and press releases to the Fringe office for many years, the first full-scale press office opened in 1989.

The variety of services provided is a response to the staggering conjunction of journalists and performances. Registration of journalists is encouraged but remains voluntary. The press office issues accreditation cards to hundreds of journalists, broadcasters, and researchers.[25] From one-third to one-half of press cards are issued to the radio and television personnel whose numbers have been increasing. Press tickets for the shows themselves are issued directly from the office, but many journalists, registered and unregistered, pick up tickets directly from the venues. Few companies outside of the largest venues are concerned with these niceties when a reviewer appears at the box office wanting tickets.

While the box office caters to the public, the press office caters to reviewers, journalists, and performing groups. While the box office is impartial both in principle and practice, the press office is more directive. Here the primary goal is to promote festival coverage, with information provided in two directions. Artists seek to generate previews, reviews, and stories about their shows, so information about news media is extremely valuable. They seek contact names and phone numbers as well as clues to standard practices. Some groups hire special promoters to generate press coverage but this is rare.[26]

For journalists, certain kinds of information will improve the chances of finding material. It is recognized that some shows are better grist for the journalistic mill and, besides, many writers in Edinburgh for only two or three days do not relish being left on their own for ideas, particularly if it is their first festival. As a Fringe press officer notes, "There are basically two categories of press: those who've done homework and those who haven't. For those who haven't we do their homework for them. We'll provide a list of shows." This guidance extends to editors, planners, researchers, feature writers, reviewers, and previewers, as well as television and radio producers. "We try to steer people if they tell us what they want. They'll say 'what's going with dance?' or 'what new comedians are there?' We don't say what the best shows are but *what* are you after? Hone them down by genre."

Information is organized in several forms to provide a bridge between performers and press:

  1. A file of information on newsworthy events (often produced by the companies themselves), including information on photocalls and stunts as well as "mishaps, mayhem, and miracles of various sorts—accidents, weddings, births, adventures, sudden fame or infamy."[27]

  2. A diary of events such as press launches, conferences, and events organized by Fringe groups as well as the other Edinburgh festivals.

3. A photographic library containing the black-and-white photographs supplied by most Fringe companies as well as color transparencies to be used in previews, features, and reviews.

4. An audio and video library consisting of videos, cassettes, and compact disks of material provided by Fringe groups.

5. A reviews database generated by daily scanning of the major papers (all fringe company previews, news items, and reviews are entered by date and publication in a database, then pieces are cut and filed for use both by performing groups and journalists).

6. A contact list providing names of all fringe groups, their contact person, and phone numbers.

7. A database of companies and shows, which includes information about show themes, authors, place of origin, awards, famous names and relatives, strange hobbies or talents, and other points of interest.

Journalists often lounge in the upstairs press office. They scan papers, drink coffee, and chat about what they've seen. For the machine-minded press, the database provides an easier and more comprehensive search than the more traditional technique, word of mouth. Journalists search for information by keywords or topics using computers in the press office. While the most prominent critics have the freedom to select shows, others will have shows assigned to them by editors. For longer pieces, there is always a search for an angle, for links between shows that can provide focus.

Although mornings are reserved for press visits, afternoons are also open to Fringe companies who come for information and tips on getting the coverage they so ardently desire. A detailed guidebook is sent to Fringe groups before the festival, consisting of advice for planning press and marketing campaigns.[28] A media directory is included along with a special section of reviews and advice from various journalists and broadcasters. During the festival, performers can find out which members of the press have seen their show using the database of press tickets. They examine the database, looking for the reviewers, the dates the show was attended, and making note of press affiliations. Like the main office downstairs, during its peak of approximately 10 to 12 days the pace of the press office is "head spinning and relentless. The phones go literally every minute and each call is an urgent request. Meanwhile there is one person desperately needing your attention in front of you and anything from two to fifteen journalists and Fringe companies waiting to speak to you after that" (1993 Press Report, p. 43 [unpublished]).

New groups are at a disadvantage and need special assistance. Some performers have gone into debt simply to come to Edinburgh and now they are locked in competition with over 1,000 other shows, many by well-known artists. To offset the advantages of large venues with separate press offices, groups at small venues get more staff time: "For struggling groups we produce little marketing plans, for example one [group] at Randolph Studios. Their first press release was bad—no mention of previous crits and they were doing poorly. We resent the press release, to try and get the materials to target audiences." The egalitarian ethos makes itself felt, but in continual tension with the disposition of journalists to cover the performance news, not to miss "what everyone else is writing about": "I can say which shows are getting the most press coverage. . . . This has happened a lot—[journalists] looking for a 'smash hit' to cover." This tendency can create "the buzz," a process of accumulative advantage in which certain shows receive an initial coverage that is self-reproducing. News media with less space for festival coverage often restrict themselves to highly visible groups, which amplifies coverage for those that have already been previewed, reviewed, and featured:

> You get some excellent journalists and critics at the Fringe but even amongst some of them the struggle to educate goes on, the struggle to instil a sense of artistic adventure in their lazy, cynical souls. . . . We must caluculate the risks for the more wary and guide them in a direction we feel will produce a positive response. This involves a certain amount of selection but as with most of our work with the press it is selection based on the journalists's need. (1993 Press Report, p. 49)

It should now be clear that the Fringe is anything but disorganized. Although its name suggests an amorphous entity, the idea that it lacks structure or is "deliberately unorganized" is a pleasant fiction that supports the egalitarian ideology. The pressures on the box office (from spectators) and press office (from journalists and performers) occasion the perennial conundrum: how to promote *all* of the shows without seeming to promote *any* of them.

Diversity

Self-selection of groups in a context where costs are not exorbitant insures abundant variability in terms of performances. The Fringe attracts all but the most lavish and expensive productions. Participants range from groups with international reputations to companies of teenagers staging their first play. Comedians with weekly television series share venues with amateurs and "mavericks"[29] such as a Japanese millionaire producing a series of plays about "geniuses." In the early 1990s productions ranged from the standard repertoire of theater and classical music to improvisational theater, late-night performances in a traveling lorry, a nine-minute play based on a modern seaside postcard, grand-piano nose-balancing, zippo lighter and dustbin percussion, a seven-member sibling choir, and student examinations.

Discourse practices as well as administrative classifications actively maintain the genre distinctions that constitute the core of the cultural hierarchy. Sometimes it is not even clear to artists what kind of thing a particular performance *is* because of ambiguities in classification systems. But their classification decisions—the selection of a particular *category* for their show—help to determine how it will be perceived and evaluated.

In the preceding chapter we saw that classification into genres has both cognitive and organizational implications. For the Fringe, the establishment of performance classifications in the program itself was a decision to provide information and reduce complexity for spectators, since people recognize that their own preferences lean toward particular types of shows. "Genre" summarizes and compresses these expectations in terms of culturally relevant categories.

It was 1973, a full quarter century after the Fringe began, before the program included a system of categorization by genre. This "Index of Show Titles" appeared before an alphabetical listing of performing groups. The only feasible way of implementing such a system was to allow the *companies themselves* to select the appropriate genre for each of their shows from a preestablished list.[30] As a result of the inherent ambiguity that attends many performance pieces, this classification is often viewed as a strategic decision. The "genre problem" ("What *kind* of object is this?") is applicable not only to production and review but to marketing in systems with high levels of competition.[31]

The diversity of the Fringe may be measured by the large *number* of categories that are used for this index and the relatively even *distribution* of shows across categories. As Table 4.2 in Appendix D shows, twenty-three separate categories were used in 1994 to cover the gamut of Fringe offerings. Several of these are explicitly "combined" categories. Theater is the dominant genre, with over one-third of all shows, but the percentage of shows in any one category quickly drops. Comedy represents the next largest genre, with 13 percent of the total, but no other category has more than 10 percent.

Decision processes by performers that enter into such classification are opaque to spectators and reviewers but affect the mediation process. Self-description is generally accepted by critics and editors as well as the Fringe office. Editorial classification has implications because of the size of the "review hole," the space that newspapers and magazines will devote to arts criticism. Some newsmedia do not classify, preferring name-of-show headlines. But given preestablished space allocations to particular sorts of shows, some genres have greater chances of receiving a review than others.[32]

The Growth of Comedy

> Now the Fringe is just Channel 4 stand-up comedians.
> It's not really fringe at all.
> —*Scottish director*

Figure 4.2 showed that the Fringe reached a kind of equilibrium during the 1980s in terms of the number of shows and groups. The distribution of shows across genres has changed, however. The Fringe is not an independent engine that controls the flow of activity in the art world but a reflection of larger developments in the performing arts. In the recent past, first in the United States and then in London, comic forms have experienced a substantial rise in popularity. Since the Los Angeles comedians' strike of 1980, comedy in the United States grew rapidly and the growth of comedy in the United Kingdom is largely parallel. Many think it has continued longer in the United Kingdom, while in the United States it peaked during the mid 1980s when there were over 300 comedy clubs, a number that has fallen by half.[33]

The most significant changes in performance categories, based on the "Index of Show Titles" are examined from 1982 through 1994 in Figures 4.6 and 4.7. Theater remains the single dominant genre. While there was slight growth in the number of dramatic works in the 1980s, the number of shows peaked in 1988 and has since fluctuated. During the same time period a vivid change has occurred within the popular genres. Figure 4.6 shows a gradual and continual increase in the number of shows categorized as comedy from 18 in 1982 to a peak of 183 in 1993. Kevin Day, the English comedian, described this trend perfectly without any knowledge of the time series provided here: "About 1985 comedy took off [at the Fringe]; 1987 was the first big year people really *noticed* a lot of comedy. Now it's plateaued here. It won't get any bigger." What seems clear is that, consistent with the upsurge of interest on both sides of the Atlantic, "stand-up" and other comic forms that emphazise jokesmithing, one- or two-person sketches, and often music in the service of laughter have become a more significant part of the performing arts than they were prior to 1980. The pattern for comedy is even clearer in Figure 4.7, which shows this growth does not apply generally across popular forms. Cabaret performances grew along with comedy in the mid 1980s but then declined, while revue has fallen off consistently. In the early 1980s revue was more popular than either cabaret or comedy. Yet by 1990 the number of revues was half what it was in the early 1980s. In 1994 there were fewer revues than poetry readings (Table 4.2).

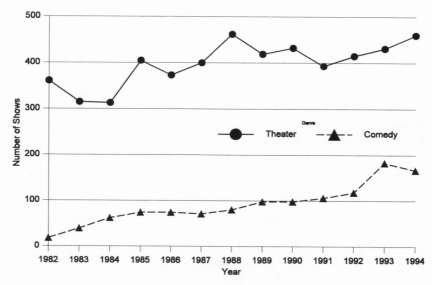

Figure 4.6 Fringe theater and comedy, 1982–1994.

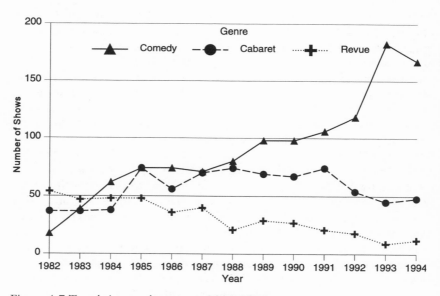

Figure 4.7 Trends in popular genres, 1982–1994.

Since classifications are self-generated some of this shift is a result of contingent assignments. That is, a minority of assignments could have been different had the group simply decided to characterize the show as theater rather than comedy or revue rather than cabaret. To this extent, classifications indicate *perceived shifts* in the popularity of genres. Yet by any measure, the number of stand-up comics who populate the clubs and spill over into the morning hours in hopes of discovery by the BBC Light Entertainment department has increased significantly since the early 1980s.

Special previews and discussions of comedy offerings are now prominent in nearly every newspaper with substantial Fringe coverage. Headlines such as "Comedy Rules the World" are common, while some proclaim that "comedy is the new rock 'n' roll." Growth and competition have promoted high levels of innovation within the form. Comedy is no longer simply joke telling and the spread of observational, storytelling, and physical comedy is the result. Most important in the British context is the rise of Alternative Comedy with a new generation of comedians who rejected both traditional sexist and racist humor and whose scorn for the Conservative government was clear (Wilmut and Rosengard 1989). This efflorescence did not mean the disappearance of traditional pub comics. Soon alternative, "politically correct" comics were joined by "anti-" or "postalternative" stand-ups who did not share their political views.[34]

William Cook, comedy critic for the *Guardian*, emphasizes that the most important aspect of the new comedy is originality: "the establishment of the comic as sole author and rightful owner of his own material is Alternative Comedy's most important achievement" (1994, p. 6). While gags and stories were common property among traditional comics, the new performers seek to create a unique comic persona from their own experience, prizing innovation and often culling jokes that seem derivative. Comics that depend on old material or the jokes of others are held in low esteem. Even critics are taken to task for "using" material in a review. The problem is, according to one English comedienne, "they describe your act and then the audience knows what's coming. That's plagiarism."

The Edinburgh Fringe has by all accounts taken on a special importance for comedy.[35] For comedians, it is the equivalent of a trade fair (Connor 1990). The highest accolade is the Perrier Award. Established in 1981 without fanfare, the Perrier was awarded to *groups* through the mid-1980s, including Cambridge Footlights, Brass Band, and Théâtre de Complicité. Beginning in 1986 the Perrier has *only* been awarded to comics and is generally viewed as the springboard for lucrative radio and television contracts. The half dozen nominees are widely publicized and

Edinburgh buzzes with speculation more intense than that which accompanies the theater prizes. The winner is announced after the second festival week at a midnight gala, receives a large cash prize, and leads a special comedy series at the Lyric Theatre two months after the end of the festival.

For many, the experience of so many renowned performance artists along with talented newcomers has made comedy the highlight of the festival. For others, comedy has undermined new and experimental theater. In terms of audience opportunities, there has been no drop in theater, as Figure 4.6 shows. But in terms of social organization, the rise of comedy is associated with a new spatial clustering.

SUPERVENUES

> Some people say the Fringe should just be comedy. Forget about theater in the Assembly Rooms and just have the comedy there.
> —*American comedian*

> There's a snobbishness about comedy. The Assembly only tolerates it. They'd still rather have Polish mime.
> —*London comedian*

In Edinburgh, part of the fun and much of the frustration is *finding* the show. In unusual places and with little time between shows, even the taxi drivers are sometimes at a loss. As the Fringe grew, year by year, another level of organization began to emerge: the growth of self-contained performance centers called "supervenues." Supervenues make it easy for spectators to stay in one place rather than move between venues. They allow more groups access to scarce space in the city center. Like any contract with a venue manager, it means performers can devote themselves to performing. They do not need to know that the steps up to seats must be at least 3.6 inches wide, at least 11 from back to front, and at most 6 inches high.

The most lucrative supervenues represent a departure from the overall Fringe policy of nonselectivity. Centralization of advertising, ticket sales, and planning as well as the marketing of the venue itself are provided as a service to groups for a fee and reflected in generally higher ticket prices. It is no accident that the growth of comedy occurred in tandem with the success of these "suborganizations." Just as the central Fringe office was a product of growth in size and the need for information, venue entrepreneurs have been successful in providing spheres of organization, "mini-Fringes," for media and spectators. These performance centers reduce uncertainty for audiences and, equally important, for first-time groups. Appearance at a top venue is perceived as a "guarantee of quality" and a tremendous advantage for performers whose shows are included in its program.[36] The *Guardian/Observer Guide* to the Edinburgh Festival (1994, pp. 37–38) provided what now amounts to standard advice.

> The Edinburgh Fringe is notoriously unpredictable, with pockets of brilliance in venues way off the beaten track and a huge number of entries remarkable more for their enthusiasm than their expertise. So how do you blow the wheat from the chaff and decide which shows to book? . . . If you're only there for a couple of days, it's even more difficult, and you need some rule of thumb. First tip is look to the venue. The competition for the prestigious Assembly Rooms means that you can be pretty sure that all its shows will be up to scratch.

The development of supervenues generates strong feelings and has been criticized as not representing the true spirit of the Fringe. In one important sense, they are a microcosm of the Fringe itself, but they do not take all comers, controlling the groups that appear. One English comedian expressed a common view: "The Gilded Balloon, Pleasance, and Assemblies are really a separate comedy festival. Audiences assume if you're not there, you're no good and people in the business know you've got to be at one of those three."

The development of autonomous suborganizations may be traced back to minifestivals such as the 1970 New Edinburgh Arts Complex at the Heriot Watt Student Union. When venue-sharing practices became widespread in the late 1970s, groups and entrepreneurs began to provide a variety of services and multiple performance spaces at one location. In 1982, the Circuit housed up to thirty-eight companies in a giant tent near the Edinburgh Castle, while over fifty shows were produced at the Assembly Rooms. Together they composed almost one-quarter of the Fringe program.

By the mid 1990s, the main supervenues are the Traverse Theatre, the Assembly Rooms,[37] the Gilded Balloon, and the Pleasance. Apart from the Traverse, the reputation of these venues is linked to comedy rather than to traditional theater. They contain multiple performance areas, from the intimate to the spacious, featuring several simultaneous productions, and dining and drinking facilities. In 1993 the Assembly Rooms, the Gilded Balloon, and the Pleasance not only produced independent programs, but a combined program as the Stella Artois Comedy Festival. To many, this represented an elite Fringe, a view reinforced by the fact that a bus shuttled between the locations.[38]

New acts fortunate enough to land a supervenue slot have a large advantage. One year two American stand-up comedians, both unknown in Britain, were scheduled to fill supervenue time slots made available owing to cancellations. In spite of their omission from the main Fringe program, both were quickly playing to large audiences and reviewed by the major media (one was even short-listed for the Perrier Award). This attention is mainly attributable to their inclusion in the supervenue programs, the ready audience created around the venue, and the effectiveness of its publicity.

Each supervenue has a separate press office that sends out press releases and promotes its shows beginning in early summer, sometimes with a London publicity meeting. Staff members are able to be much more active in promoting their own artists than the main Fringe press office:

> Someone may come from the *Financial Times* or the *Daily Telegraph* for one day and ask me "I have three hours, what should I do?" I tell them what to see and say don't waste your time on others. I gain credibility that way and they'll come back [to me] again. . . . My influence is only the first week. After that we do very little hassling. It's short-term people who need advice.

Supervenue bars are known for their high concentration of performers, critics, scouts, directors, and personalities. Even those located in distant venues will often make a trip to the Assembly Rooms or Traverse, simply to hear "the buzz."

The historical development of the Fringe in the preceding chapter has been followed here by a discussion of its modern organization. In the next, I ignore time and enter the realm of myth before describing the review process in action. One of the points the Fringe office seeks to communicate to prospective performers is a warning that their appearance is likely to be unprofitable. What, then, is important? The experience, the personal contacts made, and the reviews obtained for the show, which serve as concrete *tokens* of that experience. For artists, as well as spectators, there is always the chance of *discovery*.

1. Festival Fringe Society, 180 High Street, Edinburgh.

2. Main workroom of the Fringe office. (*Left to right*: Laura Mackenzie Stuart, Kathleen Mainland, Hilary Strong, Jean Dickson)

3. Fringe press office. (*Left foreground:* Stuart Buchanan; *left background:* Alison Forsyth)

4. Fringe Club, Teviot Row House, Bristo Square.

5. Opening press reception. (Performers and critics crowd the Debating Hall at the Fringe Club)

6. Main offices, the *Scotsman*.

7. Tweeddale Court, Royal Mile.

8. The *List* office, Tweeddale Court.

9. Main newsroom of the *List*.

10. The *List* office. (*Left to right*: Lila Rawlings, editor; Robin Hodge, publisher; Mark Fisher, theater critic)

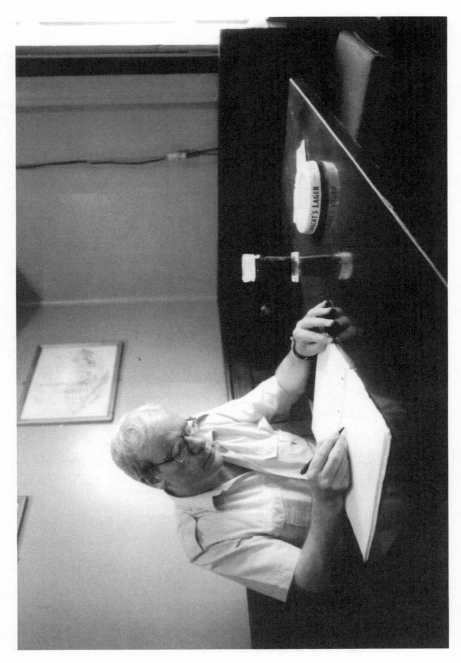

11. Hayden Murphy, the Oxford Bar, Young Street.

12. Courtyard of the Pleasance against the backdrop of the Salisbury Crags. (*Left foreground*: Christopher Richardson in white hat)

13. Assembly Rooms.

14. Courtyard of Gilded Balloon II (Old Traverse Theatre) off the Grassmarket.

Chapter Five

MYTH OF THE FRINGE

> There's no doubt about it. Hits can be made during the
> festival. Things snowball. Good reviews, an award—our show
> got a Fringe First—the national critics come. [The actress]
> might get a film or a tele . . . all sorts of things.
> —*Scottish director*

> We have six spotters. They go out kissing frogs. If they
> spy a prince, they report back to me.
> —*Editor,* Independent

A BOVE ALL, one myth explains the concentrated drive for attention in the presence of such risky opportunities for profit. It is
not the peculiar property of the Fringe, or festivals. It helps to
produce and maintain the motivational structures characterizing all art
worlds. Myths, in the concrete contexts of their reproduction, are not
abstract, free-floating idea systems but frameworks of situated, locally
produced discourse. In this chapter I consider some aspects of myth as
well as the review process itself. For the ideology of "discovery," of the
"identification of quality" in both highbrow and popular performance
genres, grounds the festival system. But the review process is a matter of
assignments and deadlines, newsrooms and subeditors.

What is different about the Fringe? Only that the field of discovery is
so wide. The dramaturgical approach of Erving Goffman, originating in
the 1950s, viewed people as actors in elaborate if often unconsciously
staged performances. His fieldwork was in the Shetland Isles, in the far
north of Scotland, but surely he passed through Edinburgh in August.
The lines between performers and audience blur here as nowhere else.

MYTHS AND BOUNDARIES

During the first week of the 1990 festival all the papers carried two photos. Muammar Qaddafi was pictured in his striped concrete bunker,
arms outstretched in a shiny jacket and cheap holiday shirt, looking like
nothing so much as a carnival barker. Saddam Hussein was on the front
page, grinning like some maniacal uncle at a young British hostage

named Stuart and patting him on the head. The "real world" had become a Fringe show, competing with a thousand others for newspace.

An arts festival is an extended system of interaction experienced on
two levels. Personally, it is a history of encounters with people and performances. Vicariously, it is experienced through tales told, myths, expectations, plans made and unmade. The socialization of newcomers involves learning the patterns and images "representative" of culture.
Such learning is ideological and mythological. The archetypes of experience and expectation are the complex possibilities that *have* occurred, at
least in the collective memory and, hence, may befall one. In Fringe subculture, the identification of "types," taking people as kinds of people,
even taking on a persona for oneself, occurs more readily given the sheer
density of artists and performers and the backdrop of the city itself. It is
easy to act in the presence of actors.

Buskers line the High Street and the Mound. Leafleters crowd the
walk around the Fringe office, smiling and thrusting. The ticket queue
is a captive audience. The opportunity is well used by touts reading
aloud from *Scotsman* reviews, musicians and perfomers serving up scenes
and songs, acrobatics and demonstrations. Acting troupes from shows
tucked into secret closes and wynds leave the venue to buttonhole pe-
destrians on the street, offering free tickets when sales lag. Nuns on the
lookout for a performance are asked what show they are promoting. The
unwritten rule is to keep moving, or risk being mistaken for an avant-
garde theater piece.[1]

The Fringe has been described as twenty-one consecutive New Year's
Eves. One festival the comedian Arthur Smith held "alternative tours"
of the Royal Mile. With an audience of 200 at four o'clock in the morning, he asked one of the castle guards to do some slow marching in exchange for a joint. To everyone's surprise, the squaddie took it, only the
first strange event in an evening of unexpected revelry. As Smith tells the
story:

> The police broke it up in the end, but it had been a real laugh and people were
> trying to give me money. I said, "Oh no, I don't need the money—if you
> want to give me money, put it in that bloke's hat." There was this old, pissed,
> homeless bloke, lying there asleep by the cathedral. Fifty quid must have gone
> in. . . . I love the thought of him waking up the next morning. (Cook 1994,
> p. 247)

The chance that a Fringe performance is the turning point in the career of an artist is like the good fortune of a sleeping drunk. This small
likelihood makes little difference.[2] There is, indeed, a chance. One performer claims getting a review from the *Scotsman* cost his group three
years and $37,000—and was worth it.[3] In the competitive environment

of the Fringe, myths reflect with precision the ideologies that provide "reasonable" or "accountable" vocabularies of action in other art worlds as well: the audience as earnest and hungry for experience but ignorant or misguided; the performer as worthy and deserving through the privation of creative effort; the critic as cynical journalist or jaded intellectual, but a potential savior.

Although the idea of mediation locates critics "between" audiences and artists, in a more fundamental sense audience, critic, and performer are linked in an interdependent fate, each mediating the interaction of the others. Performers rely on both critics and audiences for their success. Spectators depend on the critic for assistance in selecting shows as well as the performers on whose shoulders their enjoyment or edification finally rests. The critic depends on a readership, as well as something to review, developing relationships with directors, producers, and actors over the course of time.

Any full participant in a subculture should be able to rehearse its mythology, at least as a signal of membership.[4] I paraphrase Miles Kington for a concise statement:[5]

> When the Fringe started in 1948, there were only four performers: Alan Bennett, Dudley Moore, Peter Cook, and Jonathan Miller. They were doing a new play by a hitherto unknown writer called Tom Stoppard. On the strength of a *Scotsman* review, the show played to packed houses and transferred to London's West End. Now, a million people flock to Edinburgh each year and poster the city, while the BBC and assorted scouts comb the talent at the Assembly Rooms for the next John Cleese and Derek Jacobi.

None of this is true—apart from the presence of talent scouts.

Talent aside, artists should experience poverty and hardship, sore throats and overdrafts,[6] at the beginning of their careers. The romantic image is not only a vision of the artistic career, but a motivational process. Penury creates the will to succeed and weeds out the unworthy. A dialectic of genius and discovery provides the fulcrum through which events and reactions are interpretable. The "empty show" challenges the critic to love or hate because it is either an offense to cultivated sensibility or an unrecognized gem, an opportunity that must be trumpeted to the performance world. Performers, in their fashion, employ conventional and ready-made justifications for empty houses, which are not at all uncommon.[7] The number of shows is so large that there are not enough spectators to fill every house. Even free tickets, a sure way to draw an audience in most settings, are often useless.

Often, within days of the start of the Fringe, a bit of folk knowledge circulates among performing groups that the average number of spectators at Fringe shows is only seven. In fact it is seven times higher than that. But the number seven, unfounded though it is, permits a reasonable inference for the many groups whose audiences may be only a dozen or less: they are doing quite well, in spite of the visual evidence that houses are virtually empty.[8]

The concentration of shows, their qualitative and generic variety, and the ideology of discovery produce the stereotypical performance addict: a beady-eyed Fringe hound combing the reviews and the program in the lounge bar in a brief respite between shows. It represents the search for excellence.[9]

> It's 6:00 P.M. and we could get there in time for the Sam Shepard piece at the Festival Club. But I've never heard of the group. The Traverse Theater is a sure thing, but there's a good chance we can't get tickets and we'd be out of luck getting to anything else. The best bet would be to go see Red Shift at the Pleasance—the reviews weren't too good but it's a new translation of a classic—then we could stay there for the Miles and Millner cabaret at 8:30. That will end just in time to get to the Gilded Balloon for some late night comedy. But it means we'll have to leave the Molière for tomorrow.

Not a blind follower of reviews, he arrives with some awareness of prior reputation, both for groups and venues:

> Cranking himself up on malt whisky he had careered like a pinball from venue to venue: soaked in sweat before arriving, soaked in sweat in the steamy theatre, topping up the lost liquid with pints and pints of lager. His conversation was a medley of shows missed, or seen and part-remembered, or might have seen, or maybe heard about. Eyes darting this way and that, like someone expecting somebody, unnaturally bright one moment, dull the next; talking frantically, then lapsing into voyeuristic silence.[10]

The occasional Fringe Marathon lends droll recognition and a competitive form to this persona through a sponsored competition: a prize is awarded to the individual who can see the most shows in twenty-four hours.[11]

Among the number of genuine unknowns about the performance is the prospect of being, one's self alone, a large share of the audience. This is disconcerting for many and I recommend that you fantasize yourself the director or perhaps a talent scout. The burden of evaluation weighs heavier, sometimes, in the pause after the curtain than in the blank sheet confronting the reviewer. The magnitude of differences between shows leads observers to compare Fringegoing to playing the slots, panning for gold, and other metaphors of randomness. For the audience and critic, the "jackpot" is unrecognized excellence; for the performers, the full house and the rave review. The presence of scouts and theater managers in large numbers enhances the plausibility of the scenario.

"The reviews haven't appeared." The belief in the power of the critic to ferret out genius is supported by a few unique and decidedly outlying events. The most important is the "discovery" of *Rosencrantz and Guildenstern Are Dead*, launching Stoppard's successful career, still told by performers, playwrights, and directors.[12] As "everyone knows" there are brilliant actresses saddled with abysmal material and dreadful performers corroding jewels of dramatic excellence.

The hope is that bad (unrecognized, poorly attended, still unacclaimed) work is simply uneven, that inessential characteristics have underwhelmed positive attributes, that the judicious reviewer will spot the luminescent core. The "right to fail" with risk-taking and creative artistic performances is earnestly and ideologically guarded, in contrast with West End and Broadway commercial reasoning. The plausible dissection of a finished performance into multiple responsibilities allows the ideology of performance "potential" to work as an incentive structure.

The myth of discovery is as essential to the role of the critic as to the romantic artist.[13] Brooks Atkinson averred that although he was sometimes credited with "discovering" Geraldine Page, he never had the insight to see what she or anyone else was going to become (Greenberger 1971, p. 167). He did, however, praise her in his reviews. What makes it possible for critics to "discover" playwrights, actors, and directors is what makes it possible for fortunetellers to foretell. Sometimes, for whatever reasons, the critic is right. Selective memory creates a bias toward rightness. Given the number of reviews and their variability, it is inevitable that someone will be right. I consider the actual variability among reviews in Chapter 7. The sources of the discovery myth are explored further in Chapter 9.

The performance bias, wherein every action in Edinburgh could be a Fringe performance, has its counterpart in the review. If the homeless residents around the Grassmarket have been brought inside a venue to act their own roles in a show—as they were in 1990—then what about those that are still on the street? Are they simply a competing show? Only if there are spectators, with interpretations to proffer, and critics to judge. I argued in Chapter 1 that cultural objects must be "differentiated" as art, but the Edinburgh audience—partly, perhaps, because so many of them are artists—is extraordinarily flexible. The boundaries of art are rendered ambiguous, as the border of performance softens and flexes.[14] The critic, as discourse specialist and definer of roles, creates by *construing* action as performance. In the remainder of this chapter I take a qualitative look at the process that generates critical text.

The Newsroom

> Fringe groups call us up and they seem to have the impression
> we're providing a service to them—they've busted their ass to
> come here and think we're obliged to cover them. That's not the
> way it works. We're feeding off them to sell a magazine. Look
> at this issue—maybe a hundred professionally produced
> photographs, all provided free of charge.
> —*Assistant editor,* List

Arriving in Scotland I'm apprehensive about my new job, reviewing for
an Edinburgh events magazine called the *List*. It has been said that the
only qualification for being a reviewer is going to see plays every night
of your life. One London critic claims to have seen 4,000 shows.[15] That
rules out most of us, but immersion in the Fringe is the next best thing.

What can one write about so many shows, so close together? An
American reviewer asked how it was possible for the Edinburgh critics to
review so many shows: "I mean, how many things can you say? Don't
they run out of adjectives? The acting was splendid, brilliant, luminous,
radiant, dazzling, effulgent, clever, unique, intelligent. The show could
only be characterized as incompetent, inept, ineffectual, faulty, substan-
dard, inferior, mediocre, second-rate. Don't they start repeating themselves?"

For peace of mind, I figured to rely on the amateur shows: we'll be
matched up that way. Or the comedy. I'll know if it's funny or not.
There are almost a dozen American stand-ups, following the great and
largely unexpected success of Will Durst and Emo Philips. The British
critics won't know as much about that. At least I can do comedy. Or the
kid's shows. If only I had brought my kid. I dutifully submitted my list
of preferences to the editor.

By the mid 1990s there remain only two relatively comprehensive
sources of Fringe reviews. Best known is the *Scotsman*, whose critics
phone or fax reviews to the receiving desk without much opportunity to
interact. The *List*, normally a biweekly magazine for central Scotland, is
published weekly during the festival. The building has housed publishing firms since 1806. It is designed and organized as a special kind of
newsroom devoted solely to arts and entertainment.

Every tourist in Edinburgh strolls the Royal Mile on the way from
castle to palace. Halfway down the High Street the John Knox house
intrudes bluntly into the road. Apart from visitors to the Scottish Poetry
Society and the Saltire Society for cultural heritage, few turn right into

Tweeddale Court, where the Marquis of Tweeddale once occupied the largest and most elegant home within the city walls of old Edinburgh.

First built by Neil Laing, Keeper of the Signet for the Scottish king, the oldest door retains its 1576 inscription "The Feir of the Lord Preserveth the Lyfe." It was remodeled by Charles II's architect for Holyrood Palace, Sir William Bruce, sold in 1670 and occupied by the Tweeddale family until 1791, then used as the headquarters of the British Linen Bank (Gifford et al. 1984). By that time the Old Town of Edinburgh had become so rough that bank patrons were increasingly reluctant to make the trip there to transact business.[16] Occupied from 1806 to 1970 by the publishing house of "Oliver and Boyd," Robin Hodge renovated the building and began publishing the *List* in 1985.

While Edinburgh is not known for its dramatic tradition, its intellectual, literary, and publishing credentials are impeccable. In the drawers of the room where reviewers enter copy, the names of Oliver and Boyd's distinguished correpondents are still visible: Walter Scott, James Hogg, John Galt, J. G. Lockhart, and Thomas Carlyle. Perhaps the modern writers for the *List* may be forgiven their compositional haste. Mark Twain, whose scorn for our state capitol in Baton Rouge grew with each trip up the Mississippi, attributed all architectural monstrosities and bad literature to Sir Walter Scott. But the spirit of Sir Walter, who tried to write himself out of debt and died doing it, is a fitting muse for festival critics.

The *List* is different from the *Scotsman* because its editors and reviewers occupy three newsrooms. Writers enter reviews into several computers and editors compile sections on art, books, classical music, clubs, film, folk, jazz, kids, rock, sport, television, theater, and dance. During the festival most of each issue shifts to festival coverage and more critics are hired. The rule is that reviews may not actually be *written* on the machines, but the policy is sometimes honored in the breach.

It is the main office in the middle of the first week of the festival. Two teenagers beat me to the reception area. With seven outside lines one cannot still the phone just by answering.

> *Young man*: We've come to inquire about street selling.
>
> *Nikki*: Yes, fine. You buy the magazines from us, then return the ones you don't sell. A couple of rules: no selling in Princes St. Gardens and not in Waverley Station either.
>
> *Claire*: [*answering phone*] Hello, the *List*? [*Turns*] Alastair, it's Robert from the Fringe office on line three.
>
> *Alastair*: We don't have a photo of Black Mime Theatre. This piece needs a photo. Hey, Mark, did you get any faxes? Paul says he sent his reviews and they're not here.

Eddie: [*hanging up*] That was the antipublicist, making sure he gets no coverage every year by being offensive to every journalist here.

Susan: [*answering phone*] Hello, the *List*? Who's speaking please? [*Turns*] Mark, it's "Thirteen O'Clock Productions" on line one.

Mark: Hello, this is Mark Fisher. That's the *Black Ambulance Gang*, is it? You haven't seen a *List* reviewer at the show? I feel pretty certain someone's been down there. I'll just be sure to check that. There may even be a piece that's just come out in today's issue. Thanks very much, I've got someone on another line just now. [*Hangs up*]

Eddie: Haven't we done that already?

Mark: I said it was the worst show on the Fringe. Listen, we need at least one or two more shows for the "Hit List." Seen anything good?

Eddie: There was a Scottish comic down at the Pleasance. Really preposterous, I couldn't believe it. The guy was deconstructing comedy with fortune cookies and it ends up being a pub quiz. Put it in.

Mark: There's another comic. He does a bit about being at university and he asked the audience who'd been to university—everyone in the whole place raised their hand.

Thom: Bethan, seen anything?

Bethan: Not much yet. I did see *Meeting Cassandra* at Demarco's. You know, one of these arty things. This one by an Israeli group. I didn't really understand it—you had to know classical mythology and allusions to all sorts of things.

Thom: That was that one woman show?

Bethan: Yeah, really pretentious. She's rolling around smearing lipstick on herself in all sorts of contortions. Well, I've smeared lipstick, too.

Thom: Did you review it?

Bethan: Yeah. Didn't have a clue.

The Black Ambulance Gang: The accolade of worst show on the Fringe is one that should be awarded with care and consideration. So check back with me in two weeks' time. Suffice it to say *The Black Ambulance Gang* is a serious contender. You don't have to search far to find bad acting in Edinburgh at this time of year, but the supreme glory of Thirteen O'Clock's production (for it is so bad that it is almost good) is that you can see bad acting all over the city. Because *The Black Ambulance Gang* is performed on a coach. It's a tragical mystery tour characterized by halfhearted improvisation, unconvincing performances and ramshackle direction made all the more enjoyably dreadful by the knowledge that with a decent script and a bit of rehearsal it could have been quite successful. One for bus-spotters and lovers of trash. (Mark Fisher, *List*, 19 August 1993)

Meeting Cassandra: Tortured, passionate, physicality: Tmu-Na Theatre's *Meeting Cassandra* works the myth of the Goddess and Apollo into a highly wrought one-woman tour de force. Antonia Smits seduces with an intensity

augmented by stage minimalism and stark lighting. Slow motion and exqui-
site detail inform Smits movements. She gestures her way through sensuality
and power struggles, torture and nostalgia with poise. Echoes from famous
historical liaisons resound through the piece. . . . Infused with conceptual lay-
ers of interpretation and inner wisdom. An aesthetic delight. (Bethan Cole,
List, 19 August 1993)

The bulletin board in the main office is located where the Marquis
once warmed himself by a large fireplace. There is now a huge computer
printout, ten feet wide, in a dozen vertical strips. I scan it thoroughly,
but my name doesn't appear. My list of requests has been lost, most of
the shows have been assigned, another American has been assigned the
comedy, and the kid's shows will be done by a special editor. Of three
dozen requested, I get one.

The Review Process

Folk theories of evaluation, treated in more detail in Chapter 7, rarely
consider the *process* by which critical discourse appears in print. Performers and publics hope that knowledgeable, careful, and evenhanded critics write the reviews that praise and censure. Many forget about the editors—a big mistake.

Editors are concerned with the inscription and flow of text—getting
copy in and out. "Beware the arty staffer," says the *Associated Press Man-
aging Editors' Guidelines,*[17] aware that a reporter fresh from the crime
desk may be better at producing for deadline. Although a review is distinguished from a feature item in form and content, both fill a news
hole. Reviews of a play or movie must be timely or they are not worth
printing. Critics often attend opening nights and their reviews are expected to be in by the next day. Deadlines are no worse for a reviewer
than a reporter, and most critics do not fulminate over them.[18] With an
average assignment of several reviews a week and other journalistic tasks,
there is little preparation time. Far from delving into the background of
plays or the careers of performers, a general *lack* of background knowledge is the norm. Hayden Murphy of the *Scotsman* even characterized
his perusal of two biographies as "cheating" before seeing a play on the
life of Emma Hardy.[19]

As I will show in the following chapter, favorability is not as important as the sheer appearance of the text in a widely circulated newspaper,
so editorial decisions are often more important than the evaluations of
critics. A critical notice may not appear because it is not commissioned.[20]
It may be commissioned and rejected. And it may be altered in form or
occasionally even content before its appearance in print. These kinds of

outcomes are affected by the review process. The selection of shows for coverage is an interactive process involving editor and reviewer, based on a recommendation by one and an agreement (sometimes grudging) by the other. If anyone has the power to make or break a show, it is the editor rather than the critic—the one who selects the text and not the one who produces it.

Selecting shows for review is of the utmost importance and not always best left to critics. In the preceding chapter, press agents were shown to guide critics to certain shows, but this applies more to non-Scottish reviewers. At the *Scotsman* and the *List* shows are usually assigned by the editors. This protects them against greenhorns like me who are susceptible to foolish promises. Once I promised to review a show after being cornered by the director: "It's an important new show about breast cancer by a group from London. The playwright died a few months ago, just after completing it." This intrigues me because breast cancer runs in my family. The players in this show were all friends of the deceased. "It's a tribute to her memory and a consciousness-raising experience for the audience." Yes, I would come. It sounds like a dedicated group and it should raise the important issues.

Wounds is a complete disaster. I have never seen a worse piece of theater. It's not just the quality of the acting, but the play itself. One woman in the audience sways and appears to faint during a ravaging "lung biopsy" scene. I think she really *is* a spectator but you never know.

The company has rewritten the original script slightly after the author's death to reveal a greater reluctance by her friends and family to care for her in the last stages of her illness. A miserable and depressing illness followed by a miserable and depressing death. The patient rejects treatments proposed by her doctors, involves herself in numerous forms of quackery, and dies after kicking her husband out of the house and, presumably, writing this play. Is there a message here?

The company, to my utter amazement, asks the audience to stay for a discussion afterward. Are they going to hand out promotional literature for the Hemlock Society? My own experience of the death of three aunts and my mother's cure is so far removed from their friend's bleak world that I immediately race for the door. A review of this pathetic show would be inadmissable, negative or otherwise. The *List*'s editor had suspected as much.

The *Scotsman* is the "review bible" of the Fringe and publishes more criticism than any other source. With only two permanent members of the arts staff, and two part-timers, most of the reviewers are freelance journalists.[21] After the Fringe program appears in late June but before the festival begins, most reviewers submit preference lists. These lists range from several to one or even two hundred shows.

The *Scotsman*'s arts editor, working with an assistant who will take over much of the daily assignment function, creates a diary listing each show by its opening date. Owing to the overlap of preferences—theater reviewers in particular tend to select the same well-known companies—the arts editor meets with the critics and makes preliminary assignments, giving the plums to the most experienced reviewers. Companies with established reputations (regardless of show) and those eligible for Fringe First awards are given priority: "We recognize what's likely to be an important show and assign the most experienced and best reviewers to them. But good reviewers aren't simply the most experienced ones, some of the newer ones are the best."[22] The *Scotsman* eventually reviews over half the shows that appear.

> All of the rational performing groups get covered: not the once only shows or the medical students doing "Womb with a View" or "What's Up Me Doc" somewhere in Morningside. The audience already knows it's going to be coarse and funny and they don't need us to tell them that. We might not cover some parochial, amateur groups performing for their friends and relatives.

The initial listings, established before the festival, are subject to daily changes. Owing to scheduling difficulties, the fact that the arts editor is himself a critic (hence often out of the office), and the sheer size of the project, the list of shows that are eventually reviewed changes. The preferences of critics and even actions by companies and publicists also affect the final set of reviews: "It makes a difference if they call more than once and are quite pleasant and sincere on the phone. If they're arrogant, I won't be as inclined to assign someone to the show." Reviewers schedule shows themselves, calling in advance for tickets at the busiest venues and simply showing up for others. They are sometimes asked explicitly to review a particular show for a certain daily edition.

At the Fringe, the complaint is often heard that no one has been to review the show. In fact, most shows get reviewed, though not as often as they like. Popular artists sometimes feel slighted in favor of "straight" theater. If so, this might be the result of editorial and critical selections.

Do editors or reviewers exhibit a preference for highbrow genres? I acquired press records from supervenues at the 1990 Fringe to find out whether reviewers—or the media they represent—were more interested in theatrical offerings or comedy/cabaret. As we saw in Chapter 4, because of the volume of shows as well as the demand for its tickets, the Assembly Rooms maintains a separate press office and checks credentials more rigorously than most venues. The number of press passes issued for each show as well as the names and organizational affiliations of their recipients were available for each day of the run.[23]

I found no evidence to suggest that the press is more interested in highbrow than popular shows. All of the differences are small, both relative to the number of shows considered and in practical terms. The average number of press passes distributed for premiers was 7.4 for comedy and cabaret and 6.7 for theater. But since the former tend to have shorter runs (one or two weeks rather than the full three), critics have more reason to review the opening.[24] When only the longer runs are considered, theater and comedy/cabaret distribute similar numbers of press passes. For the first five shows as well as the entire run, the numbers of press attendees are virtually identical.[25] When we restrict interest to the local print media (Edinburgh and Glasgow), a slight emphasis on theater is evident, but it is not large. The largest difference is in the opening performance, where an average of three reviewers cover theater and two cover popular shows.

Such small differences do not provide evidence that the audiovisual and print media prefer either highbrow or lowbrow shows in these large venues. If anything, they are scrupulously fair. Whether this fairness derives from the assignments reviewers get or personal curiosity combined with a press card, it is not possible to say.

Returning to the *Scotsman*'s review process, draft reviews are delivered to the main office directly, by fax, or delivered over the phone to the copy desk.[26] The copy is in, but it must still get to press. Copy takers route files to the arts editor, who is first to examine the reviews, may do some initial editing, and send a few forward with next-day priority. Three to seven percent of reviews written are unpublished for four general reasons.[27] Most are not "rejected" outright. Submitted late or subject to queuing problems,[28] the review is "purged" from the system when the show closes. Sometimes there are duplicates (two critics have been assigned to the same show). Finally, some are "editorial" rejections. They are considered too poorly written for simple editing to suffice, or, occasionally, rejected *because* of an evaluation.

What kinds of editorial bias appear in the *selection* of reviews once they are received? In spite of anecdotal evidence and widespread suspicions by performers, directors, and sometimes reviewers themselves, the positive and negative evaluation biases built into the selection process tend to offset one another. Given a large number of performances to review, it is possible to reject the negative ones and still fill the review page.[29] (A "performers" orientation, in which the editors act functionally as promoters of local groups, entails this as well.) Although it is rare, some reviews are indeed rejected because they are, in the words of a *Scotsman* arts editor, "hysterically hostile":[30] "Some reviews that are irresponsibly hostile have been suppressed. They express the criticism too violently or too uncleverly. This is almost the same thing as just being badly written."[31] But there are obvious costs in paying a cadre of reviewers *not* to write publishable material. Moreover, negative reviews provide much of the entertainment value for the readership. The rejection of negative reviews occurs rarely, perhaps 1 to 2 percent of the total written.[32]

Most reviews are edited again by the dreaded but extremely useful "subeditors." Their manifest function is to clear and correct text. Because they tend to be anonymous or, at least, shadowy presences, subeditors are a frequent scapegoat for flaws, mistakes, and sundry embarrassments. They edit the text, add fonts, and after the compositors have laid out the copy, cut the "overmatter" to finalize the page layouts. None of the critics I interviewed said that editors made significant changes in their reviews, though it is sometimes alleged that the subeditors will chop off your last sentence.[33] This viewpoint is not shared by the subeditors, who have little direct contact with the critics: "You get cynical being a subeditor. Sometimes you read reviews from the same person that look like the name of the show is just changed. . . . I try to vary the sentence length, cut out the dribble and repetition. . . . [We] save the reputations of reviewers all the time by correcting their blunders."

Although evaluations are seldom modified in standard reviews, summaries of reviews offer great scope for editorial involvement. Someone must decide which part of the review to reprint. Reviewer judgments in shorter reviews are positively shifted by such selection.[34]

Whether a review appears is affected by the size of the review hole. It is influenced by editorial preferences for certain shows, though not for high or low art as a whole. It is affected by the requests of reviewers and shaped by their interaction in organizational contexts. But these factors are seldom considered by participants directly concerned with the success of a show. For them the idea of a chance encounter with a discerning judge is more important, one who singles out *their* show, *their* performance, whose public illumination of talent will set them apart, the first step on the road to fame.

PART THREE

THE TRIANGLE OF MEDIATION

Chapter Six

DO CRITICS MATTER?

> *Hydra*: The Critics will Condemn your Piece for want of a Plot. . . . Pray what is the Plot? . . .
> *Pasquin*: . . . The Plot, Sir, is the filling of this House— don't you see how thick it is?
> —*Charles Macklin,* Covent Garden Theater; or, Pasquin Turn'd Drawcansir *(1752)*

T HIS CHAPTER takes a systematic approach to the question that is central to the idea of cultural mediation: Do critics matter? In one sense the answer is, Of course. Critics matter to performers, and reviews are almost never good enough. But in my interviews with artists there was one overwhelming curiosity: do critics matter so far as the *public* is concerned? This issue affects not only the performers themselves but producers, directors, backers, and distributors: if the critics like it, will people come? After discussing audiences in general and the festival audience in particular, I estimate models of attendance for highbrow and popular shows.

PUBLIC AND SPECTATOR, SPECIALIST AND AFICIONADO

It is sometimes useful to draw a distinction between those that can and those that do. Where the arts audience is at issue this is a matter of what is often termed "consuming," but it seems more natural to call it "witnessing" or "experiencing." Those for whom the performing arts are experientially accessible are the "public" in the sense of a *potential audience*. The "spectators" are those who *attend a particular show*. These groups are not undifferentiated masses nor are they sets of socially autonomous individuals, a point I will consider further in Chapter 9. For the art world, the trick is converting a vast public into paying spectators.

For the analysis of taste and the development of cultural products, classifying the audience has remained fuzzy. Schemes such as Adorno's dividing the musical public into the expert, the good listener, the cultural consumer, the emotional listener, and the resentment listener are generally impossible to implement for everyone but their originator (1976 [1962], pp. 4–12). Herbert Gans correctly points to the importance of *involvement levels* of spectators: when levels of interest are extremely low, one is foolish to make a big analytic fuss about the societal impact or meaning of a product. For the analysis of the product itself, the kind of involvement is often critical.

Members of the theater public, for example, may be characterized as falling somewhere on the continuum from never having been to a play to active involvement in a theater career. What implications does this have for the response to various performance genres? For the process of mediation, what is important is the location of the spectator within a network of specialists or aficionados, that is, her position within the "social circle" related to the art form (Kadushin 1976). The closer to the center of production, and hence the greater the involvement with the art form, the smaller the impact of cultural experts and authoritative assessors of quality. The "core" audience of specialists and aficionados is by no means impervious to social influences but the "taste-making" function of critics is unlikely to apply to this segment of the audience.[1]

Here we must avoid the danger of confusing "within" and "between" genre differences. The audience for high-status genres should not be confused with the "serious audience" (Becker 1982, pp. 47–50). "Core" members of the audience for *any* genre know more about its history and development, can compare its styles and artists, are able to predict trends, and so forth. This is just as true of comic book collectors as opera buffs, but the former are still involved in a lowbrow genre. The less involved—and much larger—public is subject to mediative processes of a different nature. There the difference between high and popular art forms is visible in the different roles of critics. Neither specialists, those occupationally involved with the art form, nor aficionados, committed and knowledgeable consumers, are much influenced by critics.

Aficionados may also serve gatekeeping functions, but this kind of cultural discourse is informal and private rather than published or broadcast. For example, heavy consumers of art films are highly educated, tend to be employed in prestigious occupations, and, like avid readers of romance novels, are often relatively *un*discriminating. The nature of the picture is not terribly important to the selection decisions of such consumers because they attend every one available (Austin 1989). Critical discussions may be read and digested, but aficionados feel themselves as qualified to render judgments on the merits of particular films as reviewers. One would not expect any systematic influence of reviewer evaluations.

Although they are similar in their relative judgmental sovereignty, the difference between specialists and aficionados is conspicuous in their diametrically opposed views of originality. Originality is usually a prime concern of specialists even in popular art forms, but not per se of any particular interest to aficionados, who often clash over the issue.[2] There is no relation between originality and occupancy of high status in the hierarchy of cultural genres. Yet it is always a main concern of performers and specialists who must *relate original works to works in the canon*.[3]

Most research on audiences takes as its primary focus the characteristics of individuals. Studies of cultural activities often begin with a sample of the general population and ask how people spend their time (Blau 1988a). Like a coarse sieve, they sift and separate users into general demographic and attitudinal categories, letting much of the interesting variation through. Studies of specific art forms or audiences, because they begin with a restricted population, provide a level of detail unobtainable in sample surveys, but cannot make any claims about the behavior of audiences in general nor do they say anything about the reception of particular cultural objects.

At the most general level, we would like to know the reasons people become involved in art worlds and the ways in which they do so. The first part of the answer is accessibility. One cannot attend performances if there are none about. One cannot read texts that are not distributed.[4] Modern societies have the greatest number and variety of both genres and performances in history, but there are still a good many complaints on this score.

The second set of reasons relates to visibility. Even if they are available, one cannot attend performances if one does not know about them. *Routinization* cuts through a variety of other requirements here—the Greater Dionysia occurred every year at the same time and Athenians planned accordingly. *Advertising* plays a role by producing awareness and curiosity. In the early French theater, audiences were gleaned through harlequins and acrobats in the public square (Wiley 1960). Not long after, the poster came into use, followed two centuries later by the more elaborate apparatus of television, radio, and print media. Still more important is *talk within networks* of people who communicate with and influence one another. Such talk is the subject of Chapter 9.

Critical reviews, even if they had no other function, are a form of advertisement. One easy way—too easy, in fact—of indicating their impact is by asking people. A 1975 survey by Lou Harris (Americans and the Arts) found that 40 percent of the sample reported that critics affected one's choice of entertainment. These respondents were typically frequent attenders, affluent, and well educated (English 1979, p. 117). Older people reported less influence than younger. Another 1973 study found that 43 percent reported critics were somewhat or very important.[5]

Accessibility and visibility are structurally prior to social class as a determinant of participation. The possession of money and leisure time are of no use otherwise. The most comprehensive recent survey of audience studies shows that education and income are related to attendance at theater, with education the more powerful predictor (DiMaggio and Useem 1983). Baumol and Bowen, surveying a large sample of spectators throughout the country in the mid-1960s, were able to paint a relatively clear portrait of the performing arts audience for theater, symphonies, opera, ballet, and ensembles—all highbrow forms. Nearly two-thirds of the audience were professionals, over half of the males had graduate education, and the median income was twice that of the urban population in 1960. As they put it, the audience is composed of "*exceedingly* well-educated persons" (1966, p. 80). Blue-collar workers accounted for only 3 percent of the audience, as compared with nearly 60 percent of the population at the time.[6] In the mid-1970s, a study by the National Research Center for the Arts found that about three-quarters of the college-educated had attended the theater in the past twelve months, while less than 18 percent of those without a high school degree had done so. In New York State, only 2 percent of the theater audience was blue collar, while 55 percent were managerial or professional.

Conventional wisdom has it that the relationship between education, income, and participation owes to two kinds of constraints: the ability to purchase culture and the ability to understand it. In addition, there are matters of prestige involved: "status climbing" and its interactional rewards (or dangers). One's presence at the opera or theater became a fashionable extension of "salon" life and symbol of upper-class taste as early as the seventeenth century (Lough 1957) and continues to be so today (Gans 1974).

At the individual level, there are several speculations to account for frequent consumption of certain genres. These range from the most general kinds of "escapist" motivations (Bentley 1964), through well-formed social-psychological theories (Austin 1989), through factors such as the design of the theater building, location, and performance times (Bennett 1990). But all of these factors are nonspecific, first-order influences, helping to explain certain *general* types of cultural participation. They tell us nothing about why some *particular* performances are viewed rather than others (selection). They say nothing about the responses of those who, for whatever reasons, become witnesses (reception). And they are subject to the general problems of survey research. Since unpopular performances seldom go any further—and virtually never become parts of the cultural canon—it is important to understand the conditions that provide infant works with the opportunity for adulthood and, rarely, immortality.[7]

Here, in the context of specific artworks, individual and social decision processes play a primary role. Here it is that the influence of cultural judgments is manifest through assessments that circulate via print or persons. Unlike gossip, dirty jokes, urban legends, and stories, tales of performances do not course widely through networks of social relations,[8] but tend to pause one or a few removes from their source.

WHO GOES TO THE FESTIVAL?

Are audiences for the Edinburgh festival unique in certain ways? Are Fringe audiences different from audiences for the official festival? Available information does not lead one to believe the festival audience is unique or peculiar. What is peculiar is the concentration of people, not their personal characteristics.

The best information on audience characteristics comes from a Scottish Tourist Board survey of nearly 6,000 interviews with visitors to the nine major Edinburgh festivals. Conducted in 1990 by a Scottish consulting firm using both personal interviews (n = 2,473) and self-completion questionnaires (n = 3,480), the estimated audience of 1.3 million is generally more female than male, under forty-four years old, and middle class.

For the Fringe itself 1,604 questionnaires were analyzed.[9] The audience consists of a slight majority of women (53 percent) and is slightly younger than that for the other Edinburgh festivals. Thirty-one percent of spectators are under twenty-four and 37 percent are between twenty-five and thirty-four years of age. In terms of British occupational categories, one-third of the audience is middle management (grade B), while 41 percent are supervisory, clerical, and junior management (grade C1). Nine percent are skilled manual workers (C2) and only 7 percent are in the lowest two occupational types (DE). International Festival audiences have slightly higher social status than Fringe audiences, with higher percentages of spectators in grades A (7 percent to 4 percent) and B (38 percent to 33 percent).

Fringe audiences are mainly British but there are large differences in estimates between the Tourist Board survey and the 1992 Fringe office figures. Both agree that the Fringe audience is more Scottish than English and the overseas component is small.[10] Fringegoers are more likely to come from England than visitors at the International Festival, while Continentals make up less than 10 percent of the audience. Overall, audiences for both "official" festival and Fringe are similar and consist predominantly of Scots and English.[11]

Given its reputation as a feast of performances, we might expect Fringegoers to be more serious about the business of spectatorship than those at other festivals. Over half (57 percent) of nonlocal visitors report that the Fringe was their "sole reason for coming" to Edinburgh and an equal number reported that their visit was an "independent holiday."[12] Of spectators at eight comparison festivals, spectators at Fringe shows were *least* likely to say they would not attend other shows at the festival (6 percent). Nearly 90 percent had a copy of the massive Fringe program and over one-quarter of those interviewed said they would see ten or more shows. Fringe shows are typically attended alone (24 percent) or with one other person (48 percent).

Since the analysis presented here uses 1988 attendance figures, a small study conducted that year by a geographer is also relevant.[13] About half of those questioned come from Scotland (38 percent from the immediate Edinburgh and Lothian region) and one-third from England. The remaining 18 percent hail from western Europe, Asia, the Commonwealth countries, and North America, somewhat higher than other estimates, but again, contrary to popular belief, there are not many Americans. Fewer than 5 percent were from the United States (down from an estimated 9 percent in 1977).[14] More than half of Macrae's respondents were not visiting any other place besides Edinburgh and only a small minority of these were day-trippers. Over 70 percent stayed at least four nights and one-third stayed *eight or more nights*.[15] These surveys, while flawed, indicate a young, middle-class, British audience with a relatively high interest in the Fringe.

SURVEY RESEARCH

Much can be learned from surveys and often they provide the best data available. I report the results from such an audience survey in Chapter 9. But I doubt they are ideal for assessing the effects of critics because people often do not know what has influenced them and, when they do, often fail to report it accurately. The quality of the evidence collected varies, as many respondents can attest. And those who say that survey research removes the "human" element would do better to hope than to complain.

I encountered the Tourist Board Survey at Marco's Leisure Centre in the person of a splendid Scottish matron. Apparently—though I have never understood it fully—some karmic law operates to guarantee that if there is a questionnaire of any kind to be completed, I am selected for the sample. This may be because I am a sociologist.

Marco's is a large venue within hopping distance of Scottish and Newcastle's Fountain Brewery. It has neither the architectural charm of the Pleasance or the Assembly Rooms, nor their proximity to the tourist trade. In fact, Marco's is really an athletic club. Up to five performance areas insure a lively crowd of theatergoers, while the locals weave through tables of performers and pints for racketball and weight training. I had seen the interviewers in various places around Edinburgh and now considered it my duty to sit down and take my medicine from this gentle soul. Her thick white hair and pleasant countenance had soothed many a Fringegoer that day. Had she turned out to be mother of the exalted Hume, it would not have surprised me.

She had found it prudent, if less effective for the purposes of her heartless employers, to seat herself somewhat away from the turmoil of trade. Instead of counting the patrons, she was offhandedly reading Fringe posters and sorting blank questionnaires. My appearance startled her.

"Are you rushing somewhere just noo?" she recovered.

We began slowly, but skipped past the series of questions on "daily expenditures during the Festival." I informed her that I was not paying for my lodging but instead contributing to the Improvement Fund of the Methodist Church on behalf of my hosts. A Fringe group had ruined the stops of the church organ to the tune of £2,000 and they were needing replacement. By the time she had finished beaming and praising me for this, I not only considered her as my own grandmother, but was even tempted to give my maternal surname so that I could tell her I was a MacDaniel as well. The fact that she missed the next page of questions seemed inconsequential as she inquired "Dae ye tak porridge with yer breakfast in America?"—a matter of greater personal interest.

Still, as we came to a series of questions that required me to "agree or disagree" on a five-point scale, I could not resist a surge of professional concern. She had reversed the scale and was checking "disagree" boxes instead of the "agree" boxes. One other thing puzzled me.

"Dae ye agree strongly," said she, with a magnificent roll of r's, "or disagree a wee bit with these other things. Wait. Just a wee second. Here we are—'Ticket prices are higher. Somewhat higher. Than expected.'— Wha dae ye think?"

"I disagree strongly. They're always high."

"Very nice." Reading her form upside down, I see she circles a "6." "The next one. Let's see. Here we are. 'I have gone to fewer shows than expected. Because of the tickets.' The prices of the tickets, ken?"

"Disagree strongly. I don't pay for them."

"Why that's lovely, isn't it? So ye can gie the money to the kirk!"

Maybe not. But she circles another "6." This worries me because such questions usually have fewer options. "6" might be a "don't know."

"Ma'am. It's none of my business, but shouldn't that be '5' instead of a '6?'

She peers intently at the questionnaire, eyes widening, then flips her pencil to the eraser end: "Ach, I dae better wi' my spectacles, but I left them at hame."

AUDIENCE AND CRITIC AT THE FRINGE

Attendance counts are superior to survey data in assessing the impact of reviews because the effects of other factors can be controlled. Self-selection combined with diversity in the range of Fringe shows allows estimation of meaningful quantitative models. Consider again the contrast between the Fringe and the "official" festival, which shares with other potential research sites a number of problematic characteristics. At the official festival, groups are selected by the administrator, at least partly on reputation for excellence within a narrow range of performance categories. They are virtually guaranteed audiences through advance sales to travel agents and many have established international reputations. These features limit variability in genre, reputation, and audience size.

Self-selection of Fringe groups insures variation in performances. The Fringe Society guarantees nothing except a show. Reviews, if they have any effects at all, could be expected to have an impact here.[16] Critics in Edinburgh are attributed substantial power: the discovery myth implies their influence over audiences. Reviews may make *more* of a difference at the Fringe for the simple reason that one can expect a Broadway or London play, even a very bad one, to reflect the significant amount of money and effort that goes into professional productions.

At the Fringe it is possible to pay six quid to see one performer engaged in what looks like the first rehearsal for an unfinished play still searching for a director. Sometimes it is not even in English. Relative to word of mouth, one might expect critics to be influential.[17] To an extent that does not exist anywhere else in the world, the Fringe approximates a perfect market arrangement, with buyers (audiences) and sellers (performing groups) operating in a competitive environment where substantial information is provided by the advance program.

Further, since the number of Fringe performances is predetermined, runs are not generally lengthened when they are popular or cut short if no one comes. This is a major boon for examining the effects of reviews. On Broadway, a producer may withdraw a show because of the expectation that negative reviews will lead to financial loss. This assumption may or may not be correct, but artificially limits the size of the audience.

For most of the analysis in this chapter, I use information from the 1988 Fringe.[18] The program advertised 913 different shows, including 50 exhibitions, by 473 companies from 22 nations.[19] Over 90 were from overseas, with the rest divided evenly between London, Scotland, and the rest of the United Kingdom. Professional (40 percent) and amateur (44 percent) groups are represented in roughly equal numbers, with the remainder mixed (16 percent).[20]

Productions ranged from the standard repertoire of theater and classical music to improvisational theater sports, a two-person opera based on the life of Hieronymus Bosch, eight five-minute plays in one show, a cabaret about the rise of Marilyn Monroe from the grave, and the Zen meditations of a nude artist's model. This heterogeneity was reduced to seventeen types in the program "Index of Show Titles"—including theater, comedy, opera, cabaret, orchestral performances, poetry readings, jazz, folk music, and children's shows (see Table 6.1 for complete listing).[21] Shows are assigned to categories by the groups themselves.

Size and diversity are structural constraints that affect the behavior of performers, public, and mass media. For the performers, competition for audiences is intense. From 103 to 492 ($\mu = 378$, $\sigma = 123$) performances were available each day. At peak times the daily guide listed over a dozen simultaneous start times for shows on the Fringe. For the arts consumer this unparalleled degree of choice can be equally problematic. Many tourists arrive specifically to attend a large number of performances, as we have seen. How will they decide what to see? What heuristics can they use?

Two basic strategies are available. First, they can apply a *restrictive* strategy. Based on knowledge of past festivals, one's interest can be narrowed to established performers or groups that have been enjoyable in the past. Some spectators and critics restrict their experience to the supervenues because of their feeling that the "best" acts will be there. This is the reason for widespread concern that the establishment of a special program for the three largest venues will undermine risk-taking spectatorship.

Alternatively, consumers can apply an *information-gathering* strategy based on the acquisition of current information (asking friends, reading reviews). Friends are the "best" source of information simply because one often knows their tastes. Yet a strong qualifier applies. Although one's friends tend to like the same "kind of thing," tastes within "kinds" vary. An equally important aspect of relationships, reserved for Chapter Nine, is *joint attendance* at performances. The decision to go to a show is often one made together—if not democratically, then by some other means. Flexibility and influence here are more important than taste, which implies attendance at many events that would not be "chosen" if people acted independently. The influence of the social network of family, friends, and co-workers is obvious, but still poorly understood.

Visitors are not likely to have much of a social network in Edinburgh. Even with a passel of art-loving friends, it is not likely that they could see everything at the Fringe—at least not soon enough that *you* could see it all as well. The print media attempt to fill this demand for information by an increase in space devoted to the arts during the festival period and the number of critics prowling Edinburgh is enormous. Some of these reviewers are well-known arts journalists, but some are hired for the festival, recruited from the news desk, art schools, or the arts-conscious public.

We have seen that the *Scotsman* is the leading source of covereage for the festival, reviewing 41 percent of Fringe shows in 1994. The more locally oriented *Evening News* has recently taken an aggressive role in reviewing.[22] The *List* expands its coverage to weekly festival editions. In the late 1980s and early 1990s, two weekly tabloids (*Festival Times* and *Review88*) were exclusively devoted to festival coverage. Several national papers (e.g., the *Independent*, the *Guardian*) establish temporary offices in the city, and virtually all of the others send correspondents. But no single source reviews all productions.[23] In spite of frequent complaints to the contrary, all shows have an opportunity to be reviewed, and the majority are reviewed at least once.[24]

I use Fringe audience data to ask (1) what kinds of show are preferred when people have such a wide range of performances choices available every day? Next I turn to the questions that are crucial to the idea of cultural mediation. (2) Is there a relationship between the kinds of reviews received by a show and the size of the audience? (3) To what extent are there different effects (in Bourdieu's terms, "distinct sensibilities") for different performance genres? The mediation argument suggests that high-status genres should exhibit such an effect, while popular genres should not.

ARE LOWBROW GENRES MORE POPULAR?

An extraordinary level of pickiness is needed not to find anything interesting at the Fringe. To what extent do audiences gravitate toward specific types of performances? One would expect that "popular" genres have larger audiences than "highbrow" genres.[25] This empirical expectation is implied by the term I have generally used to refer to lowbrow forms. Northrop Frye declared that comedy is more popular than other types of drama because of its greater concern with social integration (1957).[26] This notion is attractively sociological but a trifle cerebral and, worse, probably wrong. Comedy is more popular than tragedy because it is funny. More generally, "popular" art is based on unmediated responses. No status enhancement is gained through association with it, but response is personal and immediate.

Table 6.1 in Appendix D indicates the range of performances that were offered at the 1988 Fringe, their relative frequencies, and their relative popularity.[27] The column on the left lists those genres that are considered "high" art while the righthand column lists "popular" genres. Most shows at the Fringe are theater. Apart from dance, no other high-status genre offers even a dozen shows. Although comedy is the most frequent popular category, these shows are more evenly split among musicals, revues, and cabarets.

Table 6.1 shows that the best-attended genres tend to be popular. Performances of popular music—rock/blues, folk, and jazz—are first, each averaging over three dozen tickets sold at the central box office.[28] Comedy, musical, and revue are next. Although the average number of theater tickets was less than ten, opera, mime, and dance averaged about the same ticket sales as the popular genres. It is not the case, then, that all popular genres are better attended than all highbrow genres. However, the popularity of opera and dance may be due to the relatively few performances in these fields (e.g., only three operas were available). Among popular genres, cabaret and, particularly, children's shows were less well attended.

The averages for *all* shows in the last row of the table indicate that highbrow shows sold less than half as many tickets as popular genres. For audiences and genres at the 1988 Fringe, "popular" genres are indeed more popular.[29]

DO REVIEWS AFFECT ATTENDANCE?

In the absence of an audience, the success of an artwork or artist is likely to be minimal.[30] If a review is a kind of selection mechanism for certain kinds of art, the evaluation should affect the likelihood of attendance. Highbrow mediation implies that the more positive the review, the larger the size of the viewing audience. But for all art the mere appearance of a review, independently of anything it says, is a kind of "objective advertisement" or "notice" for an artwork.

A test of the idea that reviews affect attendance requires indicators of audience size and the number and favorability of reviews. I used records maintained by the Fringe office to develop two measures of attendance. Tickets are sold both at the central box office (about one-third of all sales) and at the venues themselves. The first indicator is the total ticket sales for a production, which combines both main office (centralized) and venue (distributed) ticket sales. But since less than half of the performing groups report their venue sales to the Fringe office, such complete attendance information is available for only 61 percent of all shows. This measure, while comprehensive, is biased in favor of the more stable and established groups that maintain and report sales records (e.g., those with administrators; those that do not disband after the festival).[31]

A better indicator is the number of tickets sold at the Fringe box office. Reflecting advance ticket sales (up to a few hours before the performance) rather than total attendance, the main advantage is its availability for all productions. For purposes of comparison, models are presented for each dependent variable separately.[32]

Review coverage of a show varies in terms of how *favorable* it is and how *much* of it there is, that is, the visibility of coverage.[33] Visibility indicates *whether* a cultural object receives the attention of critics, while favorability indicates the *kind* of attention it receives. That is, favorability indicates whether the evaluation is positive or negative. Each factor may affect audiences for the performing arts but favorability is especially relevant to the hypothesis of cultural mediation.

Table 6.2 in Appendix D shows the results of regressing the two measures of ticket sales on review visibility, favorability, and a number of other factors (see Appendix A). The same variables are statistically significant in predicting each dependent variable, and the magnitudes of the unstandardized OLS coefficients are similar as well.[34]

The model that includes all ten variables explains half of the variance in Fringe box office sales. Excluding the effect of venue,[35] the nine-variable model explains 63 percent of the variance in attendance. In each case, the only factor not contributing significantly to the prediction of attendance is the youth of the company. Capacity, national reputation, the number of reviews (both in print and in the audiovisual media), the length of the show, and the start time are positively related to audience size. Originality is negatively related to size.

The cultural mediation argument is supported by the positive coefficient for review modality, indicating that the more positive the critical evaluation of the show (and the earlier it appears) the larger the audience in attendance. But it is not a particularly large effect. The number of reviews is related to attendance much more strongly than their favorability. Which suggests, as agents are wont to say, that all publicity is good publicity.[36]

DO REVIEWS MATTER MORE FOR HIGHBROW SHOWS?

> *Sneer:* And do you think there are any who are influenced by [reviews]?
> *Puff* : O lud, yes, sir.—The number of those who go through the fatigue of judging for themselves is very small indeed.
>
> —*Sheridan,* The Critic

The evaluative function of reviews appears to be less consequential than their role in providing visibility. If instead of attending to aesthetic judgments, readers simply employ and use the review as a source of information, then critics are less important.

Glowing reviews of distressing subjects may serve to warn off an audience. Negative reviews of subjects with high cultural interest may still promote attendance depending on the way cultural objects are classified by genre. The mediation hypothesis does not attribute critical power across all positions in the cultural hierarchy. Contrasting views on the relationship between high and popular culture have already been distinguished in Chapter 1. I recapitulate them briefly here because of their differing predictions on the effects of reviews.

The "cultural convergence" view emphasizes the diminishing differences between the realms of high and popular art. Arenas of high and popular art that were once distinctive have lost their separate identities (Blau 1988b, pp. 285–86; J. Blau 1986b; Gans 1985). Concentration of wealth no long promotes elite art, while both popular and elite cultural institutions flourish in cities with low inequality and high education (Blau, Blau, Quets, and Tada et al. 1986). Whether classification systems are viewed as becoming more differentiated (DiMaggio 1987, p. 452; Gans 1985) or simply blurred and flexible (Levine 1988, pp. 243–56), genres have become less hierarchical. The "cultural convergence" hypothesis predicts no difference in the mediative process for different genres. Even if, as Table 6.2 shows, reviews mediate the reception process through their effect on attendance, we should not expect genre differences.

The "cultural capital" view stresses the relationship between art and class reproduction, in Bourdieu's terms, relationships of "distinction" (1984). Cultural consumption is taken as a marker of class differences. Participation in high culture, with its monopoly of "sublime purposelessness,"[37] is therefore important as a means of mobility and symbolic affiliation with high-status groups (DiMaggio 1982a; DiMaggio and Mohr 1985). Divergent underlying "aesthetics" are produced by socialization and educational experience (Bourdieu 1984, pp. 1–44). The implication is that class interests promote the continuing differentiation of "legitimate" and "popular" taste, but it is not clear whether critical discourse should have any effect for higher statuses, independent of formal education and influence.

The "cultural mediation" view holds that the distinction between high and popular art does not rest exclusively on the kinds of people who consume them. High social status is associated not only with consumption of high art, but of *more diverse* art (Feld, O'Hare, and Schuster 1983; Blau, Blau, and Golden 1985; DiMaggio 1987). Frequent consumers of most cultural objects tend to be middle class, but different discursive processes characterize the ways in which opinions are created and sustained for high and popular genres. I have characterized participation in higher art forms as a kind of bargain in which one gives up partial rights to one's own opinion in exchange for status. Views are more often mediated by experts and educators than in lowbrow forms. The "discriminating" and "popular" aesthetics described by Bourdieu are better for characterizing ways of relating to different genres than they are as descriptions of the behavior of different positions in the stratification system.

This view of high and popular culture generates different expectations for the mediative function of critical discourse, that is, the opinions of experts. The discriminating sensibility associated with "high" art depends on the continual generation of "legitimacy" associated with critical evaluations. This aesthetic is distanced from the naturalism and direct perception of the popular disposition. One measure of the distance is the authoritative expertise provided by others who are "discriminating." Common features are defined and contrasted with other artworks, helping to circumscribe the boundaries of correct taste both by including and excluding works based on aesthetic criteria (Duncan 1953) and by suggesting performance characteristics that are valued.

By this reasoning we would expect that the public for high art pays more attention to reviews. For "legitimate" performance genres such as theater, reviewer evaluations should be associated with attendance. The audience for "serious" work, simply put, is more likely to read reviews and to follow their recommendations. Contrariwise, the popular aesthetic reserves a diminished position for reviews and remains largely unaffected by them. This is not to say they go unread or unappreciated in terms of content or value. They simply become part of the complex of popular culture without systematic influences on consumer behavior.[38]

Highbrow and popular genres are examined separately in Table 6.3 (see Appendix D). Standardized coefficients are presented in order to compare the magnitude of effects *within* each model. Again, from half to two-thirds of the variance in attendance may be explained by this set of independent variables. As in Table 6.2 capacity, reputation, duration, and review frequency exhibit positive net effects in all four equations. Originality of production has a significant negative effect in each model except total sales for popular shows.[39]

The effects of media coverage and youth status are not consistent across the models for Fringe box office and total sales. Audiovisual coverage (as well as youth status) is more important for popular genres when the dependent variable is Fringe box office sales. Showtime is, on either criterion, important for highbrow shows but not for popular shows.

For testing genre mediation arguments the most important comparison is between the coefficients of favorability for each genre type. The second to last row of coefficients shows that modality is positive and significant (p = .01) for highbrow shows only. This comparison is consistent for Fringe box office and total sales, though the difference is not as great for total sales. That is, for highbrow genres such as theater, positive reviews are associated with larger audience sizes, but not for popular performances (e.g., comedy, cabaret).[40]

Again, comparing the size of the effects, the best predictor of audience size[41] is the sheer number of reviews published in the four major Edinburgh papers. The prior reputation of the performing group and the show (known performances) are also important, followed by show length (the longer the better). Somewhat less important, but still significant, are media coverage and youth status (for popular genres) and, for highbrow genres, start time and review modality.

The impact of reviews is primarily through the visibility they grant rather than through the evaluations they tender. A common synonym for a "review" is a "notice," which is exactly what they provide. Even the simple count of reviews received is a fairly good predictor of audience size.[42] More important than *what* the reviews say about a production is simply that it has been noticed and reviewed by critics in a variety of public forums. This viewpoint is expressed by the performers themselves but for a different reason. Even mediocre or negative reviews are better than no reviews at all because they can be "carved up" (strategically edited) to present a show in a favorable light. Potential audiences respond less to the evaluative component of reviews than to their descriptive component.

Reading or seeing reviews in a number of places highlights the importance of a show and maintains its salience for potential spectators in ways that may be more effective, but with much the same function, as advertising. This visibility effect is somewhat less powerful, but still significant, outside the print media through radio and television coverage.

Reputational processes, set in motion long before groups enter the competition for festival audiences, are a second crucial asset. This result is consistent with another effect of reviews, namely that *prior* reviews, by drawing the attention of audiences and producers, may have helped to generate the visibility and career trajectory that carries over to the present festival. Still, all else equal, for the purpose of capturing a public, good notices are not worth as much as prior reputation.

Artworks themselves, not just groups, have reputations. Although I was unable to evaluate these reputations directly, the negative coefficient for new plays suggests a liability of newness for the performance of unknown works. If anything, the Edinburgh Fringe has a reputation for innovation, risk taking, and an "adventuresome" audience. Yet these results show that consumers are generally disinclined to view new work,[43] at least in a festival situation where there is an abundance of choice. For original shows, the reputation of the group and the reviews become quite important.[44]

In terms of the comparison between highbrow and popular genres, two differences in the factors that affect attendance are shared for both indicators of participation. Unexpectedly, for highbrow but not popular genres, *later* start times are associated with larger audiences. Griswold, in her account of the nineteenth-century London theater, attributes part of the loss of the affluent audience to a postponement of the dinner hour that conflicted with performance times for many theaters (1986, p. 132). At the Edinburgh festival, audiences for highbrow genres are less willing to attend early performances as well, probably because of this "consumption" effect.

These results are consistent with the persistence of cultural hierarchy through the operation of critical discourse as a mediator of experience. If the underlying "aesthetics" identified by Bourdieu are interpreted in terms of the distinction between highbrow and popular genres, then the differentiation of "legitimate" and "popular" taste might be framed as a difference in how people select kinds of performing arts. Since the discriminating sensibility associated with "high" art does not depend on direct perception but rather the refined evaluation of aesthetically relevant production features, the critic plays an important role in the definition and maintenance of performance standards. Expert judgments are relevant to consumer participation and perceptions in "legitimate" genres but unnecessary to popular genres.[45]

In the latter, aside from imparting information about the performance, reviewer appraisals are not important. Although reviews may be read and used, the judgmental function is ineffective.[46] So the relationship between the favorability of reviews and attendance should differ by genre if this difference in processes of selection were occurring.

The positive association between reviewer evaluations and audience size for highbrow but not popular genres is consistent with *both* cultural mediation and cultural capital arguments, though it is not specifically predicted by the latter. But since I have no measure of the socioeconomic status of the audience for specific shows a "compositional" explanation cannot be ruled out.

In Bourdieu's view, discriminative processes are class-related, such that higher positions in the stratification system are associated with the pure aesthetic, lower positions with the popular aesthetic. *Individuals*, as carriers of aesthetics, respond to participation opportunities in specific and consistent ways. Theatergoers at the Fringe attend cabaret as well. But do they *participate* in the same way for each genre? A less individualistic and more situational conception of the popular and pure aesthetics views them as dispositions that come into effect for different kinds of artwork. For highbrow genres, critical opinions are valued and assimilated.

For popular genres, direct and unmediated participation is more likely, regardless of class background. Viewed as "mere entertainment" without cultural and symbolic pretensions, comedy and musicals need no authoritative aesthetic vision to legitimate their worth. Gans's characterization of lower-taste publics as lacking an interest in the "correct" responses to art is accurate, even if the "public" is drawn from diverse occupational and educational strata. For genres such as revues and cabarets as well as soap operas, the world of everyday experience is sufficient ground for understanding and appreciation.[47]

Yet, for these same consumers, high art may be approached differently, as an "enchanted experience" for which training in school and university is supplemented by the estimation of cultural legitimators. The cultivated disposition is brought into play when considering art forms regarded as serious. Form replaces content; relational and comparative features grow in importance over direct perception; elements of the artistic traditions are referenced that require critical interpretation. There is no point wasting time on theatrical productions known to be of inferior aesthetic value—better go to a movie with stars you can count on.[48]

INTERVIEW WITH THE CRITIC

Not everyone finds such results convincing. One critic was at pains to demonstrate their imperfections. The place was the courtyard of the old Traverse Theatre in the afternoon. The critic, accompanied by an attractive middle-aged woman, was an English gentleman in his mid-sixties, well dressed and titled, with a penetrating gaze—the kind of person who could plausibly wear a cape.[49]

Critic: Now tell me, young man, what is the object of your study?

Sociologist: I'm looking at the relationships between critics, audiences, and performers. Mainly critics, and their effects on audiences.

Critic: Yes, yes. Well. And what sort of study will this be?

Sociologist: It's a sociological investigation of the role of critics. I'm asking them about the review process. I'm talking to performers about them. And looking at whether their reviews have any impact on how many people go to see a show.

Critic: And according to you, what effects do they have?

Sociologist: Well, taking other things into account, not much, actually.

Critic: Yes, yes. . . . Well then. . . . Interesting. Of course, you can't predict human behavior.

Sociologist: Sir?

Critic: Human behavior. No one knows, really. I mean, that's all rather been discounted, hasn't it.

Sociologist: How do you mean?

Critic: The very idea. Men . . . and women [*looks to companion*] are quite unique creatures.

Sociologist: I suppose I'm not following you.

Critic: Well it couldn't be simpler, could it? You can't predict human behavior. You can't get inside the human mind.

Sociologist: Frankly, you can predict a lot of it. And I'm not trying to get inside anyone's mind—except maybe my own. That would be psychology more than sociology.

Critic: . . . How can you know how a person reads a review? I may read a review one way and you may read the very same review, by the very same critic, and see very different things.

Sociologist: Absolutely, sir. But most people can tell if it's a good review or not, don't you think?

Critic: And then, young man, they may or may not go to the show. Take, just for instance, Peter O'Toole's *Macbeth*. I—and every other critic—heaped piles of scorn on it—it was an absolute joke. And everyone went to see it—packed houses, you know—just to laugh at it and see how bad it was. No sir, you can't get inside the human mind. You can't tell how they'll respond.

Sociologist: Maybe they were just going to see Peter O'Toole?

Critic: Utter nonsense. How can you predict human behavior with a survey?

Sociologist: I'm not doing a survey. I'm simply relating a number of things—like the reviews—to the size of the audience for various performances. That's not a survey.

Critic: No difference, really. There's no saying why a person goes to a show. They may go because they know someone in it. They may go because they're interested in the play. Why it's ridiculous! It simply can't be done. There are just so many things, so many reasons.

Sociologist: Of course. That's why there's always unexplained variation. You can't predict things perfectly, but that doesn't mean you can't predict them at all.

Critic: This kind of behaviouralism just isn't feasible. That was proven years ago. You can't predict things like this. The human mind is a marvelous thing. You couldn't predict as much as 1 percent. Maybe 2 percent if you were lucky. And on the Fringe, in Edinburgh, I'd stake everything that wherever your models were developed, they won't work here. The Fringe audience is too fickle.

Sociologist: But I'm doing the study here. Here at the Fringe. That's where I got my information.

Critic: How very unfortunate for you. No amount of numbers will get you around the fact that you're dealing with peoples' preferences, peoples' *prejudices*, for God's sake. You can't know these things—why, what makes you think you can put a *questionnaire* on someone's *seat* and find out what they're *thinking*.

Sociologist: I'm not putting questionnaire's on seats and I'm not trying to find out what they're thinking . . .

Critic: . . . because your methods, and the methods of all these behaviouralisms don't take the critical *judgment* into account. I assess a show based on the other shows I've seen. I have seen over two thousand shows. Sociology has no way of dealing with that! Sociology is a contradiction in principle!

Sociologist: Sir, with all due respect, you are an extremely ignorant man.

Critic: I say, this is all absolute rubbish . . .

Sociologist: You know *nothing* about sociology. Your ignorance is so thorough you don't know when it's on parade. You probably haven't read a book of nonfiction since you left college, if you went to college. The point is not to get into anyone's mind. The point is not to insist that critics are robots or audiences are sheep. The point is to see *if* there are any *patterns* in the relationships between the reviews people write and the size of the audience for the show. You define what you're interested in—like shows on the Fringe or arrogant critics. Then you've got to define a dependent variable—like how large your audience is or how hard your head is. Then you've got to eliminate all the confounding factors you can think of. You know nothing about the *assumptions* being made here, the techniques used, or the theory involved. . . .

Critic [*rising*]: Sorry, we'd love to stay, but we've got to be off just now to see a show.

Chapter Seven

CRITICAL EVALUATION

> Some would maintain one laugh throughout a play.
> Some would be grave and bear fine things away.
> How is it possible at once to please
> Tastes so directly opposite as these?
> —*Henry Fielding*, The Universal Gallant

ACTORS, DIRECTORS, spectators, and critics themselves often speculate about why reviewers like—or say they like—particular shows. I begin this chapter by considering these "folk theories," commonly held views that purport to explain why reviews are good or bad. Next, I turn to the question of whether some shows really do have an edge when it comes to getting reviewed. Fringe notices are used to show that popular art is reviewed more favorably than high art. Is this because highbrow shows are, in general, worse than popular ones—that is, do reviewers really like them less? This issue is crucial, because if the answer is yes, then the evidence for highbrow mediation is based purely on factors external to the review process itself.

Internal evidence of mediation would only be provided if highbrow shows were reviewed *differently*. Through interviews with the critics and comparisons between informal evaluations and their published judgments, I show that critics *like* high art just as well as popular art but *write* more critically about the former. They are simply more reluctant to praise high art—in other words, they have "standards." In the last section, the way is paved for an examination of performers' views in Chapter 8 by examining the extent of agreement among critics.

FOLK THEORIES OF EVALUATION

Several theories professing to explain critical evaluations enjoy currency. They are offered in everyday contexts as explanatory devices. They may be viewed as "folk theories" in the sense of accounting mechanisms, conventionally produced and accepted in ordinary talk. They are accountable only to the mundane reason of the art world (Pollner 1987).

In mundane talk it is often the "exceptions" that require explanation. Particularly acidic reviews and ill-tempered critics are the subject of animated discussion among performers. Folk theories are employed in the serious business of criticizing the critics, determining whether to "believe" an evaluation, rationalizing negative reviews. If a good indicator of the significance of a phenomenon is the extent to which it is "theorized" in ordinary discourse, then the critical review is surely one of the art world's most important artifacts.

One important theory emphasizes the *predispositions* of reviewers to make positive (or negative) judgments. This includes partiality to certain works, authors, and performers and can occur because of editorial pressure or illicit incentives. If not out-and-out bribery, reviewers are at minimum caught in a web of personal favors and obligations grounded in the professional relationships that their "parasitic activity" entails.[1]

Although most reviewers cannot aspire to such largesse, gifts constitute a wellspring of potential coloration. Music reviewers receive dozens of free albums per week; artists give critics paintings that are resold. Large advertising budgets by publishing houses, theater groups, and film companies are a persistent prod (sometimes editorial) to critics who constantly give negative reviews to their output.[2]

One "experiment" bears on this question. Some twenty years ago John English surveyed a group of critics and included a quarter, offering to treat them to coffee as they completed the survey. One-third of his respondents returned the quarter.[3]

Another theory is rooted simply in the informal social networks of the reviewer: "It's not how good you are, it's who you know." Just as friends of the playwright packed the house for shouting frenzies in the eighteenth century, the sentiments of reviewers are tapped when assessing the work of friends and rivals.[4] Best of all, if you can get the job, is reviewing your own work. Walter Scott praised his own *Waverley* novel at length and Anthony Burgess created a minor scandal by reviewing his own "Poetry in a Tiny Room."[5]

We might go so far as to say that reviewers as a class exhibit differential susceptibilities to the genres they cover. In the late 1950s Kurt Lang produced the first modern study of reviews focusing on evaluations. He noted that the "severity" of reviews varied for different media, increasing from theater to movies to television. One interpretation of this finding is that the smaller and denser the art world, the more likely the reviewer is to have personal ties with the artists and the more favorable the review will be. This is consistent with relatively generous theater reviews[6] and relatively harsh television reviews (where reviewers are particularly unlikely to know the artists themselves), but book reviews were even more positive than theater reviews.[7] Is the book world even smaller and more interconnected than the theater world? Or is it that since book reviewers are more likely to be authors than reviewers in other fields are to be performers, their general esteem for the reviewed objects is greater?

Gifts, pressure, and social network processes can be forms of bias. But if "bias" is augmented to simple "preference" then it is the best-seasoned folk theory of all. Reviewers may be "expert consumers," but within their assigned genres display recognizable cultural tastes. Part of their evaluation is attributable to these dispositions, but since they can operate at the level of the subgenre, artist, and style, they remain a fruitful area of theory.[8]

Like scholarly debates, folk theories often involve diametrically opposed views. Two examples of this are alternative views of the nature of "critical consensus" and what might be termed "satiation effects."

The first view of consensus is that critics are pack dogs at heart. Elite or influential critics establish the "line" on a current object or performer, which is then picked up by workaday journalists. Or perhaps the first review to appear influences the remainder.[9] According to one first-time performer "From what I've seen at the festival, one or two reviews kind of get the ball rolling." A somewhat inverted argument is often put forward with respect to both performance and plastic arts reviews. Though critics want to follow a leader, what they fear most is *extremity*: hence reviewers seek to *conceal* their opinions out of nervousness and uncertainty. They fear being wrong, out of step, or lacking in judgment, as determined by other reviewers and subsequent generations. Stylistically, they wax ironic to mask their commitments and disguise their judgment.

But directly contrary to this is the notion that critics revel in their uniqueness and love nothing more than voicing the lone dissent. A Scottish director expressed one version by way of a story: "We couldn't put a foot wrong for eighteen months. All good reviews. Won every award. Then the *Scotsman*'s arts editor was heard to say 'it's time they were taken down a notch.'"

According to this theory critics prize independence, but awareness of other opinions is likely to generate opposing reactions, redounding to their own professional advantage. As the sole antagonist or proponent of a new show, a critic can heighten his visibility, particularly with the promotional (or irate) assistance of the producer.

My own interviews indicate a high level of commitment to the idea of evaluative autonomy: one keeps one's own council until one's review is on paper. During the Edinburgh Festival, most critics have little time to read the reviews of others. The volume of newsprint is as daunting to the critic who is curious what others think as it is to the public. Routine reviewing work during other times of the year is less frenetic, but here the professional ethic makes itself felt: "The Edinburgh reviewers usually catch the last train after seeing a show in Glasgow. We sit there together, me and [*Guardian* critic], [*Scotsman* critic], and [*Evening News* critic]. We're all thinking about our reviews, we're all dying to talk about the show, and we talk about everything under the sun—except the show." I could find little support for the idea that reviewers pay much attention to other critics in formulating their own views, but the belief is functional for performers who have received a string of bad notices.[10]

A second pair of theories explaining judgments emerges from the fact that critics see a very large number of shows. This sheer volume of experience alters the evaluation process. There is good reason to think that people who see many shows will react differently from those who see only a few. What is the effect of this surfeit of experiences?

One notion is that standards sink lower and lower over time, such that critics wind up praising mediocre work.[11] But another claims that critics become jaded and hence progressively harsher, comparing works with the best they have seen or impossibly high standards (mis)remembered from years past. Cultural mediation implies that both "standard sinking" and "jading" should be attributed most often to critics of high art.

WHICH SHOWS GET THE BEST REVIEWS?

Do critics treat high and popular works differently? If the idea of cultural mediation is valid, they should, because critics are key players in the reproduction of cultural hierarchy. When works are labeled as highbrow or popular, is the reaction of critics predictable? I suggest that it is, but not in the way some might expect. The obvious possibility is that popular works will be condemned for their lack of complexity, their reliance on superficial devices and sentiments, their eager manipulativeness.[12] But the idea of cultural mediation suggests the opposite: popular works will be forgiven sins for which legitimate performance art would be taken to task. In the next two sections I evaluate this idea. The evidence for this claim is indirect but confirmatory.

What kinds of shows receive better evaluations? I use the *Scotsman*'s reviews because of its history, coverage, and prestige. As we have seen, the national dailies have limited coverage of the Fringe. Special purpose newspapers and magazines, while they are widely read in Edinburgh and cover a diversity of shows, do not have the reputation, distribution, or visibility of the reviews appearing in the *Scotsman*.

The objective is to predict how positive or negative reviews will be from the structural properties of performances *without any information about the content of the performances themselves.* Structural properties are the publicly available features for all shows, factors that can be defined for all kinds of performance art. Undoubtedly, if one were to attend the shows and view their contents explicitly, predicting reviews might be easier. But that approach was unsporting, even in the eighteenth century. As John Gay wrote, "they can scarce be called critics who must hear and read a thing before they will venture to declare their opinion. Anybody can do that."[13]

The *Scotsman*'s evaluation is used as a dependent variable.[14] Shows that were not reviewed at all are excluded, leaving a total of 406 shows. Better reviews are at least weakly associated with the following factors:[15] higher priced tickets, earlier opening dates, older shows, greater media coverage, better-known groups, sold-out shows, and past awards won.

Note that these empirical associations are indifferent as to an interpretation of "bias" (judgmental predisposition) on the part of reviewers or features that happen to be associated with the "quality" of the show, if we could identify such a thing. The fact that prestigious groups get better reviews could mean that critics were biased in their favor, or simply that their performances are different.

More generally, no matter what structural feature is shown to be associated with more favorable reviews, it can always be argued that the reason for the association is that the specified feature is itself related to quality, hence naturally associated with more positive evaluations. I note that this might also count *against* an interpretation in terms of quality as such features become progressively mysterious and ad hoc. But the knockout punch against objectivist views of quality must ultimately be conceptual rather than empirical.

The preceding list is problematic because many of these features are also associated with each other and hence do not explain unique variation in the *Scotsman*'s published evaluation. If, for instance, sold-out shows are typically performed by nationally visible groups, then it may be wrong to say that reviewers rated sold-out shows more highly, *independently* of their performance by such reputable groups. Reputation, in other words, may be solely responsible for this association.

After eliminating the variables that have no independent effect, Table 7.1 (in Appendix D) shows the results of regressing the *Scotsman*'s evaluation on four factors, each of which contributes to a prediction that is much better than we could do simply by chance (p = .0001) but still explains only 7 percent of the overall variation in critical evaluations ($R^2 = .07$). Each predictor variable is significant at conventional levels. The magnitude of the effects are roughly equal, as indicated by the standardized coefficients in the last column.[16]

Table 7.1 shows that popular shows tend to receive more favorable reviews overall. The unstandardized coefficient in the first column can be interpreted as follows: if we know *nothing more than the genre* of a show, we can already guess something about the kind of review it is likely to get. Comedies, cabarets, musicals, and the like will, on average, be rated .3 higher on our five-point scale than highbrow shows. Not only are popular shows better attended, as the previous chapter showed, they are more popular with reviewers as well. Is this because highbrow shows are, on average, worse than popular ones? That is, do reviewers really like them less? I return to this question in the following section.

Three other factors help us in guessing how favorable a review is likely to be: the national reputation of the group, the television and radio coverage received by the show, and its date of opening. While each of these factors is included in the best predictive model for all shows, they are not all significant when we predict reviews for highbrow and popular shows separately, as in Table 7.2 (Appendix D).

A comparison of the first and second halves of Table 7.2 shows that media coverage and reputation are important to the prediction of reviews for highbrow shows. The magnitude of their effects is larger than in the full model. However, they are insignificant for popular shows. Groups with strong national reputations and, particularly, shows with high levels of media attention were more likely to get positive reviews in the *Scotsman*, but only when they were theater, dance, mime, or one of the other "high" performance arts. If these factors represent specific "biases," then reviewers exhibit them to a greater degree in high art.

Well-known groups, assuming their reputation is independent of this particular festival and established in advance of the offerings under consideration here, have a better chance of receiving a good review. Whether this is due to better funding, advertisements, professionalism, or, as one reviewer had it, the quality of the whisky during the interval, we cannot tell. But it is more significant that the advantage does not seem to be conferred on popular performances. Whatever its source, the *Scotsman* reviewers, though they write more favorably about comedies and cabarets, are neither impressed by credentials, nor influenced by unmeasured factors associated with reputation.

The same argument applies, albeit with more uncertainty, to media reporting. The degree of media coverage might be related to favorable highbrow reviews for several reasons. First, reviewers might be unconsciously swayed, though they do not ever admit it, by radio and television coverage of an event. Second, a good review in the *Scotsman*, important as it is to performers, might be important to coverage decisions by the audiovisual media. Third, since audiovisual media tend to prefer larger, more "newsworthy" stories such as international companies and star appearances, the association may simply reflect a similar tendency for reviewers.

The *absence* of certain effects is just as important to the interpretation of media coverage. I collected two measures of other journalistic coverage: the sheer number of reviews by the four major Edinburgh review sources and the number of reviews by other local and national papers. Although larger *numbers* of reviews in other locations are associated with favorable reviews in the *Scotsman*, when television and radio coverage is controlled, neither measure is significant. This implies that it is not sheer media coverage that is important, because newspaper reviews should show some effect as well.

Since popular shows do *not* demonstrate either media or reputation effects, is there any structural feature we can use to predict them, or are they subject only to unmeasured factors, such as the personal histories of the reviewers? Only one variable is significant: the opening date of the show. Popular shows that began *earlier* in the festival had better chances of getting a good review. This does not appear to be due to any absolute preference for shows appearing at the beginning of the festival. There is no such effect for highbrow shows.

It is tempting to say that popular genres are more quickly exhausted (or exhausting) than highbrow. While London reviewers tend to come to the festival for a few days and return, most Edinburgh reviewers see large numbers of shows during the three-week period. Increasingly, amusement becomes difficult. Cabarets seem smokier and audiences less tolerable. Reviewing the next dozen stand-up comics constitutes a too conscious effort to stay entertained. Subjects that were funny at the outset lose their potency. In plain terms, diversion becomes a chore. One reviewer put it in explicit terms: the later you see the show, the harder you are to please.

For theater there is no apparent "exhaustion" effect. Do reviewers simply have more energy for highbrow shows? This interpretation is arguable: it may be true that reviewers have no more stamina for theater than comedy. That being the case, what could account for the lack of any measurable effect? Probably the fact that as *critics* they do not feel as free to dismiss shows simply because they did not enjoy them. Scrutinizing—whether forced or free—adds balance to the review, evident in the absence of an exhaustion effect.

DO CRITICS SAY WHAT THEY THINK?

Popular shows, as a general rule, get better evaluations at the Fringe. Does that mean they are preferred by the reviewers who write them? If so, we should conclude that there is no evidence for highbrow mediation in the review process itself. Such evidence would only be provided *if highbrow shows were reviewed more critically*. This point is difficult to address directly with published reviews or questions, but it is straightforward to ask, Do reviewers say what they think?[17]

Through a comparison of published reviews and interviews with the reviewers themselves, I show that the answer turns out to be no. Most important for the idea of mediation is the comparison between reviews of highbrow and popular works, where there seem to be two conceptions of criticism operating, often in the very same critics.

If the review process affects the text but not the evaluation, can one assume that the printed judgment connects with—"reflects" in some sense—the subjective judgment of the critic? We might posthaste say no. There must surely be a distinction between the complex psychological experience of an artwork at the time it is witnessed and the expressed *evaluation*, which may or may not appear in a review. Various types of bias or preference could effect such a difference. Further, expressive competence is not a constant for all critics. Reviewers vary in their ability to commit reasons to textual forms and render them intelligible.

But let us ignore these subtleties and focus on the question of more interest to publics, performers, and the idea of mediation. Do critics give good reviews to works they don't like very much? Do they damn artists for the sheer pyrotechnical fun of it? If these were consistent patterns, it might seem to doom the critical enterprise by undermining credibility. Critics, like philosophers, are *supposed* to love the good and hate the bad.

It is impossible to address this question simply by asking the critics themselves. Most of them can and will cite specific occasions on which they relaxed standards or stiffened up at a particular show. But it would be highly suspect if they admitted to any persistent *systematic* bias in favor of one thing or another. The Fifth Amendment, that honorable American institution, should apply to Scottish critics as well.

So I approach the question indirectly. Let us distinguish between "subjective" judgments of the work and judgments that appear in the media. We can then ask *how closely the printed review corresponds to the subjective judgment of a reviewer*. In the absence of the analyst's couch, we have no access to the "real" judgment of the reviewer—if such a thing exists at all. The subjective experience of the performance—variable in its demands and relations, constantly shifting in aspect and effect—remains always a mystery. But within the constraints of method and good sense we can compare the reviewer's stated evaluation of a show to the review that eventually appeared. That is, we can compare informal and formal judgments.[18]

To discover the extent to which these judgments corresponded, I conducted a series of interviews with reviewers for the *Scotsman*.[19] All who had written twelve or more reviews were interviewed five months after the festival. The rationale for this length of time was to insure that the reviewers remembered the *show* (which, perhaps surprisingly, they did in all cases) rather than the *review*, which they wrote shortly after seeing it. In a very few instances, phrases or content from the original review were remembered, but generally not. I obtained these informal ratings for 319 performances from the fifteen most prolific reviewers.

Each reviewer was asked to rate the performance on a five-point scale, from very negative to very positive ("3" was neutral).[20] Published reviews from the *Scotsman* were rated by two judges and averaged for a measure of the extent to which a performance received a positive evaluation. Review "bias" was expressed by the *difference* between reviewer (i.e., informal) ratings and the *Scotsman* ratings—written by the same reviewers, of course. If we subtract the *Scotsman* rating from the informal rating, then a positive value indicates that informal judgment is more favorable than the published judgment, while a negative value means that the published review is more favorable.

Table 7.3 in Appendix D shows the results of a direct comparison for all available Fringe performances for each judge separately and the combined score. The association between formal and informal evaluations is high and positive in each case. Roughly 60 percent of the variation in the *printed* review may be attributed to variation in the *judgment* of the reviewer—far less than perfect.[21]

In about 63 percent of the cases (203/319), some difference exists between the scores.[22] But there is no reason to fuss over every small difference. Since scores may be positive or negative, an *average* difference of zero would obtain if published reviews are no more likely to be favorable than informal evaluations. The negative sign of the difference in Table 7.3 means that the *reviews themselves* are, on the average, more positive than the expressed opinions of their authors about the shows they reviewed. The magnitude of the t-score indicates this is unlikely to have occurred owing to random variation in scores. Compared with the printed reviews, the personal judgments of their authors are actually more negative—that is, there is a "positive bias" to reviews.[23]

Before we conclude that reviewers generally have hearts of gold, we should ask whether this pattern occurs across all performance genres, or whether it is restricted to some specific categories of performance. Cultural mediation entails differences in the importance of critical discourse by position in the cultural hierarchy. Reviewers themselves should be biased *in favor of popular forms*.

Table 7.4 in Appendix D shows the correspondence of evaluations (combined score only) for six genres on which ten or more scores were available. Approximately two-thirds of all comparisons between informal and published reviews diverge. In all cases, the average difference is negative, indicating more favorable public reviews. Although the differences for musicals and dance are not statistically significant (these comparisons have relatively few cases), the other differences are reasonably large.

The largest difference scores appear for comedy (–.36), cabaret (–.89), and children's shows (–.66). By contrast, there is a relatively smaller positive bias for theater (–.19). The last two rows of Table 7.4 show that, while the *proportion* of differences is about the same for highbrow and popular shows, the *magnitude* of the difference is greater for popular genres (comedy, cabaret). Published reviews of popular genres diverge *more* (and more positively) from the stated judgments of their authors than do those for highbrow genres, represented primarily by theater. The difference score for those cases in which evaluations differ is more than half a rating point for popular performances, whereas it is less than .2 for highbrow performances.

The implication of these differences may be summarized by comparing the averages for highbrow and popular shows in four ways. The difference in the average informal ratings for the two types of show is trivially small.[24] That is, critics *think no more highly of popular shows* than they do of highbrow shows. But this "equality of judgment" does not apply to the published reviews. The average notice for a popular show is significantly more positive (3.86) than the average notice for a highbrow show (3.50). The difference score indicates why this is the case: published reviews for popular scores diverge much more from the actual evaluation of critics than they do for highbrow reviews. If one excludes those cases (n = 118) where there is no divergence between informal and formal judgments, the difference is even larger, amounting to one-half of a rating point (.82 – .31 = .51).

Why are highbrow and popular judgments differentially biased? We cannot directly show that a difference in the distinctive discourse norms associated with high and popular forms is responsible, but we can rule out some other explanations. One possibility is that there is a difference in the *kind of critics* that review various kinds of shows. Critics, like most people, are mildly generous. It might simply be the case that the kinds of individuals who review popular genres, whether they go by choice or assignment, are kinder than those who review highbrow genres.

A breakdown of the difference scores by individual critics revealed that six of the fifteen (accounting for 134 reviews) had a relatively high degree of bias, with published reviews more positive than their private opinions.[25] Do these reviewers account for the relatively greater bias in reviews of popular than highbrow shows? They might do so by virtue of two processes: (1) either by *reviewing* more of the popular shows, such that popular performances receive more positive reviews overall, or (2) by being *more biased* toward popular shows.

There is little indication that either process occurred. Popular shows accounted for 38.8 percent (52/134) of the reviews by these six critics. For the remaining reviewers, popular shows accounted for 35.1 percent (65/185). Those whose published reviews were most likely to deviate from their actual evaluations were not (much) more likely to encounter popular performances in their critical forays.

Nor is it possible to conclude that these six reviewers were individually more biased than their counterparts. In only one of six cases does the reviewer clearly exhibit more bias when reviewing popular than highbrow shows.[26] Further, the two reviewers for which lowbrow genres were heavily overrepresented had difference scores only slightly above the average difference score for lowbrow shows.

One of these six—the only one of the fifteen—revealed a bias in the other direction. This reviewer was more critical in his published reviews than in his expressed opinions. In the opinion of both editors and his fellow reviewers, he was a "weak" reviewer, either "unwilling to express an opinion" or "favorable towards everything." His style was tepid, descriptive, and safe. In the interview situation, however, it appeared that he had actually *liked* and liked a lot, vitually everything he had reviewed. But his reviews were "neutral." This neutrality was no more—or less—a reflection of his opinion than other critic's reviews.

Taking this evidence into account, it does not seem likely that a difference in the kinds of people covering highbrow and popular shows accounts for differential bias. But perhaps characteristics of the shows themselves, or the performers, are responsible: to what extent are reviewers biased toward or against shows and performers of various sorts? By examining the effect of genre taking these other factors into account, we can at least test the possibility that it is the association of genre with other factors rather than genre itself that facilitates bias.

Several other factors seemed likely to affect the degree to which one's actual opinion might diverge from the evaluation that eventually appeared. Some of these factors were freely discussed by the reviewers interviewed, while others seemed likely by virtue of my own experience as a reviewer.

1. The number of printed reviews.[27]
2. The originality of the performance.
3. The group's reputation on the Fringe.
4. The number of lines in the review.
5. The youth of the performing group.
6. The locality of the group.
7. The time of the performance.
8. The length of the performance.[28]

I estimated a simple model to predict bias (the extent to which the published review differs from the informal judgment). None of these factors is significant *when the genre of the work is taken into account.* If we know that a performance is "popular" (cabaret, revue, comedy, musical), we would want to bet that the average reviewer will be more lenient with her judgment than if it is highbrow. No other measured variable makes a difference. Relative to the critic's expressed liking of the show, highbrow works tend not to get as big a break. To put it squarely, reviews of lowbrow works are more likely to be positively biased.

The method I employed may be at fault in the following way. Since I waited, of necessity, before collecting the reviewers' informal opinions, perhaps the time lag produced the differential results for highbrow and popular shows.[29] Perhaps critics write about the immediate (emotional, visceral) experience, so that the published reviews actually do reflect their judgments *at the time,* but the "retention quality" for comedy and cabaret is less than that for theater. This possibility would be more compelling if the later (informal) ratings for popular shows were less than those for highbrow shows. During the interviews critics did not remember the comedy any better or worse than the drama.

The finding could also be due to personal associations between critics and art world participants. Those who are more integrated into a network may be more favorable in their notices. If popular reviewers know more comedians, cabaret artists, and rock musicians, perhaps they contribute published reviews in which positive sentiment prevails over actual judgment. Popular reviewers, in other words, would be less willing to say what they think. But the sheer volume of reviewing during the Fringe and the large number of nonlocal groups makes this unlikely: reviewers simply have little time to chat and worry over social relationships at the Fringe. And most critics express greater interest in theater than they do in popular performance.

The remaining interpretation is provided by the idea of critical mediation. Critics take their own job more seriously when they set out for highbrow shows, which amounts to much the same as taking "the show" more seriously. I doubt that there is more "consensus" about highbrow shows. As I have argued, there are no "principles" on which consensus could be based and, in any event, the application of principles is never straightforward. A critic who can find nothing to criticize in a dramatic performance is doing *more* than just giving a work the benefit of the doubt. Such an individual is not being a proper critic. Hence, there is not the same degree of divergence between public and private judgment.

Critics are not really more enthusiastic about the popular performances they see than the highbrow shows. But there is, we might say, *greater benefit to the doubt.* If, for lowbrow shows, the experience is thought to consist of personal and immediate enjoyment, what is good for one is not good for all. In contrast to the multiplicity of aesthetic criteria that might be applied to drama—after all, it is quite likely the object has failed in one or more senses—the clarity of popular shows means that reviewers can rely on the audience for assistance if they choose. One critic talked about the "pull" he felt in writing reviews—

> being aware that the audience is looking for a good night out. Do I say "the audience will have an OK time" knowing the audience liked it—and you yourself stayed awake without boredom? Or [do I] criticize the play and say it could be so much better from the standpoint of theater. But it seems churlish somehow—especially if it's a local group in a church hall.

Reviewers, when they attend popular performances, are more likely to want to "represent" the public. They may be lukewarm about this role, but they are more reluctant to employ the justificatory arm of censure. Was the production unprofessionally unfunny? Well, perhaps it was meant to be. The critic is a sport, too.

There may be minor institutional incentives for a "tolerant" approach to popular genres. Pauline Kael was fired as McCall's film critic after panning *The Sound of Music*. In the summer of 1990, the staff of *Entertainment Today* was reorganized owing largely to its unfortunate and visible condemnation of *Pretty Woman*, which subsequently became the hit of the summer and was precisely the kind of movie such a publication is meant to recognize. In the 1990 Fringe, a critic for a London daily wrote a scorching review of comic Ennio Marchetto and was sacked after the show became one of the main festival hits. In fact, it is quite difficult to think of cases where negative reviews of highbrow shows have been followed by adverse consequences. The Scrooges of theater are simply critics.

Another kind of evidence of this tendency may be found in iconographic representations of text. A reviewer using such a system has, in effect, two judgmental opportunities. One is in the text. The other is in the explicit rating affixed to the review, expressed as one or more stars, for example. Although readers commonly view the rating as a reflection of the embedded judgment—large or frequent discrepancies would be noticeable—this need not be the case.[30]

We might call it an "iconographic bias" if there were a difference between the text and the rating. In an examination of Roger Ebert's *Movie Home Companion*, the average discrepancy is, as expected, close to zero. But if we divide movies into higher and lower statuses, there is indeed an iconographic bias: the lower the status of the movie, the greater the tendency for the number of stars given to exceed the judgment embedded in the text.[31] A reader may conclude, if she does not bother to read the text, that the critic is quite favorable toward lowbrow movies.

A last bit of evidence that critics are "sporting" when it comes to lower cultural forms comes from the comparison of reviews of *video* releases with reviews of the original films. Is a home video release a "degradation" or reduction in the status of a cultural object?[32] We might then expect an *increase* in the favorability of the reviews associated with the same objects. An examination of video reviews in *Entertainment Weekly* does not support this view—in fact, on average, the original movies receive higher ratings than the video releases. However, when we separate out the drama and documentaries, the effect reverses: video reviews are more favorable for these forms. The originals are more favorable for action, comedy, and adventure films.[33]

Evidence of iconographic and video ratings differences is not as persuasive as the difference between informal and published reviews but points in the same direction. Critics themselves display different "biases" or ways of reacting to high and popular art. It is not because the critics are different people—though we would expect a reviewer who dealt exclusively with highbrow forms to react differently to a popular performance than one who routinely covered both. It is not because there are clear and consensual criteria for quality in high cultural genres, deviations from which can be spotted by the discerning eye. And it is certainly not because critics are incapable of applying a "discriminating" aesthetic to popular forms. It is because they apply distinctive patterns of discourse—different "sensibilities"—to different bodies of performance art.

HIGHS AND LOWS

Critics are harder on those who aspire to higher status in the cultural hierarchy. Although I was not to make sense of the experience until later, I discovered this my first time out as a reviewer owing to a propitious assignment. I had been assigned to review two shows together owing to their common subject, the pornography industry.

Arriving for my first review I was both eager and nervous. What if I forget it before I have time to write it? No kidding, I mean what if I see five shows in one day and get them mixed up. This won't do at all. Assured by other reviewers that it is customary—or at least allowable—to take a few notes, I have just been to Brown the Stationer to pick up a "Challenge" notepad with a gladiator on the cover.

Reviewing at the festival, you may or may not get a press packet full of information you can pinch for the review to help you look sharp.

You're lucky sometimes if you get a program. Too many companies adopt the ridiculous practice of charging for a program that consists of nothing but their names. The difference between highbrow and popular shows is striking. For a stand-up comic there is never a program. For a classic Irish drama I have seen one of forty-four pages that included four commissioned essays.

I sit well to the back of the sloping theater at the Pleasance, to scribble in peace, to join in the "hidden mutiny of felt-tipped cyphers spider-webbing notebooks in darkness."[34] One critic I know rigidly opposes note-taking during the show. Did you ever take notes in college, I asked? Sure, she said, but that's not the point. The experience of the drama—both visual and emotional—is disrupted by writing, squinting in the dark.[35]

The dark? It depends on your seat. If you're clever, you can position yourself in the peripheral glow of some lights. I had practiced for the eventuality of attic darkness by taking a few pages of notes in the back of a comedy club in Baton Rouge the week before. Not bad, except when you use the same page twice.

This first show, *Next to You I Lie*, is by a new London group. All women. They are very ardent about their subject. With fifteen people in the audience, they stride through sequences describing the lives of London models, their relations with Mom, boyfriends, booking agents. Is it a professional company? I can't tell. Apparently a group of committed feminists. Seems a valiant effort. I enjoy this kind of thing and it should be easy to write about.

I begin taking the first of nine pages of notes on the show, trying desperately to like it. I'm not politically correct, just nervous and paranoid. I won't succumb to the lure of wanton witticisms like most novice reviewers. Nothing particularly confusing about this piece. A nice sense of the contemporary problem.

After a half hour I start to look at my watch. I've got to be getting to another show in an hour and have a couple of phone calls to make first. Maybe if I get time to collect my thoughts after the show I can draft part of the review. Now they attack cosmetics and the "makeup" process. This scene is great—you're going to take off your clothes so you add a layer of something else between you and the camera. It reminds me of the scene from the movie *Scandal*. Should I draw the comparison? Have enough people seen that for it to make sense? They seem to be implying that love itself is linked to male dominance. Doesn't that contradict the whole theme of the drama. Maybe I'm missing something. Maybe the play is missing something.

Funny. Now that the protagonist (slash that term, too litcrit) is considering doing the hard-core porn I'm thinking this is really an apple without a core (terrible joke—can't use it). Wait a second. Anyone who's ever looked at a Page Three is perverted? I doubt that. Swimsuit competitions? That's no different? Not a new theory, just a bad one. This is going nowhere.

Now they claim the reason pornography is bad is because you get *dependent* on it for orgasmic sex. Damn, I didn't know that. Didn't know that at all. Is it true? What if it's even common knowledge. What if everyone knows it except me and I look like a fool? There's been some research done, but I'm not familiar . . . I can steal from my own lectures on gender roles.

How academic! How depressing! And after I'd promised myself to leave all that stuff out of it. I need to quit thinking logically. What am I doing here? I don't want to be critic. Between scenes I scan my notes. They just summarize the play, who cares about that? Is it any good or not? If I can only figure out how to evaluate this thing. But *It Depends*, doesn't it? On what basis? Relative to what? It must be almost over. Am I enjoying it? By this time I can't even say and, besides, I've been thinking about my review so much the experience has been rather disjointed.

What about a typical member of the audience? Does she like it? Elusive glances about. Mostly women I expect. Yes, in fact, I'm the only male here. I hadn't noticed that. Or did the men slip out furtively? So much for that angle since I didn't think of it soon enough to look. It would be nice if the play had a male role in it. Well, perhaps that's nitpicky.

It's heartfelt stuff. Maybe it even comes from their own experience. The script needs work but they seem talented enough. One or two ideas here and it's got a realistic feel about it—but then I'm a sociologist, not a critic. A provocatively ambivalent view—not bad, "provocatively ambivalent," that sounds like a good phrase to use. A view of what constitutes "success" for these women in the industry and especially the problem of women defining themselves in terms that age is guaranteed to devalue. Their treatment of the way your friends and family very subtly push you, encourage you in this line of work. That it's normal folk that buy this stuff and pose for the pictures. That there are even prestige processes at work here. You know, this is positively sociological now that I think about it.

Hold on. Now I'm just reading my own lectures into it. It's not really a very deep play when you come to it. A lot of lines about "what men have in their heads" are pretty sophomoric. Do Brits understand "sophomores"? This is an exercise in preaching to the choir. All "tastefully" done. I'll say that in my review and to assure my readers—not that there will be any, but just in case—that there is no nudity. I've noticed that about the Fringe. The shows that you'd think would have it, don't, and the shows you'd never guess, do. That's too general to mention. Better just stick to the show.

Look at this fit she's throwing, what overacting. It ends with a long series of phone numbers of "glamour" modeling agencies. Endings are problematic. You could say they wanted to hammer home the point but I'd guess they just couldn't think of an ending. I don't know what it is yet, but maybe I'll get a good line out of this.

On to the next show. I've read the previews of *Onan* so I know what to expect. The gimmick is simple: two guys start a left-wing porn magazine. One actor, Robert Llewelyn, is well known on the cabaret circuit. Both performers won Fringe First awards for shows last year. They have a late afternoon spot at the Assembly Rooms, one of the most popular venues at the Fringe. The organization is impeccable: a line forms fifteen minutes before the start time. QUEUE HERE FOR ONAN.

The punters are gentled into the Wildman Room, appropriately named for this show. No seats are to be had by showtime. Anticipation is high, but there is no other reason to think it apart from the swarm of people. The show will start on time and finish on time, undoubtedly. The Assembly insists on that.

There is no set. Lights dim, not much, no time to think, the music cranks, jazzy and distracted. Feet are tapping everywhere. Lance Boil and Rick Hardkiss are the two characters. Quickly, they play a childhood scene to develop their rivalry. One wants to make a quick buck, and sees the Lefties as easy prey. The other hopes his childhood nemesis will lose his shirt and is willing to play along. Everything is in place. The audience begins to laugh almost at once. Because of the accents and the pace of the dialogue, I can't get some of the language, but you've got to laugh at Llewelyn—he mugs and spins with perfect timing. Relax. You're in the hands of a professional. The audience is *right* to laugh. The younger MacKay is a perfect complement. Every character change is pumped up by five seconds of music, loud and funky.

They transform themselves into truckdrivers who deliver *Onan*, the left-wingers' "dirty book," along with their *Playboys*. A pair of chairs bolted together is all they need for the truck.

"Do it again. Please, will you? Just do it *one* more time," Llewelyn pleads in heavy working-class tones. The audience is quiet. What's going on? Not really in character for a trucker.

MacKay, from Glasgow, pauses, then imitiates Star Trek's Scotty to a tee: "Warp factor ten ciptin? Ach, I dinne think she can make it." The audience explodes. A dumb joke, but what a setup. There'll be no tickets left by week two.

Halfway through I remember I haven't made any notes: better get a couple of quotes. But as I write them down I know they won't be funny.

"ONAN, the magazine that Looks and Cares." "Homelessness: Does it affect your libido?" Every leftist slogan is used and parodied. Porn is euphemized. The show has a punchline, too. *Onan* is a great success, but not with the lefties. Instead, the truck drivers are converted, and begin a symbolic "journey to the north" that delights Scottish nationalists, Londoners, and American tourists alike.

Afterward, I begin to wonder what this has to do with pornography. Beats me. Dirty magazines and skin merchants were used for every cheap laugh. No attempt to evaluate or analyze the industry. Frankly it was shallow and didn't pretend otherwise.

But who cares? If there was any problem, it was trouble hearing for the laughter. A botched line, or even a noise from the upstairs venue would be turned for effect and set the audience off again. If your politics were left wing, you had to take yourself pretty seriously to sit through the hour without a grin. If right, you had to love the satire. Left-wingers and New Agers are the butt: what contortions they put the language through in the search for social and political rectitude.

As I try to write the review, I find that the two shows, highbrow and lowbrow, make an uncomfortable comparison. Of course, they *can* be compared on any number of dimensions, from pace to professionalism to meaning to audience response. But the comparison does not do either of them justice. That they are both "about" pornography—that is, they take as a theme the creation and marketing of nude photos—is coincidental. They occupy different spaces in the cultural hierarchy.

To review them together requires one of two moves. Either I can accuse *Onan* of superficiality, which is truthful but irrelevant. It was hilarious. I enjoyed *Next to You* but a really positive review would be a gift—heartfelt, but not great art.

DO CRITICS AGREE?

Until now I have ignored the issue of consensus. Critics are less generous to highbrow than popular forms. But to what extent are their evaluations consistent? The issue of agreement among critics is crucial for reasons that point back to the last chapter, which showed an association between evaluation and attendance for highbrow forms, and forward to the next, where the views of performers are considered.

One reason to expect an association between evaluation and attendance is the suspicion that the former influences the latter, at least for high art. But the association might not exist because the reviewer has directly shaped the preference of consumers: perhaps the reviewer is just *predicting* the likely response of the audience.[36] Lack of consensus among reviews bears on this question because high levels of dissensus mean it is problematic to speak in general about "the reviews" being good or bad. Most people generalize when recounting reviews. They speak in the plural about "reviews" when often they have only seen one.[37] Shows may acquire reputations for reviews that are not closely related to their actual notices.

To what extent is one review likely to be representative of others? Although there are cases where all the published evaluations of a show agree with one another, to what extent is there *generally* agreement about shows? Can we speak meaningfully about a "consensus" of opinion?

The simplest way of addressing the question is to examine the strength of the associations between pairs of reviews in different sources. Table 7.5 in Appendix D provides three standard measures of association between the favorability of shows as assessed in published reviews by the *Scotsman*, the *List*, *Review88*, and *Festival Times*. Although in most cases the correlations are statistically significant, they are not large. The average correlation is .20. Put differently, the average amount of variance that is explained in the judgment of one reviewer by another is only 4 percent.[38] At best, such an association is weak.[39] At worst, cynics may find support for the chestnut that reviewers have not been to the same show.[40]

Reviewers, as we have seen, are more reluctant to praise high art than popular art. They like theater just as well as comedy, but this is not expressed in their published reviews. Put differently, they have "standards." But if critics do not agree on the merits of what they see, it is not because shared rules or criteria are the cause of judgments. The kind of standard to which they subscribe is a threshold, a commitment to be more "critical" of high art.

Perhaps we still cling to the notion that critics are *generally* similar in their judgments of performance art. Another, more intuitive, way to examine the agreement between reviews is to pool all of these comparisons and examine the actual differences between reviews. I took absolute differences between reviews for all possible pairwise comparisons between the four periodicals.

The percentage of cases in which two published evaluations agree is just over one-quarter of all comparisons. Since small differences might be due to errors in evaluating the reviews themselves (although each review was coded twice), I judged that differences of one point or less on the five-point scale were minor. Counting such cases as agreements, two reviews of the same show agree in about 61 percent of cases. And if, following the same logic, we increase our tolerance further and count differences of *two* points or less as negligible, we increase the degree of agreement to 75 percent of all comparisons.

Because a five-point scale is two points from either end to the middle, a difference of *greater* than two may be interpreted to mean that one reviewer rates the show favorably, while the other rates it unfavorably. So on average, two reviewers disagree on the worthiness of a show about one-quarter of the time. This does not seem to reflect much disagreement, unless we allow for the fact that reviewers would be likely to agree at least part of the time simply by chance. If the judgmental dice were thrown completely at random, we would expect them to praise (or condemn) in concert about half the time.[41]

But as we have seen, the critical dice are loaded slightly in favor of positive reviews, so this estimate is still too low. Reviewers are not evenly divided in assessing performances favorably or unfavorably. In our sample, they are favorable 69 percent of the time, so the odds of reviewer agreement regardless of *what* show they are reviewing are approximately 55 percent.[42] The agreement over and above this is 75 percent minus 55 percent, or 20 percent.[43] Stated baldly, critics who review the same show are only slightly more likely than critics who go to different shows to produce similar evaluations.

These comparisons have all been taken in pairs. But what accounts for differences in reviews of the same show? If there is simply less consensus on reviews of popular shows, this might account for the fact that critical evaluations do not influence the size of their audiences. If potential audiences find less consistency in reviews of popular performing arts, then reviews might have less effect because they are weighing inharmonious recommendations.

Excluding shows for which there were none or only a single review leaves 363 productions for which at least two reviews were published. Table 7.6 (Appendix D) presents the results of regressing a measure of variation[44] on genre, originality, and reputation, controlling for the average evaluation of the show. (A positive coefficient in the first [and fourth] columns indicates an increase in the likelihood of disagreement, while a negative coefficient indicates a decrease—that is, more consensus.) Popular shows are slightly, but not significantly, more likely to exhibit variability in their evaluations.[45] Although group reputation increases consensus, the effect disappears when the overall level of evaluation is controlled.

Only two factors are significantly associated with consensus. Together they explain 21 percent of the variation. The negative coefficient of the average evaluation means that more favorable reviews are related to lower variability. This is not surprising because, unless there is a good deal of consensus about a show, it's overall rating could not be high.[46] But the effect of originality is more interesting. The positive coefficient means that *new shows*[47] *are more likely than known productions to generate dissensus among critics.*

We can begin to see how the myth of the Fringe operates in more detail. The discovery myth, not only at the Fringe but in artistic circles generally, is most significant for new shows. All artists have experience performing at least some original work. Audiences, as we saw in the preceding chapter, are less likely to habituate new work, so the motivation to innovate cannot generally come from this source. And now it seems that critical reviews are *more important for new work than for established shows.*[48]

Are critics themselves biased against new work?[49] Not particularly. None of the four Edinburgh papers rate new work significantly lower than established performances, and originality was not one of the factors that influenced the *Scotsman*'s judgment.[50] But *lack of consensus may have a far greater impact on artists than simple negativity*. Dissimilar reviews provide more information than convergent notices. These vicissitudes can produce or heighten uncertainty about one's competencies and promote exorbitant levels of ambivalence about a practice that obviously has *some* effects—on morale, in any event—and may, for all the anecdotes that abound, control one's career. Critics can lead you to ruin or vault you to the heights of stardom. And to make matters almost unbearable, they do not even agree.

Chapter Eight

DO PERFORMERS LISTEN?

> *Sir Fretful Plagiary*: The newspapers!—Sir, they are the most villainous—licentious—abominable—infernal—Not that I ever read them—No—I make it a rule never to look into a newspaper.
>
> *Dangle*: You are quite right—for it certainly must hurt an author of delicate feelings to see the liberties they take.
>
> *Sir Fretful*: No! quite the contrary;—their abuse is, in fact, the best panegyric—I like it of all things.—An author's reputation is only in danger from their support.
>
> *Sneer*: Why, that's true—and that attack, now, on you the other day—
>
> *Sir Fretful*: What? where?
>
> *Dangle*: ... In a paper of Thursday; it was completely ill-natured, to be sure.
>
> *Sir Fretful*: Oh, so much the better.—Ha!ha!ha!—I wouldn't have it otherwise. . . . You don't happen to recollect what the fellow said, do you?
>
> —*Sheridan*, The Critic

IN THE TWO preceding chapters we saw that reviews have an impact on the audience for high art and that critics are more critical of high art than low. Let us turn now to performers, the last leg of the triangle of mediation. Do their views of critics depend on the position of the art form in the cultural hierarchy?

There is a general feeling, of course, that the relationship between critics and performers is adversarial. The Venezuelan critic Marco Antonio took a small part in a play in Caracas, hoping to acquire some insiders' expertise. In the last scene he was to be "shot" in the back. The prop man forgot to remove the cleaning brush from the rifle. When it was fired, the brush went straight through Mr. Antonio's heart. As Peter Hay recounts the incident, the curtain dropped and the audience applauded on schedule, unaware that "in the eternal battle between critics and practitioners the score was evened for a moment" (1989, p. 283).[1]

This antagonism owes mainly to the critic's occupancy of a position on which creators themselves depend. Hence the persistence and virulence of attacks by artists. Samuel Taylor Coleridge believed that critics are those that have failed at some other task.[2] Contemporary views are remarkably similar. Faubion Bowers characterized the critic as "a non-creative, unoriginal person perpetually exposed to inventive and innovative personalities."[3] William Goldman claimed that 99 percent of all critics are "failures . . . failures in life. . . . You get the dregs, the stage-struck but untalented neurotic who eventually drifts into criticism as a means of clinging peripherally to the arts. And most of your cruel critics come this way: they are getting their own back" (1969, p. 70). Playwright John Clifford railed against critics ("one-eyed, cloth-eared, and irredeemably malicious") until he became one himself.

The eunuch metaphor crops up frequently in this male-dominated profession. Brendan Behan, the Irish dramatist, observed them in the harem: "they're there every night, they see it done every night, they see how it should be done every night, but they can't do it themselves." Russian pianist Vladimir de Pachmann had it that "Critics are the eunuchs of art; they talk about what they cannot do" (English 1979, p. 158). The standard retort is that since they *are* there every night, they know when it is being done badly. In general, the strategy of artists is to argue that *insider* or *role-specific* knowledge is the qualification for aesthetic discourse, whereas the strategy of critics is to argue that quality filters can be applied by any knowledgeable individual.

PERFORMERS AND CRITICS

> Actors are utterly dependent on what a nonprofessional has to say. They aren't trained. . . . It's very irritating to hear claptrap. They're applauding empty theatricality. [For example] four follow spots make an actor stand out on stage. It's the oldest trick in the book and most critics don't even know it.
> —*English actor*

> Everyone—despite professing to despise reviews—punches both fists in the air and shouts, "Yabadabadoo!" when someone else gets a bad one.
> —*David Baddiel*

The venom of artists generally varies with the character of their most recent evaluation and is unremarkably absent in the wake of positive reviews. It does not seem to be attenuated by the uncertainty of performers about whether anyone in the art world is actually influenced by critical judgments. And it is far more serious if the reviewer is well known.

I conducted interviews with 81 writers, directors, and performers on the Fringe in 1990.[4] These artists were associated with 56 shows, 54 of which I witnessed. Of these 54 shows, 33 can be considered representative of "highbrow" genres (31 theater, 1 poetry reading, and 1 mime), while 21 were "popular" (10 comedy, 4 cabaret, 3 revue, 2 children's shows, and 2 musicals).[5]

Within genres, a range of performing groups were targeted.[6] Established performers were identified using the reputation ratings developed for the spectator study in Chapter 6, while amateurs and unknowns were identified opportunistically. After each interview was finished, I scanned the Daily Diary listings to determine the next show that could reasonably be reached, maintaining a balance between genres and performers at various career levels. Whether this constitutes "sampling" or merely ordinary Fringegoing is left to the reader's judgment.

After each show, I approached the group and requested an interview with the director. If the director was unavailable, the principal player was interviewed. In two cases no one was available to interview. The interviews ranged over a variety of subjects, but systematically focused on relationships with and attitudes toward critics and the review process. Only one of these informants had been a critic (briefly). One other director had written a review of his own show under an assumed name.

Since these responses rarely lend themselves to neat classification, I treat this information qualitatively in the sections to follow. Where it is illuminating, I use counts or percentage differences, focusing on genre as the main indicator of status in the cultural hierarchy in order to assess the impact of criticism on artists themselves.

If there was ever any doubt, directors and performers are keenly, sometimes excruciatingly, aware of their reviews.[7] As one actor put it, "this is art but it's also work—the better [the reviews] are, the more I eat."[8] Part of the reason for this is the purely instrumental function of reviews. Since a Fringe production is often similar to a pre-Broadway tour, preparing the way for larger venues and audiences, the value of critical notices is often utilitarian.[9] In this respect, performance criticism is important for constructing the reality of what has been. The most important reason for soliciting and collecting reviews is in terms of their effects in obtaining future funding, their potential for publicity, and their usefulness for career promotion.[10]

> We're taking this show to London, then on festival tour, so we're manipulating our criticism. If we do well here with notices, audiences don't matter as much. My contacts with the *Independent* are being used.[11]

> We use reviews as publicity material. Without reviews we couldn't get funding. It's not a proven thing [but we] couldn't get money from the Arts Coun-

cil; from the East Midlands Arts Council; from the Leicester City Council. Without reviews you aren't justified. Reviews are invaluable.

When you go on tour they're just good for marketing. I don't give a shit what [an Edinburgh critic] says.

Last year we had problems. There were no good reviews and we couldn't sell the show for touring. It didn't make any difference that we'd won a Fringe First [award] the past two years.

While these uses of reviews are important, the most common expression of "review consciousness" was the strong reported effect on morale. Several directors mentioned that an essential part of the job was "taking the bite out" of the reviews for their actors before a performance. This was particularly true for amateur companies.[12] Such a morale effect was explicitly confirmed or clearly implied by about 40 percent of both highbrow and popular informants.

In one case, a comedian of renown waited in the wings while his youthful warm-up act finished. He had won the Perrier Award for comedy the previous year. The crowd chanted and buzzed with anticipation. Just before he walked on, someone whispered that there had been a good review of his act. He paused, "What did it say?" No one knew exactly. He refused to go on—"they can wait"—while someone scurried to find a copy of the *Guardian*. Standing just offstage, someone read it to him, line by line, before he made an entrance.

When there is a negative effect on morale, it is often not simply the evaluation that hurts, but the style or formulation. According to one amateur director and performer, "Critics further their own careers by writing witty and readable things, not true things." A young professional claims that the Fringe is "a festival for writers. They start enjoying their own wit." Similarly, a more experienced professional believes that "most reviewers need to draw attention to the reviewer, not the production. The London listings magazines and TV companies have as a 'subtext' the construction of their own esteem. *Time Out*, the *Independent*. [They're] channels for a whole set of people who make their living building and taking apart artists." Even when the review is positive, some artists find this annoying. "Critics used phrases like 'the gothic enormity of the plot,' and the 'Jacobean characters.' Real old style. What kind of stuff is that?"

Sometimes, as in this quotation, artists find that critics overintellectualize and overinterpret their work in the quest for profundity. But the performer's view of the problematic and even distortionary nature of style is shared more often by critics themselves, who consider these effects quite consciously, than audiences, who respond more readily to wit and readability than analytical acumen on the part of the reviewer.

Although the pose of pococurantism, grounded in "pure aestheticism," was occasionally mentioned in an abstract way, among my group of informants *no one* claimed to be unaware of or completely unconcerned with their notices. This applies regardless of reputation, career stage, or any other factor. Samuel Goldwyn's advice, "Don't pay any attention to critics; don't even ignore them," is impossible to follow.

This is not only because most performing artists are interested in their public evaluations. Directors and performers at the pinnacle of their careers, associated with famous companies, or recognized through television and film work are somewhat less likely to read the reviews themselves. But they cannot avoid *hearing* about reviews secondhand because these are precisely the artists who are most likely to have an entourage. The individual who received the highest reputation rating at the 1988 Fringe allowed as much: "I don't buy papers. Used to when I was with the group. I wait till people tell me. [My friend] doesn't read reviews either. But people always tell you anyway, so I hear about them." In short, both high antipathy toward reviews and a short temper with friends and acquaintances would be required to avoid them altogether.

What is transmitted to the performers through others is virtually always the evaluative component of the review: "did the reviewer like it or not?" Sometimes this bears little relation to the text of the review itself. These "readings" of reviews often seem to be colored by the *first* evaluation, setting the tone or expectations against which subsequent notices are read, and by the not-so-surprising practice of sheer flattery. According to an established director of a famous company, "Sometimes people say 'I've seen the good reviews [of your show]' when they're not at all." Similar comments puzzle an award-winning comedian: "It's funny. My reviews haven't been good, but several people have come up to say, 'I've seen the good reviews.' I never let on they weren't good [but] wondered which ones they had read." The opposite—unwarranted negativity—was never reported to the performers.

These differences in reportage reflect the fundamental asymmetry between evaluations received through informal reports as contrasted with published notices. Leaving aside judgments by a performer's trusted assessors, artists rarely hear *negative* evaluations informally. As one young performer and director put it: "Audiences that don't like a show don't tell you, while those that do like it will say something." Even among colleagues the standard commendation, "loved your show," is recognized as fundamentally hollow. As a cabaret artist explains: "Actors are completely insincere with each other. They're always friendly, no matter what. Lots of us are just below the big break so we're cutthroat, beady-eyed folks. You've got to be careful in your assessment of peers: you never know if people are on the way up or on the way down." During one interview, a young Edinburgh director stopped to congratulate another director on his show. The latter did not reciprocate the courtesy, though he had seen the first director's show as well: "He didn't ask me how I liked it because there's an emerging norm among performers that you don't go up afterward and *ask*, 'How'd you like it?' If they volunteer it, that's OK. Otherwise you put people on the spot."

In rare cases a performer may receive negative feedback from audience comments that are intended as praise. The information conveyed may even influence the performer by indirectly identifying a problem. One experienced professional asserts that his most significant feedback consists in such remarks as "you're working hard up there," or "you must be tired" after the show. Though meant as praise, he interprets this as an indicator of the need to "back off the role and reduce the gestures."

In the preceding chapter I described the positive asymmetry in published evaluations, their tendency to be relatively more generous than informally expressed opinions. This is not evidence of the dearth of negative reviews. In principle at least, reviews can provide an important source of information for the performing arts world. Asked about the overall value of reviews for their own work, performers and directors exhibited mixed—not generally negative—attitudes. My informants were evenly divided on the question of whether critics had generally been helpful or hurtful. This holds for those at all career levels—amateurs, young professionals, and experienced professionals. Negative and drolly hostile responses were balanced by positive and appreciative attitudes. According to a stand-up comedian, "Those who can, do; those who can't, teach; those who can't teach, teach PE; those who can't teach PE, review. I don't know anyone who's changed a show; reviewers don't have a clue." However, an award-winning cabaret artist notes that "a truthful review is recognizable. Performers *know* what's wrong but need someone else to say it."

This division of opinion poses an interesting question for our assessment of the differences between high and popular forms. We know that for Fringe reviewers there is greater bias in favor of popular shows, with comedy and cabaret receiving a kind of generic "credit" in formal reviews that is not present in more informal assessments. I attributed this to the differential importance of discourse to some cultural forms and the more critical discursive formulas for high art. Since they receive more favorable reviews, popular performers might incline toward standards that stress the reaction of the audience over and above qualities of the performance itself.

But the idea that popular performers such as comedians and cabaret artists are more likely to advocate such standards was not borne out by my informants. I asked "What standards or criteria for evaluation should be applied to this show?" Twenty-five percent of both popular and high-brow artists mentioned the "entertainment value" of the show or the "audience reaction" as desirable yardsticks. Dramatic artists were as likely to volunteer these kinds of evaluative standards as popular artists. Perhaps more important, the latter often want to be viewed in terms of innovativeness and style:

> They should keep an open mind and suspend the expectation of constant laughter. That's not what I'm trying to do. (American stand-up comic)

> Critics should look at who the audience is [and] ask if I'm doing something new with the audience I've got. . . . My romantic exposition of gay love is new. Critics haven't mentioned this. (English stand-up comic)

> [One reviewer] said there are no belly laughs, but I'm more interested in the story line, even without laughs. . . . I despise reviewers who want me to be cabaret. I'm getting the audience involved in a complex story. It's not punch-lines. I'm interested in the whole hour—the last five minutes is the most important. I want them to judge the last five minutes. I'd like it reviewed as a theater piece, not for laughs. (Award-winning Irish comedian)

The preference for response standards over performance standards does not distinguish legitimate and popular artists. On the other hand, reviews that contain any criticism at all are often resented, a fact reiterated since the eighteenth century:

> For in the world there's not a thing so thin,
> So full of feeling, as your Poet's skin.
> —Richard Cumberland, *The Battle of Hastings* (1778)

Or, from Gertrude Stein, "No artist needs criticism, he needs only appreciation. If he needs criticism, he is no artist."

The question of standards remains rather abstract, so I asked directly about reviews from the standpoint of *usefulness*.[13] If reviewers take their critical tasks more seriously for theatrical work, as argued in the previous chapter, then we might expect a correlative difference between the views of performers: position in the cultural hierarchy should be associated with the perception of criticism as beneficial.

So are reviews helpful? *Positive views were much more often expressed by performers and directors in theater than in comedy or cabaret.* In fact, only one informant from a popular genre allowed that critics might actually be helpful to his act, as contrasted with over one-third (37 percent) of informants from legitimate genres.

Still, it is too easy to produce such opinions when they remain non-specific. They are also subject to demand features of the interview in ways that are still poorly understood.[14] A more concrete way of capturing the relationship of performers to critics was desirable. Do artists ever *use* critical remarks? Perhaps they even follow Cocteau's arch advice: find out what the critics *don't* like and then emphasize it?[15]

Performance modifications are a better indicator of the value of formal criticism to performing artists themselves than responses to a sweeping question on usefulness. All interviewees were asked "Have you ever changed a show based on the critical response to it?"

The difference in general attitudes toward critics was mirrored in the history of performance changes (and willingness to change) reported by highbrow and popular artists. Fully half of the performers and directors in highbrow genres had made some change or indicated a positive willingness to change based on published critical comments. Only 20 percent of the popular performers expressed such willingness. In the dramatic genres, these changes ranged from "minor" technical issues such as lighting, sound, reblocking, and set alterations to more significant issues involving narrative clarity, transitions between scenes, and characterization.[16] Occasionally the presentation of an entire scene was altered, either structurally or tonally.

By contrast, performers in popular genres rarely considered modifications.

> I've never made a change. I've never heard of changes being made. Some obvious things a director will note too. (Cabaret director and producer)

> I've learned to accept there will always be extremes of opinion about me. . . . [As] Radio Scotland said "it's like visiting a mentally ill relative and enjoying it." The day I start pandering to critics' whims I'll start losing whatever I have that works. The sick people that see me often say I vary it. I've only done this [act] for ten days. Tonight I improvised a lot. (Scottish comic)

This last performer, a stand-up comic, chooses a phrase coined by a reviewer to characterize his own show, but does not admit the relevance of negative comments or suggestions for improving it.

Genre is not the only important factor in the relationship of artists to critical reviews. In theater, where most of the changes occur, the *career stage* of the performer is associated with willingness to alter or consider altering the show. Is it the amateur or young professional, insecure about dramatic technique and interpretation? On the contrary, older, midcareer professionals claimed to be more responsive:

> We took notice of the first review. The early ones said the story should be clarified and shortened. [This was] after about eight shows. This confirmed what we felt and the company felt. In ensemble work you adjust the performance all the time. When I was younger, I was more defensive—perhaps I ignored the reviews more.

Over two-thirds of middle and experienced professionals expressed a positive willingness to modify performances. Among "experienced" professionals only two denied ever having changed a performance to accommodate a critical suggestion.[17] If insecurity is part of the explanation for this effect, it is professional maturation—the reduction of insecurity—that allows one to accept *selected* critical opinions as legitimate rather than the insecurity that breeds principled refusal.[18]

> We know most of the reviewers [in our city]. This personal association is interesting because they feel part of the process. When I was younger, critics were the enemy. Now it's turned around. When they know your group, they apply rigorous standards and if they feel you didn't live up to what you're capable of. And when they see you're trying to do something new, they structure the review around it. They try to support their own. (American director)

Young artists may have greater need for the reinforcement and confirmation of status that the critic provides,[19] but they are determinedly resistant to their suggestions.

POWER OF THE PAD

> I can take any amount of criticism, so long as it is unqualified praise.
> —*Noel Coward*

Though I pray none of my own critical suggestions were ever taken seriously, I am not above using the modest power conferred by the critical role now that I am more comfortable writing in the dark. Early in the festival, I had one more show to review before quitting for the night, a midnight magic performance at the Gilded Balloon. Magic is not really my cup of tea. Why did the *List* give it to me? The answer is that no one else wanted to see it, I suppose.

They're a half hour late getting the show up and running. It's really a preview and I shouldn't review it at all, but there are too many other shows to see before the copy deadline on Tuesday. Looks like it's just me and two couples. One pair seem to be friends of the headliner.

A seed of nerves begins to grow in the pit of my stomach at the sight of such a small audience. This is awful. I am paralyzed at the thought of involvement—bad experience as a child, you know. Damn it all. Only a few scattered tables and nowhere to disappear. In all, maybe ten people have appeared by the time the show starts and the venue is still nearly empty. I'm really in for it now and I can't just leave. I project my fear onto the technician: what's wrong with this guy? Why doesn't he turn off the lights in this place? What's worse, my notetaking will be pathetically obvious. Maybe I should hide my notepad.

The first act isn't too bad—a woman who contorts and mimes with wild music. No audience stuff here. I make a couple of notes, but then notice the eyes of Fay Presto on me from the wings. The next act. Card tricks. Folks in the first row help out. Fay enters and begins pouring champagne all around, which reduces her first night jitters, but not mine. No complaints yet. Her patter is continuous and all the tricks need audience assistance. I can see everything clearly—next to my table.

Suddenly, it dawns on me that I will not be asked to help. Not now, or ever. The notepad is my shield. Achilles' was prettier, but not more effective.

The act was not over, but I had seen enough. The review will not be put to paper until the next morning, but I already knew the outline. Three parts, mentioning each of the three acts. Something about the audience, which they treated with civility and restraint. Something about the tricks. Highly recommended, a casual cap to the evening. Why wouldn't you like it? And very kind to timorous critics.

CAN PERFORMERS PREDICT THEIR REVIEWS?

I made one more attempt to assess differences in relationships with critics for high and popular performers. If critical discourse matters more for high art, its performers should be affected to a greater extent regardless of their overt liking for critics. The logic of the test is as follows.

If there is any genuine consistency between the standards utilized by critics and those used by performing artists in the assessment of their own work, there should be some commonality in the evaluative judgments of performances. If there are *shared* criteria by which cultural objects are judged good or bad, then this should be reflected in either the actual judgments rendered, or the reasons for these judgments. The notion that there are common standards of evaluation, but *no common evaluations*, is not actually inconsistent on philosophical grounds, but it is too implausible to consider seriously as a sociological hypothesis—and impossible to test in any case.[20]

Concretely, it would be desirable to know the extent to which critics and artists share beliefs about the merits and problems of specific performances. To this end, I asked each of my informants (directors or leading players) about the positive and negative aspects of the work I had just seen. That is, putting him or her in the role of a critic of the show, what were the best and worst elements or characteristics of the work?[21]

During the festival, I collected (but did not read) reviews in the national and local papers for subsequent analysis.[22] The reviews were then divided into two categories: those that appeared before my interview with the artist, and those that appeared afterward. The degree to which performer views mirror or diverge from reviewers can then be assessed, as well as the degree to which similarity occurs before or after the appearance of reviews. To the extent that there are similarities with artists' views as expressed *before* the occurrence of a review, such correspondences might simply be due to common evaluative standards.[23] To the extent that there are similarities with artists' judgments as expressed *after* the occurrence of a review, it could be due to shared standards or to the actual influence of the review itself. However, if judgments are *more similar after the reviews than before* the reviews, it is not likely that shared standards are the cause of it. Such an increase in similarity or correspondence can be attributed to the impact of the reviews.

I excluded ten cases where I could find no review (six) or the artists made no attempt to evaluate their show (four), hence providing no basis for a comparison.[24] I then judged these statements for discursive correspondence by comparing the artists' comments about the positive and negative aspects of the show with the positive and negative statements of the reviewers. No strict counting rules were applied to what constituted a positive or negative aspect in the review. Rather, I took the liberal view that anything that could be construed as a basis for positive or negative judgment would be counted (e.g., "fluidity" of movement was considered a positive judgment rather than a mere description). For the purposes of this comparison, I did not consider whether the reviewer and artist agreed on whether a characteristic was positive or negative.[25]

On the basis of all reviews (making no distinctions of timing or favorability) 84 percent of the informants[26] (36/43) characterized their show with phrases or concepts that were discursively similar to one or more reviewer judgments.[27] Of the seven cases in which no similarity between reviewer and informant judgments was evident in any review, the genres were split between highbrow and popular.[28]

Other things being equal, getting more reviews increases the chance of finding similar content. So the explanation for some of the difference between the two groups is due to the simple fact that a greater *volume* of reviewer discourse increases the likelihood of similar judgments. Indeed, the average number of reviews for cases in which there was no discernible similarity was 2.14 (four of the seven received a single review), while the average number of reviews in cases where there was at least some similarity was 3.25 (only one of the thirty-six had a single review).

Taking the *review* rather than the show as the unit of analysis, a simple "similarity ratio" of similar to dissimilar reviews may be computed for highbrow and popular genres. For eighty-four reviews of highbrow shows, there are twice as many (56:28) reviews that contain similarities as those that contain no similarities. For forty-nine reviews of popular shows, the similarity ratio is near unity (25:24). The numbers of similar and dissimilar reviews are approximately even. That is, the chances of a review containing any evidence of a common assessment criterion are about twice as great for theater than for comedy, revue, or cabaret.

One might consider this finding unsurprising, arguing that there is greater consensus about what constitutes quality in higher genres than in popular genres that operate with variable and subjective criteria of excellence. If that is true, then the timing of the review in relation to the performance should make no difference: common standards should result in equal similarity ratios regardless of whether the review appears before or after the performance.

But this is not the case. In fact, *the greater similarity in the views of theater critics and performers is almost entirely due to reviews that appeared before the performance in question.* When we compare the ratio of similar to dissimilar reviews for reviews appearing *after* my interviews with the artists, it is quite close: 1.2 (17:14) for highbrow and 1.09 (12:11) for popular performances. However, the ratio of similar to dissimilar reviews for notices appearing *before* the interviews is much larger for highbrow (2.79 = 39:14) than for popular (1.0 = 13:13) performances. Put differently, the chances of correspondence between a review and an artist's judgment (even in the weak sense employed here)[29] are about even for all popular performances and for theatrical performances when the review appears after the judgment. *But the chances of correspondence for theatrical performances jump to nearly three times that of popular performances when the review appears prior to the interview.*

This suggests that reviews, even in the freewheeling context of the Fringe, have a greater impact on highbrow than popular artists. It confirms the relatively weak evidence based on the expressed opinions of dramatists reported earlier. To the extent that artists' comments are similar to reviews appearing before the interview, it could be due to shared standards or to actual influence of the review itself.[30] But if comments are more similar after than before the reviews, which is the case here for theater, it seems unlikely that shared standards are the cause of it. Otherwise we must suppose that standards are newly constructed for each individual case—which comes to much the same thing. Theatrical artists are more likely than popular performers to take the content of reviews seriously and attend to the features that critics render salient.

What kinds of review features correspond to artists' evaluations? More than one element might be shared per review here, though typically it is only one per review. Whether the review appears before or after the interview, for both highbrow and popular genres there are twice as many positive features shared than negative.[31]

Since there are more positive comments than negative ones in most reviews, it would only be surprising if there was *not* a greater number of positive correspondences. And since comments shared with notices appearing before my interviews could well have been subject to influence, we turn finally to the *kinds* of features that are "predicted" by artists before the reviews appear.

Having narrowed the textual comparisons from nearly 150 full reviews to a mere 34 shared elements, it is not difficult to categorize them. Most of the predicted positive features for both popular and highbrow forms consisted of such phrases as "energetic," "very entertaining," "use of different media," "outstanding voices," "wackiness," "mime and movement." In two cases, the "idea" of the piece was praised in similar fashion.[32] Only once did both critic and artist mention "good acting."

Seven negative features were predicted in advance of the reviews by artists, including unsophisticated humor, self-indulgence, clumsy direction, exhausted jokes, and unoriginal material. Finally, in six instances, a feature was mentioned but its significance altered and reversed. For example, the director of a little-known Tennessee Williams play said it was "lovely . . . [with] a bittersweet quality," while a review noted its "gaping hole where Williams's atmosphere of frail hopes and elusory [*sic*] nostalgia should be."

Still, artists were just as likely to miss the praise in these few cases. The director of a new play about the occult said, quite frankly, "the script is rubbish," while a reviewer praised its "excellent script." Or again, the director of a Scottish play characterized the performance as "nervous . . . the acting was patchy," while the reviewer claimed the "cast works well."[33]

The evidence here suggests that overall correspondence between the views of critics and the views of artists is quite limited. This may seem obvious to anyone who has had the good fortune to witness the oral reading of a bad review by performers. On the other hand, as one informant admitted, "if it's a good review by a bad critic, you find you can warm to him." Yet this mistakes the overall judgment embedded in the review for the discursive elements on which the judgment is based and has very little bearing on the question of critical impact.

A more serious objection is that the general infrequency of correspondence owes more to the "artificial" limitations imposed by the length of a review (or equally, an interview). If a larger volume of text had been available, more similarities would be found. Yet one might just as well consider the consequences of a lengthier comparison procedure artificial. In any case we would not expect this to affect the difference between high and popular art. The most salient aspects—good or bad—of cultural objects are more likely to be the first-mentioned topics than the well-reasoned catalog of a chapter-length work of scholarship.

In this chapter we have seen that (1) virtually all artists are aware of and sensitive to reviews because of the network of social relations within which they operate—this is true whether we are speaking of highbrow or popular genres, experienced or novice artists; (2) highbrow performers are just as likely to advocate response (audience-based) standards as popular performers; (3) artists are split on the question of whether reviewers are primarily helpful or hurtful, but dramatic artists are more likely to see reviewers as helpful than popular artists; (4) status in the cultural hierarchy is associated with willingness to alter performances; (5) critical views have greater impact on the assessment of one's own work in high art. Simply put, higher status in the cultural hierarchy is associated with taking critical views more seriously even though there are not common standards for the formulation of such views.

PART FOUR
BEYOND THE FRINGE

Chapter Nine

BEYOND FORMAL EVALUATION

> We never read reviews. We know the critics. They don't go to
> the shows an' they're 'kin pisht in the pub, like,
> when they write 'em.
> —*Fringe spectator, "Sandy Bell's"*

THE THREE previous chapters have dealt with the response of the public to critics, the nature of the evaluative process, and the views of performers themselves. In each case I sought to link differences between genres with the idea that critical discourse has increasing significance at higher levels in the cultural hierarchy. Audiences, performers, and even critics themselves respond in different ways to the process of criticism. Reviewers are more critical and performers take their evaluations more seriously in high art than popular art. Potential spectators for both high and popular art are influenced by the presence of reviews, but only in high art are they influenced by evaluations. These findings constitute evidence for the differential importance of discourse and the idea of highbrow mediation. But the impact of positive reviews on attendance is small even for high art.

The alleged power of critics seems far greater than their actual impact, even in a market context such as Edinburgh where they might be expected to have a large effect on audiences. How is it, then, that the discovery myth persists for both high and popular art? What do potential spectators actually *do* with reviews? Although no definitive answers can be given here, this chapter provides some hints and directions for future work. To do this, I turn once more to interviews with Fringe performers and then to a complementary study conducted at the Festival of Israel.

CRITICAL POWER

The views of performing artists in Edinburgh on the influence of critics could hardly be clearer. In response to the unstructured question "What effects, if any, do reviews have on audiences?" opinions were almost unanimous.[1] About half of those who held that reviews had an impact on the size of the audience immediately said that the *effects of reviews were greater in Edinburgh* than elsewhere.[2] The spontaneity and near equivalence of their responses are striking and reflect the discovery myth discussed in Chapter 5. Critics, owing both to their large numbers and the prominence of their work in displays, newstands, and posters, constitute a presence during the festival to an unusual extent.[3] Convictions regarding their influence on spectators are strong.

I have shown that the actual impact of favorable reviews on audiences is small and only applies to high art forms. So why is there such an overwhelming *belief* in their importance at the Fringe? Part of the answer lies in a detailed examination of the content of performer accounts, part in the normal limits of our observational capacities, and part in the positive functions of the ideology.[4]

Accounts

The most revealing statements following an expressed belief by artists in the power of critics resort to instances of cases in which reviews were followed by an increase or decrease in audience size.[5] Yet there are four kinds of qualifications to these reports that suggest a covert consistency between the small empirical effect reported here and the belief in the power of critics over audiences.

Six performers, when they spoke about the effects of reviews on audiences, gave examples of what should probably be called "inversion," a negative review leading to a large audience.[6]

> We were accused of coming down too heavily in one side. We didn't offer both sides—we want to be one-sided. Last year we had social workers storming out. We had pediatricians' letters of complaint in the program. Last year one bad review was on the night six social workers walked out. He said in the review that they stormed out. The next night, we had a good audience.

> Last year [the reviewer] slated and ripped the John Lennon show and people packed the house.

> In 1979 [the critic] reviewed our student revue as "obscure and blasphemous" and it sold out.

It may not be necessary to underscore the fact that shows about John Lennon, those in which the reviewer reports extreme audience reactions, or the godsend of a "blasphemous" label are liable to have an advantage in terms of audiences. This has little to do with the evaluative function of the critic.

What about the positive cases, in which a good review was followed by an increase in audience size? Part of the evidence is hearsay or indirect. Several of these accounts did not refer to shows the informants were actually associated with themselves, but only cases about which they had heard. They sometimes allowed that effects might be associated with one's career stage: "Last year we got a *Scotsman* review and sold out after that. We had poor audiences [the year before]. More people have seen us now outside Edinburgh. This year we got a poor review, but it didn't matter. Even two of five previews sold out."

Third, there is a distinction between the character of the review and the *use* of the review, in whole or part, by the company. "Last year in *Festival Times* we got a great review on Tuesday of the third week. We blew it up and got better audiences. We passed it around a lot. . . . It's 70 percent the review and 30 percent work with the review." Whether such an effect should be ascribed to the review's effect on audiences or to an increase in morale and self-promotion is debatable.

Finally, many of the performers did not really claim that the review "made" the show, but only that *some* effect, if only temporary, might have been present.

> The second day we got a good review and the audience was good.

> People read a bad one and don't go, then later they forget and go. There's a stronger review effect at the festival, [but] they forget more at the festival, too.

> In Edinburgh [critics] do have an effect, but not as much as they like to think. There are too many reviews here—you get review dyslexia. The first few days it's a lottery. They're important in the final analysis because the audience must have something to follow.

> Consistent reviews are what's important. Mixed reviews don't matter. Consistently bad reviews keep them away. [Our show] had mixed reviews and a small audience.

As we saw in Chapter 7, mixed reviews are anything but unusual.

Limits

Performers, neither more nor less than other people, are subject to a positive selection bias. Confirmatory events are accepted as evidence for the belief in the power of reviews. Yet one's spectrum of experience does not count as evidence *against* the belief. Disconfirming events are "excepted" or fail to register at the level of awareness. Performers are delighted to get good reviews, whether or not there is any change in the size of the audience. Unfavorable reviews are feared, if only for their imagined potential:

> Yes definitely [a review makes a difference.] A bad review could kill us. But there was no change in the audience after the *Scotsman* review.[7]

> I don't know if they have an effect, but a sustained attack can close it. . . .
> Critics have personally attacked me: the *Scotsman*, the *List*, the *Festival Times*,
> and the *Guardian*, all within the past week.

This comic was, at the time, playing to nearly full houses at one of the largest venues in Edinburgh. Instances that seem to represent clear and immediate increments in audience size after a positive review are not balanced by a consideration of instances in which there was no such increment, cases in which reviews were negative and the audience was stable, or even falloffs in attendance after a "belter."[8]

> Yes, they have an effect at the Fringe. The *Scotsman* review increased us to
> twenty for two nights. The *Independent* listed this for ten days and offered
> thirty free tickets for tonight. We've handed out tons of flyers. It does no
> good. We've had good reviews—except for the *List*—a good venue, and low
> audiences while "Midsummer Night's Dream" next door is packed.[9]

Only two performer accounts imply the results of the quantitative analysis that showed the relationship between critics and audiences for popular genres is different than for serious theater. "Critics do make a difference at the Fringe. It's grossly unfair because they say what they like. [This] makes a big difference for theater but not comedy." The director of a local group that had played the festival for twenty-five years said:

> No, critics don't have all that much effect during festival. Our comedy audi-
> ence is unaffected. If you're established, you need a good author and a well-
> known play, like the *Arsenic and Old Lace* we did last year. I honestly don't
> think audiences pay that much attention. People don't keep their papers. . . .
> They buy it one day but they don't study it. We used to say, "Get a good crit
> and you're made," but I think it's wrong. It's difficult to know what the pub-
> lic will go for, but you need a well-known author and a comedy.

The ideas that "people don't keep their papers" and the variation among reviews help to explain why the overall effect of reviews is small. Even if a positive review has an immediate effect it "decays" rapidly. Shows are reviewed again, increasing their visibility (which increases audiences), and the next review may not be positive. Temporary effects, combined with inconsistent reviews, would explain the small overall relationship.

Ideology

Though the character of reviews seems not to affect audiences for popular genres, highbrow and popular artists do not differ to any significant degree in their *belief that reviews are important for audiences*. Nor would we expect them to, if reviews have an ideological function that renders their actual effects irrelevant to the belief in those effects. The discovery myth implies that positive critical assessments of a show lead to increased interest or even a "turnaround" from negative to positive interest. "Discovery" is not mythological in the sense that it never occurs, but in the sense that the process of retrospective social shaping vastly overwhelms any supposed association of discovery with talent or turnaround with quality.

The easiest way to see this is by analogy. The American ideology of equal opportunity underpins another hierarchy: the system of social stratification. Examples of self-made men or basketball superstars discovered on the playground are generally available. They circulate as undisputed accounts suggesting that hard work and persistence will lead to success. The fact that it generally does not for most of those in disadvantaged positions in no way reduces the value of the ideology.

Likewise, the image of the future star setting up his own stage for a one-man show or playing to an audience of three at the Fringe constitutes an important motivational story for amateur and aspiring artists. It suggests that talent will out. Reviewers, agents, and producers all have their place in these stories. The notion that even a single critic *could* ignite one's career is a commanding stimulant.[10] The ideology of discovery implies that success might be as close as a single advocate, at the right time and place. And it might, just as you might win the lottery. It is not very likely, but any lottery player can tell you that.

SOCIAL USES OF REVIEWS

First- and second-order influences on consumers of art were defined in the introduction. First-order influences are expressed in general predispositions to like and seek exposure to certain kinds of art, the result of past socialization and educational experiences. This kind of mediation has been extensively discussed by sociologists interested in taste and the determinants of cultural capital.

Second-order influences are immediate, situational, and local, but they are not all "direct" in the sense I will discuss shortly. They predispose specifically rather than generally. I have considered one such influence extensively in previous chapters—evaluations of specific performances by authoritative assessors. These influences are crucial to the argument for a discursive approach to cultural hierarchy, based on an exchange of status for rights to one's opinion. This exchange grants critics and other experts an authority they do not have in popular art. That authority expresses itself in the triangle of mediation involving critics, spectators, and audiences.

Although the introduction of a "third term" in the process of reception may be an improvement over prior conceptualizations, it is still too simplistic. Cultural mediation is a large question and my focus on reviews—on the published expression of opinion—remains limited. Influence is not restricted to the inscribed word. To what extent do people hear and discuss the evaluations of others?

The idea of highbrow mediation means that for high-status cultural objects, as distinct from popular ones, critical evaluations should influence selection and ranking. But the more general process of cultural mediation is not limited to the printed word, the audiovisual media, or the views of credentialed authorities. Another source of influence is the views of friends and close associates who mediate the mediators. To what extent is the influence of critics indirect? Even if it is correct that experts define the nature of participation in certain kinds of art, the experience and evaluation of all cultural objects depends significantly on informal social associations. But to what degree?

A survey of spectators at the Festival of Israel allows a preliminary description of the complexity of mediation.[11] Questionnaires were distributed to the audience at three Jerusalem venues immediately after arrival for four theater and three dance performances. The items were designed to answer the following question: given the audience for a show, what is the likelihood that its members report various kinds of influences—either read the reviews in advance or hear about it from friends?[12]

The demographic characteristics of these spectators mirror those found in other audience surveys of highbrow performing arts.[13] The typical audience member is female (64 percent), about forty years old, college-educated (79 percent), and works in a professional or managerial occupation (78 percent).[14] But the audience for these performing arts is not just a narrow subset of the general population. It is even unrepresentative of the middle and upper-middle occupational strata. A large proportion of the audience—nearly one-fifth—works in a profession *connected with the theater or the arts*. Since such individuals constitute only a small fraction of the general population, the heightened relevance of events like arts festivals accounts for their high levels of participation.[15]

Under what conditions did these spectators come to constitute the audience for the show? In spite of the organizer's selection of performing groups who were said to be "internationally acclaimed," the vast majority (88 percent) had *never heard of* the groups they had come to see. Reputations must be manufactured by festival publicists.[16] Artists have, one might say, only reputations of reputations. These synthetic, second-order statuses are often sufficient for consumer ticket purchases: the festival program itself was by far the largest influence on decisions to attend the show, as reported by 58 percent of the sample.

Sometimes it is assumed that the only important attraction for attendance at the performing arts is the artwork itself. But 14 percent of the sample[17] said they *did not even make the decision* to attend. These spectators were less likely to have heard of the group, less likely to be occupationally connected with the arts, and more likely to be men. If one is mainly interested in going out on the town, or simply associated with someone who has a professional or topical interest in the show, then cultural mediation is nothing more—and nothing less—than the existence of such social relationships. Neither critics nor personal interest make a difference to their participation—unless the absence of strong aversion constitutes interest.

What must be kept in mind is that spectatorship in the performing arts is a *communal* form of leisure activity.[18] Only 13 percent of the sample came alone to the show. Sixty percent came with a spouse or relative and one-quarter of the sample came with friends. Though most people arrive in pairs, groups of up to nine people were present.[19] In all likelihood many of these pairs and larger groups engaged in some kind of *joint* decision-making process.

Joint decision making is one form of social influence and only a short step from the second avenue of influence: conversation, more generally coined as "recommendations," or "word of mouth." Twenty-seven percent of the spectators had the show recommended to them by others, and 18 percent reported that recommendations were a major influence on their decision to attend. Such an influence is not, by any means, as dominant as often thought. Yet after the program itself, these recommendations were the most frequently cited influence. How do they arise?

"Word of mouth" is a tricky thing to assess. The concept confuses two different kinds of evaluation. One year in Edinburgh, before I came to an understanding of this point, I imagined I had found a way to construct an indicator of "word of mouth." Perhaps evidence of some kind of consensus about shows could be obtained from conversations with cabbies. Taxi drivers are, by reputation, a useful source of information about activities less legitimate than theatrical performances. If you want to find out what's happening, why not ask people in a profession where they are likely to know?

A marvelous idea, I thought. A way to measure the buzz *as it buzzes*. In any case they are a captive audience: cabbies never terminate an interview before you arrive at your destination. So between performances I began to sail around in taxis and ask the drivers what had they heard about shows.

The first guy was terrific and I was convinced I had hit upon a good, if expensive, method. "Have you heard about any shows?" The driver reeled off five shows, including two I'd seen: Fay Presto and *Bouncers.* Right on target. Unfortunately, he was also unusual. After nineteen rides and sixty pounds sterling I gave up. Taxi drivers either don't know or aren't telling: "Ach, they're too drunk by the time I get them."

Of the few drivers who had heard anything, I learned that:

"*Archaos* is a salty show, ken? A bit dirty. If you like that sort of thing."

"Anything at the Pleasance. Or anything at the Assembly Rooms will be good."

"I think there's a good one at Venue 87."

"The Jazz Fest was good last night."

"I saw *Joseph and His Amazing Technicolor Dreamcoat* myself—it was quite good."

Two shows were recommended that were not even on.

The strategy was unenlightening, but I was late for a show and hailed a final cab. On my way to *Beauty and the Beast, or, the Changling,* I discovered I had misread the program. Late ten minutes is said to be OK for a professor, but not a reviewer.

"Stop here," I commanded. "I've got to change shows, I'm too late for this one."

"Are ye a critic?"

"Well, yes, but I'm too late to go in now." I rummaged through the Fringe program. "Take me to *Candide.*"

"Right ye are, then." And after a few moments, "Ye dinna ken, I'm a critic, too."

"You are?"

"Ab-so-loutely. Yer best bet would be the *Pal Joey* at George Square." He sped around the corner, turning halfway around, and erupted into "Lady Is a Tramp." Not Frank Sinatra, but much better than the rendition at George Square.

"Dae ye need more? I can gie ye as many as ye like. Nae charge."

I was suspicious. "Do you get much chance to see the shows?"

"None a'tall. None a'tall. Havenae seen ony in years, but I hear aboot them, ken? Wha kinde shows dae ye like?"

"Oh, cabaret's usually good." I had taken the hint that he preferred musical genres.

"Used ta dae a wee bit o' cabaret mysel' afore I got too old for't."

"Still got the voice, though," I said truthfully.

"Mebbe you'd like the show all aboot comedy at the Pleasance. Whauraboots are ye from, then?"

"Louisiana. Baton Rouge. It's near New Orleans."

"Loosiana, eh? I've got a gret one aboot Loosiana—want to hear a joke then?"

Oh well. He pulled over and turned off the cab for effect. "Ye ken, Jummy Stooart and John Wayne are in this pub." A choice selection. I figure it's so he can do the accents.

"The Duke says, 'Howya doin' podner, what's your name?' Jimmy says, 'Most people call me Tex.'

Duke: 'Where ya from?'

Jimmy: 'Louisiana.'

Duke: 'How come they call you Tex, then?'

Jimmy: 'Well, I didn't want to be Louise, did I?'"

After another song and several more jokes, I was late for *Candide* but I had heard the cabaret. It had proved a poor way of measuring word of mouth, but the most perfect of possible taxis.

Consider aesthetic judgments as social interactions. A "recommenda-tion" is a kind of distributed or diffused evaluation: a positive or nega-tive evaluation is transmitted from one individual to another. Such a conveyance does *not* presume that the recommender has been a witness to the production. If we are interested in the circulation of performance evaluations, we must find out whether they are diffused by people who have actually seen a show.

One can discuss art, even recommend it, without having seen it. Au-diences and performers often ask the question: "What's the buzz?" This formulation of the question implies "what shows are people talking about?" and is quite different from asking "What have you seen that's good?" or "What's worth seeing?" Let us call the latter "personal" rec-ommendations as against "social" recommendations that are simply di-rectives passed on from others.[20] As commendations, contrasted with reviews, this kind of influence is informal and private: the receiver is get-ting privileged information.

Both personal and social recommendations share the important prop-erty of being "proximate" rather than "categorical" recommendations. They refer to a specific show—*this* specific show—rather than simply the reputation of a group, a star, a playwright, or a play. They are proximate because while you may believe your associate's utterance that a show is worth seeing, you can always ask further "Why did you go yourself?" The answer to that is generally informative, for it indicates the kind of artwork that is being recommended by a person who could have been attracted to that type of show in the first place.

People discuss a variety of shows—at work, at home, at leisure. They often recommend performances without experience, performances that "should" be good. Frequently, a sufficient recommendation is the intent or the promise to attend themselves.

Consider a recommendation from me to you to see a show called *Amazons*: "Very funny. Lots of good sketches and music." You ask to know more about it. "Well, it was by the Cambridge Women's Footlights— they're a fairly new group, an offshoot of the famous Cambridge University Footlights. I wanted to see if they were any good."

The recommendation is more useful if you know my tastes. And what about you? My endorsement of *Amazons* might be a useful bit of knowledge, but especially if you are interested in student revues, the Cambridge (i.e., men's) Footlights, or you are curious, never having seen anything like it (an important residual category). All told, my recommendation is most important if you like "That Sort of Thing."

Consider, now, the *source* of recommendations.[21] A friend's "known taste" is a taste for the genre itself, or perhaps a subgenre. How many personal recommendations are from our friends? Much of our guidance on these matters is not from *close* personal friends, but from acquaintances, workmates, even casual meetings. But what is the force of a recommendation from one whose tastes are unknown? Are there indicators of trustworthiness? Such a recommendation is likely to carry as much or more weight than those of a friend whose preferences you know you do not share. Like reviews, personal recommendations include *descriptions* that are just as important in determining exposure to artworks.

One important difference between social and personal recommendations is that the former, being at least one step removed from a spectator, rarely come with any knowledge about tastes. One does not know if "the buzz" was a fan of stand-up comedy, someone who has never seen it before, or someone who generally hates it.

This distinction between social and personal recommendations applies not only to art, but to reviews of art. Through Chapters 6 to 8, I assumed reviews are read by potential consumers who make decisions about cultural objects. But reviews are also the stuff of conversation by people, some of whom have no intention of going to any such performance. It is a mistake to think of personal recommendations as independent of reviews, given that they often *incorporate* accounts of reviews. People discuss reviews as independent accounts and use them as matter for discussion.[22]

With respect to the major newspapers, 28 percent of the audience at the Festival of Israel had read a review or preview of the show—about the same proportion as those who had heard the show recommended.[23]

If television and radio reviews are included, then these *media are more frequently mentioned sources of information than personal ties*: 40 percent of all spectators came to the show with prior expectations based on print and audiovisual media.

The salience of reviews is heightened by consumer interest or prospective attendence at a show. Talking about shows and reading about them are largely independent activities.[24] For the content of the interaction between spectators, the question that may be more informative is "Did you hear about any review you did not read personally?" About one-quarter of the sample reported such indirect awareness of reviews, *about equal to the number who reported reading a review themselves*.

What does this mean for the study of critical mediation? Simply that we should not equate its effects with the text itself. To hear of a review is generally to hear a performance judgment. Of those who had a review reported to them, virtually everyone was able to say whether it was generally positive or negative. Further, hearing about a review is strongly associated with hearing a recommendation of the show. Only a few of those (15 percent) who had not heard the show recommended had heard about a review, while nearly half (46 percent) of those who had heard it recommended *had also heard of a review*.[25] Reviews are the currency of talk, published and publicly available sources with which to agree and disagree. The consequence is that recommendations are often based on reviews as well as personal experience.

We have learned that significant numbers of spectators are not involved in an individualistic decision process. In many instances people are simply along for the ride. Discussions about groups and shows are generated by social relationships as well as the media. In both cases the recommendation is often indirect—either by someone who has not seen the show, or through a review one has not read. "Word of mouth" is not a useful concept because it conflates distinct processes. It is preferable to speak of influence in the form of distributed evaluations rather than recommendations.

In this chapter I have examined two puzzles: the persistence of the discovery myth and the distributed nature of evaluation. The discovery myth is inviolate for two reasons. One is its usefulness as an ideology. It is eminently serviceable for motivating artists within uncertain markets. The other is its vagueness. Since the effects of reviews are actually small, since they are confined to highbrow forms, and since there are many confounding influences, disconfirmatory personal experience does not generally count against the power of critics. "Popularity" is most often understood by performers as market success. The devil may care why there are "bums on seats."

For spectators, on the other hand, it makes a great deal of difference whether the performance experience is rewarding. Talk about art is not confined to professional and production contexts. Critical evaluations are not processed "atomistically" by individual consumers making choices, and the use of reviews is not even confined to decisions about spectatorship. Just as recommendations may be direct or indirect, many people hear of reviews they have not read, and when they do, it is generally the evaluation that is transmitted. Evaluations are distributed through discussion networks and often transformed in the process.

Chapter Ten

DISCOURSE AND HIERARCHY

> There is not, in the truth-hour of his consciousness, a
> commentator, critic, aesthetic theorist, executant, however
> masterly, who would not have preferred to be a source
> of primary utterance.
> —*George Steiner*

> Every actor, in his heart, believes everything bad
> that's printed about him.
> —*Orson Welles*

T HE POWER OF CRITICS is not trivial, given the uncertainty embedded in the presentation of artworks. Yet it is not nearly as great as many imagine and its effects are largely confined to high art owing to the terms of the status bargain. That critics do not have the power to "make or break" should be a source of relief, even liberation—your infelicities destroyed no careers.

In this chapter, I recapitulate the argument for a discursive approach to cultural mediation. The main empirical findings of the study are summarized in terms of the three legs of the triangle of mediation: spectators, critics, and performers. Can there be a "society without critics," as proposed by George Steiner? Not so long as there are interactional rewards associated with the way our opinions about art are formed. Some policy prescriptions for contemporary criticism follow from this.

THE ARGUMENT FOR DISCURSIVE MEDIATION

There have been many attempts to account for both the *idea* of and the *differences* between high and popular art. Some consider cultural hierarchy to be a matter of "seriousness," or "legitimacy," or "quality." It is quite difficult to pin down. The differences between high and popular art might be based on the qualities of the artworks themselves, the social status of their principal consumers, or even the institutions that produce them.

Perhaps if these differences were clearer the persistence of cultural hierarchy would not be so perplexing. This obstinacy is a problem for both intellectual and structural postmodernists who argue that the distinction between high and popular culture is disappearing, that a leveling or boundary-blurring process has occurred. One argument is that the arts are now embedded in a similar set of institutions that confer widespread availability on all varieties of culture. Another specifies the ways in which postmodernity has undermined the foundations of aesthetic taste and the universality of aesthetic judgments, leading to a kind of cultural egalitarianism in which status differences should wither away.

But as the twentieth century draws to a close, the cultural hierarchy shows no real prospect of collapsing. A working knowledge of the cultural forms that carry prestige remains the possession of every socialized individual. Explanatory effort is better spent on the problem of persistence than on the problem of disintegration. Postmodernist arguments, philosophical analysis, and constructivist sociological theories are in agreement that such an explanation will not be found *within* the cultural hierarchy. Cultural arenas and the social institutions that support them are too large and diverse to sustain the argument that hierarchy exists because some cultural objects are inherently superior to others.

So the explanatory burden passes to social class, as it so often has. Distinctions that once seemed to be based on the aesthetic properties of the objects themselves are now viewed as rooted in the life conditions of individuals. The kind of people who buy, use, patronize, or appreciate a work of art are responsible for its place in the cultural hierarchy.

Unfortunately, the empirical basis for such a claim is flawed. Studies of taste and cultural consumership have shown that higher up the socio-economic ladder *all kinds* of artistic participation increase. Stated formally, the number of genres in which one participates is a function of socioeconomic status (DiMaggio 1987, p. 444).[1] Education and occupational prestige are associated with a taste for variety in art. The same people participate in *both* high and low culture, so class cannot be the only explanation for the difference.

I have proposed that the nature of cultural hierarchy is more readily understood by shifting away from explanations based on generalized predispositions in order to focus on specific kinds of participation that cultural activities involve, especially the ways our opinions about artworks are formed. The move away from dispositional and toward discursive approaches leads us toward situational practices that characterize responses to particular cultural objects. Whereas dispositional studies examine the public in terms of the social characteristics related to leisure activities, discursive approaches focus on the local reactions of spectators and situated processes. The study of cultural mediation flows from this.

Cultural mediation has generally been studied in organizational terms, as a function of the production and distributional features of the culture industry. This study has broadened the focus to the processes of selection and interpretation by reviewers and individual consumers of culture, given the mutual determination of art styles and audience response. Organizational gatekeepers constrain or promote artistic diversity by making available to the public only a few of the works that are actually created.

But within the pool of available work other social processes are at work. Production capacity for the performance arts far exceeds what most people can view, creating the problems of selection exemplified so well in Edinburgh. Institutional studies are attuned to publics because the persistence of art is more than a matter of cultural supply. The longevity or canonization of artworks is specifically a problem of reception, negotiated within social networks where spectators are central participants. Students of culture must also be attuned to hierarchy, which suggests *when* particular attention should be paid to critics as mediators of response.

The reception of artworks is a complex process. A complete account would contain answers to at least the following questions. To what extent are individuals aware of an artwork? Do they read or hear about it before they see it? How often, under what conditions, and in what forms are they exposed to it? What kind of work is it perceived to be? Do they experience it completely or partially, and with what degree of concentration or abandon? How is it interpreted and with what other objects is it typically compared? What kinds of people are influential in shaping evaluations?

One consequence of the present argument is that only one set of such questions must be answered for consumers of works lower in the cultural hierarchy. For works at the top, the same group of questions must be asked of *both* spectators and critics in order to begin an evaluation of the latter's impact. Only at this point can the question of staying power can be addressed. Will interest be restricted to a specific period? Will there be revivals? Will the work become a classic?

Cultural mediation is best viewed as *discursive intervention between art and its public*, between object and consumer. The process of mediation encompasses the way that talk and text change the differentiation, perception, and assessment of cultural objects. At higher levels in the cultural hierarchy, mediation gains greater significance and affects our relationship with culture in ways that are yet to be fully understood. At lower levels, mediation is less important and the relationship between object and spectator tends to be direct, much as Bourdieu describes responses governed by the "popular aesthetic." Because discourse is so intricately intertwined with this hierarchy, we tend to treat aesthetic objects as highbrow if secondary discourse should become important to their reception. It will be difficult to untangle the causal direction of the relationship.

Involvement in high art forms builds up cultural capital and may enhance one's prestige. Simultaneously it requires involvement in a different kind of discourse, an alternative evaluative process. Unlike that which characterizes low art forms, the consumption of high art involves the suspension of direct and unmediated perception. *Assessment practices* are markedly different for high art, principally because they are *rendered problematic.*

I argued that this is a matter of symbolic exchange, the status bargain of prestige for opinion rights. The spectator gives up partial rights of control over her own judgment to cultural authorities in exchange for the higher status that competent talk about these artworks provides. The language of "rights," while useful for the purpose of setting a course, was superseded quickly by the language of "practices." "Rights" are misleading if taken to mean that consumption of high art *must* involve recourse to experts, or that positions cannot be determined "independently" in some sense.

The elementary form of the status bargain involves dependence. One form is the dependence of one's own judgment of artistic quality on the judgment of others—those defined as knowledgeable by virtue of expertise or position. Dependence is rarely complete. More common—and all that is necessary for mediation—is the process of *taking into account* these views. By rendering assessment practices problematic, the status bargain is effected. Lowbrow participation involves nothing more than response to objects. The defining feature of high art is *response to evaluations* of those objects.

What does it mean to give up partial rights to one's own opinion in exchange for status? It is an agreement to speak and value art in ways that grant legitimacy to the discourse of experts, whose views are deemed better than nonexperts. It is to grant knowledgeability a role in the ascription of quality. In practice, one may be forced to admit having liked the wrong thing, or failed to appreciate an artwork of merit. Of course, any particular expert may fail to convince and we are well aware that agreement among experts is not high. So to participate in the status bargain is not to adopt any particular view of an artwork, but to grant the relevance of aesthetic talk and take the evaluation of art to be a matter for justification.

These assessment practices are specific to works of high cultural status and are revealed in answers to the question, How good is a work? Peter Brook described his production of *Sergeant Musgrave's Dance* in Paris, miserably reviewed by critics (1968). Plagued by poor attendance, he offered three performances without an admission charge, whereupon it was performed to wildly cheering audiences.

Could it still be said that the performance was poor, given the wild cheers? Certainly so, if the actors were unprepared, delivered lines sloppily, missed expressions of affect, and so forth. Yet it would be difficult to contend that the wild cheerers did not enjoy themselves. They cheered because in no important sense could they be wrong about their experience of the performance. But that does not warrant the conclusion that the performance *was* good, because theater is high art, a genre for which talk and text are relevant. Cheers, even if genuine, are insufficient to conclude that the performance was good, independent of other evaluations. To participate in high art, one must give up the equivalence of liking and quality.

For low art, appreciation cannot be mistaken. To say something is good is to say that one likes it. This leads to a predicament for reviewers of popular art, where discourse makes little difference. Since no justified response is required, a reviewer who does not like a show may just as well say so. If the audience likes it, one may adopt the stance that the untutored masses simply appreciate the wrong things. This is little more than grousing and better just to make the best of it with some fancy penwork.[2] As we saw in Chapter 7, this way of resolving the predicament is actually atypical: reviewers are substantially more forgiving where lowbrow performances are concerned. Paradoxically, in granting spectators this influence over their formal evaluation, critics abandon the simple responsiveness that characterizes those they seek to represent.

This argument leads to the speculation that authoritative assessors should be increasingly important as we ascend the cultural hierarchy. Since judgments, interpretations, analyses, and characterizations by critics provide the raw material for the status bargain, secondary discourse is not parasitic *where high art is concerned*. Critics are not referees, however much the use of a notion of "intervention" has this unfortunate connotation, because they are not extrinsic to the artistic process in the modern world.

Critics are participants in the process that generates and reflects differences in types of culture. I have proposed that the key to understanding the distinction between high art and low lies not in the class background of the patrons but the *process of mediation* by experts. The same people participate in both highbrow and lowbrow genres but not in the same way. Discourse practices are central to the alternative modes of participation that characterize the modern world. The triangle of mediation involving artist, critic, and spectator maintains a cultural hierarchy.

HABITUS AND TASTE

The idea of cultural mediation draws inspiration from the arguments of Pierre Bourdieu and Herbert Gans while differing in important respects. Bourdieu's sociology of distinction is limited in two ways. First, in denying the strong association of class and taste, cultural mediation emphasizes the local production of value over predispositions. There is no evidence for the habitus as a tacit, shared sensibility other than the results it is said to produce (Turner 1994). Second, if there are dual sensibilities for approaching culture, they are not based on a distinction between education and naiveté. The intellectualized, discriminating aesthetic may originate in education, family background, or, as with Molière's *bourgeois gentilhomme*, in a mindless attempt to ape the nobility. But the popular, or unmediated aesthetic is not the province of economic poverty. It is widespread throughout the social system (for relational work, release, simple leisure) as a nondiscursive assessment practice.

Herbert Gans, more than most other students of culture, appreciated the role of critics and characterized the high-culture public as the only culture dominated by creators and critics (1974, pp. 75–81). "Critics are sometimes more important than creators, because they determine whether a given cultural item deserves to be considered high culture, and because they concern themselves with the aesthetic issues which are so important to the culture" (p. 78).

Lower-taste publics, on the other hand, serve as their own critics because television, their main form of participation, is not subject to formal criticism. In addition to the old taste cultures, Gans suggested that a new taste culture has emerged, cutting across upper and lower-middle culture. This culture borrows more from lower cultures and attracts both upper-middle and lower-middle classes. The middle-taste public consumes a wide variety of art, and it is not of a piece. In these ways his argument parallels cultural mediation, but Gans's main concern was the defense of popular taste against its highbrow detractors. It is precisely the strong association between taste publics and taste cultures that cultural mediation denies.[3]

THE EVIDENCE

In this volume I have examined the idea of cultural mediation using the Edinburgh Festival Fringe as a primary laboratory. The Fringe is the most concentrated collection of performances in human history and bears more scrutiny for that very reason. It encompasses the entire spectrum of art, managed—but not selected—within a unified organizational framework. If Edinburgh is the Athens of the North, the Fringe is surely the Greatest Dionysia.

The advantage of the Fringe for examining questions of cultural hierarchy is diversity within a common organizational framework. The spectrum of performance genres is represented, while the central administrative organization maintains a principled—indeed, one could say "postmodern"—fairness in supporting shows. If there is any performance context where there should be *no* differences, any place where there should be *no* evidence of cultural hierarchy, it is at the Fringe.

Using genre as the main indicator of hierarchy, I looked for evidence that would suggest differences in discursive practices for high performance art. Since mediation involves three sets of social actors, it seemed reasonable to expect consistent differences with respect to critics, artists, and spectators in the production of and response to criticism. In general, the results summarized here indicate the presence of distinctive discourse practices that help to maintain differences between high and popular genres.

AUDIENCES

1. Lowbrow shows are better attended than highbrow shows in situations of abundant choice.

2. Larger audiences are associated with more reviews and more favorable reviews. Better reviews, particularly when they appear early in the run of the show, are conducive to larger audiences. But the favorability of reviews is not as important as the visibility they provide.

3. Reviews are not the only important factor in attendance. Critics do not, in general, have the power to "make or break" a show. Larger audiences are associated with the reputation of performing groups. There is a liability of newness for original shows.

4. The *"gatekeeping" function of reviews is important for highbrow genres but not popular genres.* While the sheer appearance of reviews generates larger audiences for all kinds of shows, their evaluations (positive or negative) are only important for higher cultural forms such as theater.

5. Attendance most often occurs in groups. Reviews have an indirect impact through the processes of social recommendation and distributed evaluation.

CRITICS

6. Reviews are inherently judgmental. In all groups of reviews I examined, evaluations were bimodal (with very few "neutral" reviews) and positively biased (more good reviews than bad).

7. Critical assessments, expressed informally, are about the same for highbrow and popular shows.

8. But *critics write more critically about highbrow shows*. No other factor, apart from genre, is associated with this difference between informal and published evaluations.

9. Audiovisual media coverage and better reputations are associated with more favorable reviews for high performance art, while popular genres show an "exhaustion effect" (the later it appears in the festival, the worse the review).

10. Critics do not generally reach a consensus on merit, and reviews of high art are no more consensual than reviews of popular art. Reviews of the same show exhibit evaluations only slightly more similar than one would expect by chance alone.

11. Reviews of new work are not significantly more negative but they *exhibit less consensus* than reviews of older works.

PERFORMERS

12. Critics have a substantial impact on the morale of artists, to the extent that it can even be somewhat disturbing when reviews are sympathetic. Artists believe in the effects of critics on audiences and use reviews instrumentally, so superlatives are quite important.

13. Artists in high cultural genres are more likely to find critics helpful, more willing to modify their art based on critical response, and more likely to *modify their views based on critical opinion* than popular artists.

14. The nature of accounting practices, limited observational capacities, and its motivational function for performers explain why the discovery myth is strong in spite of limited and sometimes contradictory evidence.

In sum, differences in the critical process for high and popular genres are characteristic of audiences, artists, and critics themselves. The idea of mediation provides a simple account of the observed relations, while institutional and class-based approaches have little to say about critics and performers, however they might attempt to explain consumer preferences. The thesis that high-status genres exhibit distinctive mediation processes ought not be confused with the notion that popular art is "beyond or beneath criticism." Scholarly and analytical discussions of works throughout the entire cultural hierarchy can be useful in their own right. But studies of popular art forms (e.g., the classical and hardboiled detective story), however perceptively they analyze the "artistry of escape" (Cawelti 1976), make little difference to anyone interested in buying the latest Elmore Leonard mystery.

I caution against interpreting the result that critical evaluation has an impact on viewership in high art as indicating that this evaluation is directly reflected in audience perceptions. Higher attendance should not itself be taken to indicate appreciation.[4] The results in Chapter 6 show that potential spectators take the views of critics more seriously in high art. I have not shown empirically that critical judgment directly affects spectator judgment in high art and I doubt whether this is the case in any strong sense. It may be that future empirical work will establish such a relationship, but the hypothesis of discursive mediation does not require it.

Why? The status bargain does not involve a kind of microversion of the reflection mechanism that has flawed functional and Marxist approaches to culture.[5] The dependence that characterizes high art is a dependence on secondary discourse rather than a dependence on a *particular* judgmental outcome. Subsequent studies may determine the social conditions associated with convergence in evaluations of spectators and critics, but the degree of dissensus among critics is a major constraint.

In terms of reception, reviews of new work are important. The character of reviews for new work has more impact on the audience than reviews of established work. Quite naturally, performers are extremely concerned with these notices. Jack Klaff, the English actor, described this process for an experimental show in Edinburgh:

> I was scared to do more than four shows. I want the constructive criticism. But some is destructive of new work. It makes you feel you can't take a risk. The fear caused by journalists "not getting it" hampers the true spirit of art, the boldness of art. The better the work, the more unready the critics will be.

Critics are not significantly harder on new work, but their proneness to disagree explains the intensity of feeling about critics as well as the discovery myth discussed in Chapters 5 and 8. Since most artists perform original work, and since audiences are less likely to habituate new work, the motivation to innovate cannot generally come from spectators.

Artistic innovation occurs under conditions of risk and uncertainty. Here critics are *most* likely to disagree. If artists came to believe, owing to consistent negative notices, that critics are simply wrong, then the triangle of mediation would be much less volatile. Dissensus has greater impact on artists than simple negativity. In terms of feedback, dissimilar reviews are actually more valuable than convergent notices, particularly since spectators are less likely to provide negative appraisals in informal discussions with artists themselves. These conditions mean that critics have their greatest impact at the point of greatest anxiety. Judgmental disagreement on a continuum with only two poles means that artists generally receive some confirmation of their own hopes, suspicions, beliefs.

In brief, genre tells us when secondary discourse matters. Works of art are simply too numerous, and cognitive capacities too limited, for particular works to have a value independently of the *kind* of thing they are seen to be. Categories of events or objects, rather than particular works, define the cultural hierarchy. Quality judgments make sense as comparative statements about the worthiness of particular objects within genres even though the process is not constant across levels of the hierarchy.

The fundamental importance of genre should not imply that cultural objects may always be simply, quickly, or permanently recognized as belonging to a unique category. The frustration of critics when faced with new genres is a response to boundary questions, the profanation of the sacred by the intrusion of foreign elements. Eighteenth-century critics, obsessed with classical forerunners, were perturbed and bewildered by opera, which seemed at best a kind of Aristotelian "spectacle" with music, dance, and pageantry. While opera grew ever more popular, critics debated its value and tried to determine standards for it, often simply criticizing its plot as legitimate drama (Gray 1931, p. 20). When American musical theater emerged from the extravaganza and variety show, critics emphasized the stars, the costumes, the scenery, and the dancing with little or no mention of the music or lyrics and no attention to the direction or play (Engel 1967, pp. 170–71).[6]

The debate over architectural postmodernism, the mixing of elements from a variety of forms and styles of art, is associated with claims about the breakdown in standards of quality and simultaneously the promise of pluralism and equality (Zolberg 1990: pp. xi–x, 188ff.). As a form of innovation, blurring, blending, and refusing a generic identity is an old and risky strategy, particularly where higher and lower forms are at issue. The debate over dramatic epilogues in the eighteenth century reflected this concern, as suggested by Dr. Johnson, who objected that the "salutary sorrow" of tragic scenes was too often "effaced by the merriment of the epilogue."[7]

Performances that mix forms are subject to criticism from the standpoint of either, while artists hope for two advantages. Combinations can build appreciation by attracting proponents of different sorts of work. Since genres automatically imply comparisons, slipping between forms is a strategy for avoiding such comparisons. John Gay's play *The What D'Ye Call It* (1716) reflects this motivation:

> I would have these criticks only consider, when they object against it as a tragedy, that I design'd it something of a comedy; when they cavil at it as a comedy, that I had partly a view to pastoral; when they attack it as a pastoral, that my endeavours were in some degree to write a farce; and when they would destroy its character as a farce, that my design was a tragi-comi-

pastoral. . . . Yet that I might avoid the cavils and misinterpretations of severe criticks, I have not call'd it a tragedy, comedy, pastoral, or farce, but left the name entirely undetermin'd in the doubtful appellation of the What d'ye call it.[8]

Consider now the relative scarcity of "What d'ye call its" and it is clear how strong the bias is in favor of conventional forms. The vast majority of artworks in every era fall within the ritual classification system in readily recognized and easily assignable categories. These categories provide the basis for comparisons and the raw material for the discourse of standards.

It is wrong to think that critics "identify" quality, though this remains the prevailing form of aesthetic discourse, and, indeed, the form that maintains the cultural hierarchy. They "create" or "construct" quality through their identifications and ascriptions of it. Their right to create quality is based on the ideology of standards. The justification for authority, of experts whose opinions are worth taking into account, is not simply that some people have *more* aesthetic experience than others. If that were true, the couch potato who rents three movies a night would be the best critic. Quality of judgment justifies recourse to experts. If the judgment is to be more than subjective—at the Kantian extreme, to pretend to "universality"[9]—it must be principled.

I have argued that the ideology of standards is a key feature of highbrow discourse, but in particular its inherent ambiguity between two senses: (1) rules (criteria, principles) of judgment, by virtue of which the user can tell good art from bad; (2) thresholds of comparison, below which works must not fall in order to merit praise. The Age of Criticism shows that the usefulness of an ideology of standards need not imply agreement on the nature or application of particular principles. The existence of principles was more important than the principles themselves.

DeLaurot, a critic of the Old School, distinguished between "arbitrary negation and negation founded on a definite value" (1955, p. 5). The former, he felt, was the only form of negative criticism. As long as a "justifying criterion" exists, there is true criticism. But any "act of arbitrary refusal" can be justified by a valued generalization of some feature of its description. The justification of a criterion is as problematic as "arbitrary negation." Arbitrary negation or approval is a feature of popular art assessment and requires no special discursive practice. For high art, standards are a flexible rhetorical resource employed to elaborate assessment practices. They are generally implicit owing to the length of reviews and the transparent difficulty of justification. As long as criteria are hinted or hidden, the issue can be successfully glossed. Indeed, a variety of *different* standards could lead to the same particular judgment. And after all, who wants an aesthetic treatise as a preface to every review?

Inevitably, in order to make justificatory sense of aesthetic experience, the issue of within-genre comparisons comes to involve thresholds in high art. A threshold, like a set of aesthetic principles, is a rhetoric of judgment. Occasionally standards are alluded to explicitly when discussing thresholds. Conceptually, a threshold requires some underlying dimension but more often than not it is nothing more than "quality." When the critic compares the present work with the experience of works past, the present work simply falls short.

The rhetorical power of the threshold standard derives from the reluctance of the audience for high art to be caught endorsing *just anything*. If distinctions cannot be drawn, why then, anything is as good as everything else and there is no profit to be had from liking the right artworks. That is an intolerable consequence, since we feel strongly that all art is not created equal. But if our opinions are ungrounded, the implication is that we are nothing more than participants in popular culture. Even those who would not be caught dead with aesthetic principles in their pocket routinely employ threshold standards in the discourse of high art.

The uncertainty and frustration that come from too much self-consciousness about standards is described by Liah Greenfield in her contrast between the art worlds of figurative and abstract painting in Israel. The former, with its traditionalist aesthetic, is unconnected with the abstract, avant garde art that dominates museum exhibits and critical discourse. Spectators in the figurative art public either read no criticism, or skim the pages of the weekend supplements.[10] They do not know the names of the critics and are unconcerned with their views: "the main characteristic of the figurative art public is its self-confidence" (1989, p. 146).

The conceptualist art public values originality, but critics display a reluctance to play their traditional role. Interviews with Israeli painting critics, almost all of whom favor abstract art, did not reveal adherence to a judgmental critical ideal. In general, they avoid direct evaluations and defer to museum curators for legitimation of "interesting" work. These critics reject the idea that there are criteria by which art may be judged or even, for that matter, identified.

Modern critics in the plastic arts have been hypersensitized by an awareness of changing styles in painting. Too familiar with relativistic conceptions grounded in Marxist and Wittgensteinian philosophies, they are left without the discourse of standards with respect to which their opinions might be justified. Thus, they produce no "evaluations" of art: "The critic finds himself in an embarrassing situation. He does not know what he is, in fact, talking about" (Greenfield 1989, p. 82).

Unlike the French critics interviewed by Moulin in the early 1960s, Israeli painting critics were willing to admit profound uncertainty: they deny any obligation to describe or explain to the public the works that are their focus. Instead, they see the role of the critic as parallel to the role of the modern artist: creative, without duties to the public, producing discourse that is interesting in its own right—theorization for its own sake. The few critics who do not condemn technique and glorify innovation do not offer alternative standards.

But the spectators in Greenfield's study were unperturbed by such critical pretense. The conceptualist art public is still unwilling to commit to preferences in the absence of authorities. Although they claimed to value personalistic response to avant-garde painting, these spectators were knowledgeable about critics and curators, accepting the judgments of this group as to the artists and works most worthy of esteem. In short, they accepted the status bargain.

Standards for the evaluation of cultural objects are not shared by critics and artists in the performance art world, but the ideology of standards helps to maintain cultural hierarchy. When there appear to be standards, it is because closed networks of actors, directors, and other participants define, if only temporarily, valued performance characteristics.[11] The aesthetic view that one must simply "know" what good art is remains tenable only as an article of faith. Excellence in performance art is a complex process of negotiation among a variety of social agents. Critics enact an important role in their relations to performers.

The conceptualist critics are not worse off than the eighteenth-century wits who proclaimed their opinions from the audience of the London theaters. Modern art worlds do not suffer from an absence of thresholds, but where the existence of standards is denied, the discourse of quality suffers. When it leads critics too far from the production of secondary discourse *about* the works themselves and into more "creative" enterprises, their reviews are not as effective as guides for spectators. To eliminate descriptive, analytical, and judgmental elements of the critical review is to remove oneself from the triangle of mediation.

The findings in Chapter 7 showed that critics are harder on those who aspire to higher status in the cultural hierarchy. From the perspective of legitimate art, popular forms might be expected to fare poorly, but instead there is greater benefit to the doubt with lowbrow shows. There is no evidence for shared standards among critics except the commitment to be more critical of high art.[12] Standards need not be shared for the status bargain to function effectively.

THE PERSISTENCE OF HIERARCHY

> I think critics are really important and they're failing us.
> Theater couldn't exist without them. You need them to put
> things in context. . . . theater is desperate in the U.S.
> —*American playwright*

> But tho' he cannot write, let him be freed
> At least, from their contempt, who cannot read.
> —*William Congreve,* The Double Dealer *(1693)*

Reviewers are ideological labelers, opinionators, taste makers, symbolic framers of events. Judgments are explicitly produced as a public genre for consumption and referral. In Austin's terms, they construct communication ammunition for the social setting (1983b). The effects of these judgments and the conditions under which they occur beg incorporation into sociological theories of participation in art and models of cultural hierarchy. Besides their relationship with the public, critics provide grist for scrapbooks and advertisements, moral and aesthetic encouragement for artists, motivation to modify current and future performances.

What implications can we draw for the role of the contemporary critic? The classical view held critics to be objective arbiters of quality. True Criticism was pure of heart, sound of mind, and nurtured in the bosom of aesthetic experience. The act of criticism was an unparalleled responsibility, not to be taken lightly, for it established the texture, the direction, and the public response to art. In the words of Adorno, "the historic unfoldment of works and of their truth content occurs in the critical medium" (1976 [1962], p. 149).

This burden is entirely too great to bear and leads to absurdities. One is the proliferation of secondary discourse, of critical texts on critical texts. It is easy to identify with George Steiner's powerful polemic against criticism, against the endless propagation of incestuous exchanges, "literatures," and discourses ever further removed from a source (1989). In his ideal society, all talk about the arts is prohibited. Both oral and written forms of discourse about serious books, paintings, and music are held to be "illicit verbiage." This counter-Platonic republic is exclusively for artists and their respondents. To use the present language, there is no triangle of mediation. Gone are the journalist-academics, the "middlemen, the jobbers, the keepers of salutary distance" who seek to domesticate excellence. Although discourse about art is prohibited, there would still be critics of a sort. For Steiner, the most important criticism of art is simply more art: "The 'dramatic critic' par excellence is the actor and the producer who, with and through the actor, tests and carries out the potentialities of meaning in the play. The true hermeneutic of drama is staging" (1989, p. 8).

Steiner's purpose in this fable is to illuminate what he considers to be our current *misère*, the "dominance of the secondary and the parasitic." The abolition of all discussion of art except insofar as it is embedded in other artworks is held to result in "lived interpretation." The problem of twentieth-century culture resides in the way we seek to verbalize our experience, the antithesis of the ideal of immediacy and personal engagement. The secondary serves as a narcotic and protects us from the imperious radiance of primary creation.

While we can sympathize with Steiner's love of immediacy, the argument is self-contradictory. It is derived from the premise that truly creative art is itself secondary, based on the possibility of "real presence" or transcendence. Artistic work is countercreation. The human maker "rages against his coming *after*, at being, forever, second to the original and originating mystery of the forming of form" (1989, p. 204). The sin of the critic, properly speaking, is to be tertiary, for the making into being of art itself is a reproduction, a *re*creation on Steiner's view. When he stresses the impoverished "secondary" freedom of the critic, he is wrong by one.

More significant and paradoxical in light of the approach proposed here is the fact that the imaginary society only prohibits discussion of *serious* art—the very cultural products that criticism supports and sustains *as* serious. In one sense, that is precisely the kind of discussion one would want to prohibit in order to establish a direct and unmediated connection between artwork and public. It is futile, since it presupposes the consumption of art in a vacuum, independent of ongoing social relationships between people, linked to fundamental prestige processes. There is no ban on criticism for *popular* art because Steiner's vision does not descend so far down the cultural hierarchy. The ban would merely result in a reversal of the present situation, for then popular art would be subject to the status bargain, a consequence that is surely not intended.[13]

Criticism is not to be pitied, considered less worthy of our attention because of its dependence on other objects, which themselves derive prestige from the importance of criticism. It is rather to be cherished and encouraged in its manifold forms, including the one-line review summary, reprinted daily.[14] My own view is that criticism in the modern world is inextricably linked to the status of genres and therefore a fundamental point of reference in conversation about art. Such conversation is often between those who have not and perhaps will not experience the works the reviews are about. Through the display of practiced knowledgeability, through recognition of quality distinctions, through the vocabulary of standards, we participate in the discourse of high culture. Art forms cannot be "leveled" through deconstruction because internal aesthetic properties are not the source of their differences. High art cannot be made popular through better distributional practices, since class distinctions do not account for its different discursive treatment. So long as ordinary speakers in everyday situations gain status from talk about artworks, cultural hierarchy will be with us. To imagine its abolition is to dream the sweet dream of social equality.

A POLICY FOR CRITICS

With what manner of correspondent do we replace the classical critic? The most important issues for debate concern who should review, in what context, the subject of the notice, and the role of judgment. To be perfectly clear about it, I would support the following policies, were I Art King.

Spirited response is the most important characteristic of the review, as surely now as two centuries ago. There is a staleness and an arrogance that besets critics who have held their positions too long. Some critics, as well as critics of critics such as Booth (1991) and English (1979), have discussed rotating the critic's position. Of course, it would not make sense to retire a critic simply on the basis of years served. But the logic of the critical enterprise, seen as a process of mediation, suggests that an individual ought not remain a critic owing simply to a recognizable name. Critics themselves generally overrate the public interest in reading further particular instances of their work.

There are good reasons for thinking that an ever greater volume of aesthetic experience increases the distance from critic to spectator even as it decreases the distance from critic to artist. Constant exposure to a wide variety of performances so alters one's experience as to render it *increasingly unlike that of others*. In cases where a critic is only a mediocre writer, his usefulness will eventually wane. As E. B. White reminds us, the experience is hardly that of a typical spectator:

> The critic leaves at curtain fall
> To find, in starting to review it
> He scarcely saw the play at all
> For watching his reaction to it.[15]

While the novice has much to learn before entering her most productive phase, there is a point at which most critics were best advised to take sabbatical.[16]

Is there room for a return to the eighteenth-century practice of keeping critics *in* the audience, to interact with and even modify the performance itself? One degenerative form that seems with us to stay is the studio practice of "content test-screening," which uses a prerelease audience to shape both form and narrative in a film. Preview audiences are asked about the ending, the appeal of characters and music, whether scenes are offensive, and other aspects of their experience in order to maximize commercial success. Outside this restricted context, film audiences in general may be growing more participative—the viewer who seeks purity must await the privacy of the video release.

There is one direct contemporary parallel to the eighteenth-century wit and that is the heckler. Heckling is direct, unplanned interaction with a performer initiated by members of an audience. Although such interaction may be supportive (clapping, expressions of approval), it is generally antagonistic and therefore named. Heckling is now so closely associated with stand-up comedy that its origin in the theater before the development of highbrow "manners" is often forgotten. In the conventions of the stand-up genre, interaction is often initiated by performers themselves as a display of apparently spontaneous wit and can lead to prolonged exchanges.[17] But the pure heckle is initiated by the audience and is much more than an inebriated slur. Accordingly, it may be the "natural state of stand-up . . . the successful comic is someone who somehow defies its gravitational urge, that insatiable desire to drag the smart-arse on the stage back down to earth, where the rest of us belong" (Cook 1994, p. 5).

Heckling is often and unjustifiably scorned because of its association with the obnoxious drunk who won't let the comic "get on with the act." At one prominent club in London, it is actually forbidden. But stand-up comedy without the possibility of heckling is sterile. Remarks with acumen and wit can regenerate an act.[18] There is a need for the judicious heckler, or critic, in the theater as well.

Another form of direct—indeed, solicited—audience participation occurs in improvisational performance art. The forms most closely associated with the Chicago tradition reveal a microcosm of the spectrum from high to popular art within a single style. Improvisation involves the creation of a singular performance by a group of actors without script or advance planning, based on ideas generated on stage *during* the show itself. Specific varieties of improvisation differ in terms of the degree of audience participation. One form is organized as a competition with two teams challenging each other to a series of contests based on some six dozen games of brief duration. Each game involves one or more suggestions from the audience, such that several suggestions can be taken in a period of minutes, with players modifying the performance in associated fashion. The form is fast-paced and can be electrifying, with the audience invited to adjudicate the winner through laughter and applause.

In the 1960s a "long form" was created to go beyond simple improvisational games. It begins with a single audience suggestion (word/phrase/idea), opens with a monologue, a brief and visible brain-storming session at the front of the stage, or a brief dialogue by a pair of performers. These openings introduce themes that are used and reused by the actors during the course of an extended performance, with individual themes woven into the whole through opportunistic innovation. Long form is intended to amuse and delight, like competitive comedy games, but it is viewed as a higher-status type of performance art by audiences and performers themselves. Critics preferentially review long form over comedic games, though both are structured improvisations using many of the same underlying performance principles. It is unsurprising that improvisation games solicit repeated interaction with spectators, while long form entails little audience participation. The initial suggestion is seen by performers more as a way of convincing new audiences that an improvisation is occurring than a basic aspect of performance art.

What should be the subject of a critical notice, the artwork or one's experience of it? Cultural mediation and the discourse of standards might seem to suggest that high-art criticism treats the object exclusively. But that would be an oversimplification. Responses, or the ability to produce them, are equally suitable for the discourse of standards. Reviews that seek to objectify meaning by locating it exclusively in the artwork are misleading and more likely to be tedious than profound. Periodically, it is suggested that critics be licensed or held accountable as public servants for their work. Although the nationally televised presence of Beavis and Butthead[19] might tempt one to support such a measure, critics are not public servants. One needs no license to respond to art. Whether one is competent to write about it is a matter for an editor to decide and not an examining board.

Finally, what is the role of judgment in criticism? Raymond Williams proposed that we reject the habit of judgment, which depends on the "abstraction of response from its real situation and circumstances" (1985, p. 76). Coleridge believed reviews were damaging because they teach us to judge rather than to consider. But to remove judgment from criticism is to render it anemic or banish it altogether.

Judgment is fundamental to both readability and usefulness. Evaluations, as I have emphasized, need not arrive attached to a set of aesthetic principles. If most critics were like Art King or Sir Tremendous, gentlemen "who can instruct the town to dislike what has pleased them, and to be pleased with what they disliked,"[20] then one might be more cautious of the undesirable consequences of judgment. But except in rare cases they are not. My hope is that whatever the small, direct effects of critical writing, they are *asymmetrical*.[21] Although we ought to welcome any criticism that allows us increased appreciation of artworks we might not immediately experience as pleasurable, it is difficult to countenance judgment that leads to shifts in a negative direction.[22]

Negative notices, as I have shown, are better than no notices.[23] Nor is it true, as Lehmann Engel once claimed, that criticism somehow lacks "the kind of language that would allow an expression of dissatisfaction with this or that very real shortcoming without at the same time damning the entire show" (1967, p. 169). In case after case, that is precisely what reviewers do. To suggest that one might simply refrain altogether from filing a negative review for a new show is the height of nonsense.

The classical critic is quite happy to render judgments but objects to my other policies. The artwork itself is deemed the important thing. One can never have too much aesthetic experience. One should "behave oneself" in the sacred precincts of the theater.

In this fashion DeLaurot excoriated the "impressionistic" critics who wrote purely subjective descriptions of their responses without giving well-defined reasons for their judgment. Worst of all, he felt, was the rationale in which the reviewer will "render the greatest service to the public if he makes himself 'just like everybody else,' an anonymous 'average man' vicariously registering the impact of the film for the multitudes" (1955, p. 6). This—horrors!—was a different kind of criticism, a set of personal "impressionistic vignettes" altogether distant from "conscious and rational criticism founded firmly on social and esthetic values" according to the classical model. The greatest danger in critical writing was to "re-expose" the public to the standards of popular taste.

Although I have never personally met a critic who believes that the role of the critic is simply to reflect the audience, it is important not to be high-handed with respect to the relative merits of "criticism," "aesthetic theorizing," or "mere reviewing." Woe to the cultural guardian in the Arnoldian tradition, snubbing his nose at the pedestrian reviewers-for-deadline that he considers mere hacks. Journalistic reviewers have as much claim to the modern dynamic of criticism as scholars and experts.[24] Their talk is equally suitable for the dynamic of mediation.

The distinction between "reviewing" and "criticism" reflects, in the sphere of secondary discourse, the cultural hierarchy that is grounded in genre classifications, the domains of "high" and "popular" culture. Only critics can canonize because the continual production of discourse about a work renders it "legitimate" art.[25] Critics and critical discourse play an important role in the definition and maintenance of "legitimate" cultural forms but are largely irrelevant to popular forms.

Both the quantitative and qualitative results here are consistent with the persistence of cultural hierarchy and incompatible with the idea of "leveling" or convergence. They suggest the importance of discourse as a mediator of cultural experience. The process of discursive mediation is crucial to understanding the distinction between high and popular art because it is central to the practices that govern alternative modes of participation. Postmodernism, because it figures prominently as the contemporary discourse of high art, participates more effectively in the maintenance of cultural hierarchy than in the breakdown and leveling it prophesies.

EPILOGUE

Have pity, critic, for this volume
Begs a special critic's column;
One whose nature, through whose nurture
Lauds the subject's special virtue.

If the evidence you've found
Convincing, and the proofs are sound,
Then clearly, these results have shown us,
A Highbrow work commands your notice.

But if the matter of the chapters
Seemed leaden and confused, then after
Allowing some technique and know-how,
Regard it, finally, as Lowbrow.

APPENDIX A
REVIEW GENRES

Secondary discourse about art is not all of a piece. It is influenced by the primary product to which it bears the most direct relation. Reviews of artworks relate to these objects in specific ways and are *themselves* subject to processes of reception. Since reviews are dependent discourse, they exhibit commonalities with features of the genres they cover (film, theater, jazz, dance, opera, rock), and they derive their place in the status hierarchy from these primary genres. The difference between a TV film reviewer and a highbrow critic writing for a specialist art periodical illustrates this kind of hierarchy.

Chapter 5 discusses some of the constraints faced by critics as writers. Excluding cultural commentary and scholarly exegesis, there are five principal types of published secondary discourse, distinguished by scope and temporal relation to the object of the review.[1] If the "critical review" is taken as the baseline form, *previews, features, summaries, and thematic collections* may be described in relation to it.

The critical review is the central element in the mediation process. To define it pedantically, it is a published sequence of statements focusing on a single cultural object appearing concurrently or shortly after the presentation of the object. It is crucial that the review appear *after* the initial presentation of the object, although reviewers may experience this before the general public.[2]

Features such as labeling or font are often used to indicate that the text to follow is a critical review rather than another kind of art journalism. This protects and sustains the idea of judgment. Just as editorials are separated from the "objective" reportage in a newspaper, "features" and "previews" are kinds of secondary discourse that ordinarily eschew direct evaluations of performance. This segregation of explicit judgment is essential. It should not be viewed as functioning simply to maintain the appearance of "neutrality" in journalism. Equally important is that it maintains the purity of evaluation inherent in the idea of a critical review. Just as explicit values or opinions are thought to contaminate news reporting, explicit quotations and references to relationships with artists contaminate the review.

Previews appear before the introduction of the object.[3] Often responding to public interest in an artist or creator, they represent noncritical newspace for the performance—noncritical because in the absence of an opportunity to witness the performance or exhibit in question, the writer can only act as a reporter or, functionally, as publicist. Reporting, of course, may have a positive or negative cast, but inferences are left to the reader. The most negative reportage applies to productions with problems (e.g., casting, delays, cost overruns). Large budgets usually insure previews—not only in movie magazines—because the productions themselves are "events" that generate interest in outcomes, and therefore large audiences for their openings.[4]

216 APPENDIX A

Like previews, *features* consist of descriptions of new work that rely heavily on interviews with the artists involved. They may appear after the performance and are more likely to focus on the creative artists (actors, writer, director) than the performance itself. Though feature writers may have witnessed the performance, they exclude the evaluative function to maintain the boundary around reviews proper. Indeed, an appreciable level of public interest is strongly implied by the mere fact of coverage. It is rare to find a feature article containing negative evaluations of the performance being highlighted.

At the Edinburgh Fringe, previews and features begin to appear a week or more before the official festival opening. They contain more direct quotations than other types of secondary discourse and are based on publicity provided by the production company as well as interviews with artists or publicists. In the absence of controversy or serious investigative reporting, they generally have a positive cast. They contain brief descriptions of the performance, generally thematic in nature. Because narrative features are downplayed, they emphasize linkages with other artists and works, as contrasts, early influences, sources of ideas, career development, and continuity with earlier work.

Review *summaries* are brief accounts that appear after the opening based on the reviews themselves. Sometimes, as in the *Independent*'s "Pick of the Fringe" or the "Hit List" produced by the *List*, they are produced by the reviewers themselves, but they are also written by editors and subeditors. Quotation from reviewers in the form of summary evaluations are one customary form. As with previews or features, the mere appearance of a summary is often a kind of positive recommendation, especially when competition for audiences is intense. But summaries are of special interest because they represent a "transformation by compression" of the original review. Hence, they may be overtly evaluative. Essential elements are ferreted and excerpted, often to appear days or weeks afterward, residues of the initial review. One of the most concise was Robert Benchley's summary of *Abie's Irish Rose*, the long-running Broadway hit he hated: "Hebrews 13:8."[5]

Summaries are not always positive. Negative compression has a greater potential effect when it is run repeatedly. These capsules have a cumulative impact by virtue of their persistence, leading some to suppose that they carry greater weight than any other type of review. Companies sometimes call to complain that the capsule is hurting their daily ticket sales.[6]

The *collection* or thematic collection combines general and specific evaluations in a "reviewer's notebook" format. Here the reviewer is given space to review shows of choice, or assigned a theme for which various cultural objects may be relevant. For example, Joyce McMillan's *Guardian* column of 14 August 1989 treats "three fine plays about South Africa." Three introductory paragraphs discuss the sporadic preoccupation with South Africa at previous festivals. They are followed by three brief reviews each balanced with a negative qualification at the end. In the selection of these plays, the salient feature is subject matter. While artists hope to avoid the stigma of unoriginality, hitting a topical vein increases the likelihood of thematic collection, regardless of the evaluative outcome.[7]

Collections are the last stop for the performance reviewer and the starting point for the cultural critic. Thematic collections need not be "thematic" in the narrow sense.[8] The "Critic's Notebook" feature of the *New York Times* is an opportunity to create linkages in much the same way that academic criticism does, in briefer compass. In such a format, "equal time" is not guaranteed.[9] As the scope and distance from particular art works increase, thematic pieces merge with cultural and academic criticism.

APPENDIX B

METHODOLOGICAL NOTE

To test the cultural mediation hypothesis I obtained attendance data for shows at the 1988 Fringe, evaluated the reviews received by each, and estimated separate models of attendance for highbrow and popular genres controlling for other determinants of attendance.[1] The population was initially defined as all productions in the 1988 Fringe program. A "production" is considered any run of two or more performances for which a single ticket is required.[2] I excluded exhibitions, classes, workshops, free shows, and productions that contained completely different contents (artists or program) each time. The latter, like shows that are only performed once, are reviewable only after the fact.

GENRE

The Fringe program employs an administrative classification system (DiMaggio 1987, p. 451). This relatively detailed set of categories was designed to reduce uncertainty on the part of audiences and therefore employs widely accepted cultural categories ("ritual" classifications). I dichotomized these program categories into "highbrow" and "popular" types. Since there is no authoritative source for such a classification system, it is subject to dispute and revision.[3] Most important, it was developed prior to estimation of the models.[4] As indicated in Table 6.1, theater represents nearly 88 percent of highbrow performances. Shows are more evenly distributed in the popular category between comedy (27 percent), cabaret (23 percent), children's shows (15 percent), musicals (10 percent), folk music (10 percent), and revues (8 percent).

MEASURED VARIABLES

To measure *visibility*, I use the frequency of reviews in the four primary sources of Fringe coverage, including the *Scotsman* (Edinburgh's morning daily), the *List* (an arts and entertainment magazine published weekly during the festival), and two special-purpose tabloids (*Review88* and *Festival Times*). This indicates the local visibility of shows.[5] Eighty-two percent of shows received at least one review.

The number of mentions in audiovisual media serves as a second measure of visibility. Owing to limited air time and the selectivity of producers, all coverage is considered positive.[6] Only 20 percent of shows received notice on television or radio.

A measure of the *favorability*, or modality, of critical discourse—the extent to which reviews constitute a "recommendation" of the show—must take into account differential evaluations by reviewers and their publication in relation to the "run" of the show. All reviews of shows in the population were evaluated by two coders using a five-point scale such that negative reviews have negative values, and positive reviews have positive values.[7] For each of the four periodicals, review scores were somewhat positive (.3 to .4 on a scale from −2 to +2).

Values for the two scores were averaged and multiplied by a "risk" factor. Reviews published after a show closes are of no use to companies or potential audiences. Conversely, reviews published the day after opening could have a very positive (or negative) effect. Hence, a weight factor is necessary to indicate the proportion of total days on which shows *could be affected* by the review (number of days left in the show after the review per total number of days), that is, the proportion of performances "at risk" of a positive or negative review. The four weighted review variables were then summed to indicate the overall critical evaluation of each production.[8]

CONTROLS

In predicting attendance for the performing arts, several factors are likely to affect the size of audience.

Since the size of the actual audience depends in part on the size of the "potential" audience, that is, the number of tickets available, controls for the total possible sales (the number of performances multiplied by the capacity of the venue) were employed.[9]

Potential audiences may be affected by the hour of day at which the performance begins and duration of the show (measured in minutes).

New productions may experience a liability in getting audiences. Although there is no perfectly reliable measure of newness, eligibility for a Fringe First award indicates that the show has not been performed more than six times within the United Kingdom. I assumed these shows were quite unlikely to have been seen by the Edinburgh audience and coded shows 1 if they were designated eligible, 0 otherwise. Thirty-six percent of shows are "original" by this criterion.

Since youth groups might be at a disadvantage, shows were coded 1 if the title or description of the show indicated a school or university group (17 percent of all productions).

Audiences often have some antecedent knowledge of performers and may prefer groups that have some prior reputation. Indeed, since it is possible that reviewers are biased in favor of these same groups, a control for prior reputation was developed. A list of all groups at the 1988 Fringe was evaluated by nine judges, each of whom nominated groups that had already achieved national reputations in England or Scotland. These nominations were summed to create a measure of national visibility ranging from 0 to 9.[10] Twenty-three percent of shows were performed by groups with some prior national reputation.

A final measure is a dichotomy indicating whether the show is performed at one of four major Fringe venues.[11]

TESTS FOR HETEROSCEDASTICITY AND MULTICOLLINEARITY

Tests for multicollinearity, sensitivity to outliers, and heteroscedasticity were performed for each of the models in Table 6.3 (Appendix D). Variables were first standardized (the test is sensitive to scale). A heteroscedasticity consistent covariance matrix was estimated, and compared with the covariance matrix. Probability values for chi-square tests indicate that the differences are likely to be due to chance (i.e., the homoscedasticity assumption is met).

Because of the reduction in the number of cases and because, in the absence of prior research in the area, additional (unmeasured) factors may influence attendance, an examination of residuals was undertaken for the four models in Table 6.3. First, studentized residuals were computed. Next, all observations with values above $|2|$ were scrutinized and removed from the data matrix before refitting the models. Virtually identical results were obtained. Only one of these values exceeded the hat diagonal cutoff value—adjusted for sample size and the number of parameters fitted $(2*p/n)$—for each model.

Because of the importance of favorability, I computed a measure of the change in the parameter estimate for this variable produced by deleting each case (Dfbeta). Again, for observations with large residuals $(> |2|)$, I deleted those with values exceeding the proposed size-adjusted cutoff of $2/\mathrm{sqrt}(n)$ (since none exceeded the general cutoff value of two) and refitted the models with virtually no change in the parameter estimate for modality. Finally, I redid the analysis using one equation and dummy variables for genre. Indeed, the interaction of highbrow genre and review modality is significant in the expected direction (beta = .09, p = .01). This applies both with and without adding the interactions of all the other variables with genre.

To test the possibility that the lack of significance might be due to inflated variance in the parameter estimate for popular genres, collinearity analysis was performed. Variance inflation factors for modality of 1.46 and 1.49 (for Fringe box office sales and total sales, respectively) is well below the accepted range of 5–10 and less than the VIF for the model as a whole. Eigenanalysis of the correlation matrix (i.e., excluding the intercept) shows no large condition indices (less than 3 in all models) or small eigenvalues, indicating multicollinearity is not a problem.

APPENDIX C

NOTE ON THE STUDY OF MEDIATION AND RECEPTION

Classical theories of culture ignored reception and fail to provide a framework for understanding its products. Since Aristotle, functionalist views of art have been based on the idea that art undergirds the moral order of society, showing people how to behave correctly and depicting the inevitability of punishment for immorality. The cultural products of a society were said to emerge from its social structure and hence could be seen as informative and prescriptive at the same time. Performance art was allegedly concerned with the survival of the social system, functioning instrumentally "as the medium through which a community repeatedly instructs its members in correct behaviour" (Goodlad 1971, p. 7).

A more sophisticated functionalism provides for cultural hierarchy by allowing that not all cultural products reflect their social origins. Popularity is simply more likely for works that do so, particularly where they successfully follow established formulas, or genres. Functionally relevant works must be broadly in line with the desires or concerns of the viewing public. As opposed to those favored by innovators and intellectuals, they will be basically conservative in orientation.[1]

Marxist views of culture are not far removed. Hegemony theory denies that cultural products can be functional, since conflicts of interest are embedded in the social structure. Cultural industries are controlled by elites whose ideologies are perpetuated in the interest of historically specific class relations. Cultural objects are a subset of tools used to maintain political and social control through the production of false consciousness in subordinate groups. Contradictory class positions or positions that are peripheral to primary production technologies—such as artists and intellectuals—may be subservient to capitalist class interests *or* work against them.

The similarity of functionalism and Marxism is their subscription to a "reflection" mechanism that views cultural objects as mirrors of underlying structures. Although these structures must necessarily be implemented through the efforts of individual artists as well as the culture industry that promotes and disseminates art, cultural hierarchy itself is an expression of the social system. No wonder that criticism, or secondary discourse, was only of passing interest. Culture was itself epiphenomenal.

The present work shares with contemporary sociologies of culture a rejection of the idea of culture as a set of abstract, underlying principles and a focus on the observable properties of cultural objects (Wuthnow and Witten 1988). Both structuralists and institutionalists deny the assumption of classical theories that consciousness can be controlled or reflected in any consistent fashion. They emphasize the diversity of groups that create and utilize art. Cultural products are constructed within the framework of social interaction and their origin and reception are viewed as variable and contingent matters (Mukerji and Schudson 1986; Blau 1988a).

One important corrective to the deficiencies of classical theories is the widespread usage of the idea of "symbolic exchange." This notion has been employed by theorists with such different intellectual ancestries as semioticians and American symbolic interactionists. Semiotic models focus on the reciprocal ties between producers and users of cultural objects as mediated through those objects. In the process of "transfunctionalization" the immediate function of an object is transcended by its use within a particular social group, creating a second-order meaning to the object (Gottdiener 1985). The idea of critical mediation suggests that the nature of the social process that produces meaning depends on position within the cultural hierarchy. The symbolic exchange of prestige for opinion rights is the primary characteristic of high art.

Complementing the critical analysis of signs and signification is the "production of culture" approach, incorporating elements of the context in which culture is produced (Peterson 1976; DiMaggio 1987). Its guiding insight is that cultural objects are generated by agents whose interests are bound together through a variety of systematic processes. From the small group to the historical, social, and economic structures of society, these studies are "institutional" by virtue of their attention to organizational, environmental, and network contexts (Wuthnow 1988).

Stemming from Paul Hirsch's work on entrepreneurship in the book publishing, record, and film industries, R. A. Peterson's studies of literature and popular music, and Paul DiMaggio's examination of cultural entrepreneurship in nineteenth-century Boston, institutional studies go beyond the production context itself to consider cultural objects, artists, and audiences. The present focus on mediation is quite consistent with this tradition, since a full account of the production of culture includes its mediation by gatekeepers such as critics (Hirsch 1972).

During the past quarter century, approaches known as "reception theory" and "reader response" theory have enjoyed wide popularity in literary studies. Yet these discussions have been based on peculiar kinds of response. Most commonly they are the *assumed* responses of a "mock reader," an "informed" reader, an "implied" reader, a "superreader," and on to "inscribed" and "encoded" readers with various standardized competencies (Booth 1961; Iser 1980 [1974]; Tompkins 1980; Fish 1980 [1970]). Alternatively, the evidence of classic works and historical audiences is problematic since the only available interpretations are from published critics who constitute a very unrepresentative group. The "reader-response" approach is more accurately termed the "critic-response" approach, often as far removed from the typical audience member as Art King is from the delinquent custodian of *A Grand Scam*.

Whatever the flaws of reception theory, its legacy reinforces the argument for the expanded study of cultural mediation—that the production of an artwork is only a midpoint in its trajectory. Since the vast majority of works of art are lost or quickly forgotten, never again to be performed, viewed, or experienced, the reception history of a work should concern us more than the creative process behind it. Secondary discourse about artworks contributes to their staying power and is deeply implicated in the maintenance of cultural hierarchy.

APPENDIX D

TABLES

TABLE 4.1
Geographical Origin of Fringe Companies, 1994

Area	Number	Percent	Area	Number	Percent
Scotland	171	29.2	Europe	15	2.6
England	322	56.7	Africa	7	1.2
Wales	10	1.7	India	5	0.8
Northern Ireland	2	0.3	Australasia	4	0.7
Eire	2	0.3	United States	48	8.1

TABLE 4.2
Fringe Shows by Genre, 1994

Genre	Number of Shows	Percentage
Cabaret	48	3.8
Children's shows	46	3.6
Clubs	8	0.6
Comedy	167	13.1
Dance	24	1.9
Exhibitions	78	6.1
Folk/Ceilidh/Scottish	95	7.4
Free shows	11	0.9
Jazz	23	1.8
Latin/world music	17	1.3
Mime/physical theater	17	1.3
Miscellaneous	16	1.2
Art/film	8	0.6
Multimedia/performance art/film	8	0.6
Musical	43	3.4
Opera	2	0.2
Orchestral/chamber music	43	3.4
Poetry and readings	13	1.0
Recitals	83	6.5
Revue	12	0.9
Rock/blues	47	3.7
Talks/lectures/workshops	8	0.6
Theater	466	36.6

TABLE 6.1
Audience Size by Genre at the 1988 Fringe

Genre	Number of Shows	Percent	Audience Size[a]
High art			
Theater	331	87.6	9.8
Opera	3	0.8	25.6
Mime	5	1.3	23.0
Dance	15	4.0	17.6
Orchestral[b]	6	1.6	11.2
Recitals[c]	9	2.4	8.1
Poetry[d]	2	0.5	1.0
Performance art[e]	7	1.9	4.4
Totals	378	100	10.3
Popular art			
Comedy	68	26.6	23.7
Musical	27	10.5	24.4
Revue	20	7.8	20.6
Cabaret	59	23.0	16.0
Folk[f]	27	10.5	37.1
Jazz	7	2.7	64.7
Rock[g]	9	3.5	79.0
Children	39	15.2	9.5
Totals	256	99.8	24.1

Note: Exhibitions, free shows, and single performances are excluded.

[a] Audience size is indicated by number of tickets sold at the Fringe box office divided by the number of performances. Number of cases on which averages are based is slightly smaller than the total owing to missing data.

[b] Includes chamber music.

[c] Includes vocal music.

[d] Includes readings.

[e] Includes miscellaneous and multimedia.

[f] Includes Scottish and ceilidh music.

[g] Includes blues.

TABLE 6.2
OLS Regressions Predicting Natural Log of Attendance

Predictors[a]	Fringe Box Office Sales			Total Attendance		
	b	s.e.	prob.	b	s.e.	prob.
Capacity[b]	.23	.03	<.001	.23	.03	<.001
Reputation	.16	.02	<.001	.11	.02	<.001
New show	−.78	.09	<.001	−.47	.08	<.001
Duration[b]	7.62	1.5	<.001	4.6	1.5	.002
Show time	.02	.01	.03	.03	.01	.008
Media coverage	.22	.08	.01	.24	.06	<.001
Youth status	−.18	.11	.11	−.13	.11	.23
Venue[c]	−.33	.12	.01			
Favorability	.07	.03	.01	.08	.03	.004
Review frequency	.30	.04	<.001	.25	.03	<.001
Intercept	2.36	.23	<.01	4.16	.22	<.001
R^2	.50			.63		
n		624			379	

[a] Unstandardized regression coefficients are followed by standard errors and probability values for t-tests.
[b] Coefficients multiplied by 1,000.
[c] This variable is included in the model for Fringe box office sales only (see text).

TABLE 6.3
OLS Regressions Predicting Natural Log of Attendance: High and Popular Genres

Predictors[a]	Fringe Box Office Sales				Total Attendance			
	High		Popular		High		Popular	
	B	prob.	B	prob.	B	prob.	B	prob.
Capacity	.27	<.001	.28	<.001	.31	<.001	.37	<.001
Reputation	.20	<.001	.26	<.001	.24	<.001	.17	.001
New show	−.28	<.001	−.15	.002	−.22	<.001	−.09	.09
Duration	.19	<.001	.16	<.001	.11	.01	.12	.01
Show time	.10	.01	−.06	.24	.10	.02	.02	.69
Media coverage	.06	.15	.12	.04	.11	.02	.14	.02
Youth status	.01	.84	−.10	.04	−.02	.67	−.06	.24
Venue	−.09	.04	−.12	.02				
Favorability	.11	.01	.05	.38	.12	.01	.08	.17
Review frequency	.37	<.001	.29	<.001	.35	<.001	.29	<.001
R^2	.52		.51		.64		.66	
n	372		252		215		164	

[a] Standardized regression coefficients followed by probability values for t-tests.

TABLE 7.1
OLS Regression Predicting Evaluations in the *Scotsman*

Predictors[a]	b	s.e.	prob.	B
Reputation	.09	.04	.03	.11
Media coverage[b]	.29	.13	.02	.12
Date of opening	−.03	.01	.04	−.10
Popular genre[c]	.30	.15	.05	.10
Intercept	3.85	.26	<.001	
$R^2 = .07$				
n = 406				

[a] Dependent variable measures how favorable the *Scotsman* review was for each show, on a scale of 1 to 5, where 5 is most favorable. See Appendix B for variable descriptions. Unstandardized regression coefficients are followed by standard errors and probability values for t-tests. The final column gives standardized coefficients so that the magnitude of the effects may be compared.
[b] Television and radio coverage only.
[c] See Table 6.1 for genres included as popular.

TABLE 7.2
OLS Regressions Predicting Reviews for High and Popular Genres

Predictors[a]	b	s.e.	prob.	B
Highbrow shows				
Reputation	.13	.06	.02	.15
Media coverage[b]	.41	.19	.03	.14
Date of opening	−.02	.02	.29	−.06
Intercept	3.62	.32	<.001	
$R^2 = .07$				
n = 264				
Popular shows				
Reputation	.03	.06	.62	.04
Media coverage[b]	.17	.17	.34	.09
Date of opening	−.04	.02	.04	−.18
Intercept	3.85	.26	<.001	
$R^2 = .05$				
n = 142				

[a] Variables and measures as in Appendix B.
[b] Television and radio coverage only.

TABLE 7.3
Comparison of Informal Ratings with Published Evaluations

	Number of Shows	Average Rating	Std.
First Judge	406	3.60	1.5
Reviewer	319	3.24	1.3
Difference	319	−.30	.94
Correlation Between Scores = .79[a]			
Second Judge	406	3.65	1.5
Reviewer	319	3.24	1.3
Difference	319	−.34	1.0
Correlation Between Scores = .73[b]			
Averaged Rating	406	3.63	1.5
Reviewer	319	3.24	1.3
Difference	319	−.32	−.32
Correlation Between Scores = .78[c]			

[a] t-value for difference score = −5.67, prob. = .0001.
[b] t-value for difference score = −5.78, prob. = .0001.
[c] t-value for difference score = −5.96, prob. = .0001.

TABLE 7.4
Informal Ratings and Published Evaluations by Genre

Genre (no. of shows)	% of Ratings Unequal	Difference Score	t-value	prob.
Theater (183)	61.7	−.188	−2.81	.001
Comedy (36)	58.3	−.361	−2.14	.039
Musical (15)	60.0	−.067	−.32	.751
Cabaret (31)	74.2	−.887	−4.87	.0001
Dance (12)	66.7	−.125	−.56	.586
Children's (22)	72.7	−.659	−2.97	.007
All highbrow (202)	63.3	−.198	−3.11	.002
All popular (117)	64.1	−.526	−5.68	.0001

Note: Revue (7), opera (3), mime (2), folk (1), jazz (2), rock/blues (3), and performance art (5) are included in the totals. I was unable to get any information on orchestral (0), recitals (0), or poetry (0).

TABLE 7.5

Measures of Association between Reviews

Reviews Compared (no. of shows)	Pearson	Spearman	Kendall
Scotsman vs. Festival Times (190)	.18	.21	.16
Scotsman vs. Review88 (223)	.33	.30	.24
Scotsman vs. List (185)	.15	.21	.16
Festival Times vs. Review88 (195)	.27	.20	.16
Festival Times vs. List (135)	.16	.20	.16
Review88 vs. List (166)	.13	.10	.08

Note: All measures significantly different from zero at the .05 level except those in the last row.

TABLE 7.6

Model Predicting Review Variation

Predictors	b	s.e.	prob.	B
Average evaluation	−.23	.03	<.001	−.42
Popular genre[a]	.07	.06	.24	.06
Reputation	−.01	.01	.27	−.05
Originality	.12	.06	.04	.10
Intercept	1.54	.11	<.001	
R^2 = .21				
n = 364				

Note: Shows with two or more reviews are included. Dependent variable is the Mean Absolute Deviation $|X - \overline{X}|/N$ where N is the number of reviews for each show, ranging from two to four. See Appendix B for descriptions of originality and reputation. Unstandardized regression coefficients are followed by standard errors and probability values for t-tests. The final column gives standardized coefficients so that the magnitude of the effects may be compared.

[a] See Table 6.1 for genres classified as popular.

NOTES

PREFACE

1. The term is attributable to Hayden Murphy.
2. Reprinted in *Science, Technology, and Human Values* 19 (1994): 366–85.

INTRODUCTION
A CRITIC'S NEW CLOTHES

1. This provocative play was written and directed by Andrew Dallmeyer. In respect of its central device it is reminiscent of Tom Stoppard's *The Real Inspector Hound*, but its more famous predecessor does not express the conflict between high and low art so well.
2. Douglas Fraser is now arts editor for the *Scotsman*.
3. Plays about plays, actors, and critics are common at the Fringe, as they were in eighteenth-century London (Chapter 2). The concentration of performances brings the mediation process to the fore. Critics and reviews are everywhere. Once, arriving from the airport by bus, I observed a giant banner above a Georgian entrance proclaiming: "ignorant, inaccurate, and willfully mischievious." Aha, I thought. The first review of the season. Strangely, it did not mention a show or a group. I searched the map for the venue and found the location was not listed. A company had reproduced the form of a review without the content: the notice did not "refer."
4. *New York Times* 16 July 1990, "And Now at a Theater near You."
5. See Brantlinger (1983, pp. 53–58) for a discussion.
6. The demand for pop culture is a simple function of population size, whereas high culture does not exist unless a threshold population is reached, then increases even faster (Blau 1988a, pp. 54–72).
7. This goes a long way toward explaining the postmodern fascination with boundaries. The sense of an amalgam of diverse forms is produced by the tendency for the same people to view the diversity and make the connections themselves. Those who are also producers then engage in cross-genre experimentation, but such experimentation is clearly high art and has little effect on the cultural hierarchy.
8. Wilde's view that the critic could be creatively superior to the artist was the culmination of Friedrich Schlegel's romantic belief in art's primacy over nature and Matthew Arnold's view that critics determine the intellectual atmosphere of a period (Hauser 1982, pp. 480–83). If criticism is the modern form of scriptural exegesis, as suggested in Chapter 2, this development might have been expected. According to one talmudic tale, God himself studies and interprets his own Torah (Henderson 1991, p. 87).
9. Since I could not settle on terms that made artists in both categories happy,

it seemed best to use those that would offend at moderate but relatively equal levels. I must admit, however, that I prefer the terms "highbrow" and "lowbrow." These terms seem to induce readier recognition of the *constructed* nature of such categories, which is appealing because as phrenological categories they were originally intended to denote inherence!

It should be emphasized that while I generally employ this common, dichotomous language, the idea of cultural hierarchy clearly implies a continuum. That is, (1) there is no sharp boundary between high and low art, and (2) there are degrees of prestige within each category.

10. It is worth emphasizing that the distinction between performance and visual art is partly conventional. Photography, for instance, is often presented in "slide shows" by amateurs and the presentation is often a routinized, sporadic performance. The photos themselves are insignificant as cultural objects until displayed and interpreted—that is, with extensive commentary and joking about people (Iwanska 1971).

11. As Russell Lynes has written, there was no such thing as a "live audience" until technology created the "nonlive" audience. Until the turn of the century, audiences were face to face with the performers who played, sang, read aloud, or lectured (1985, p. 39). Copresence has never been a dominant feature of the visual or literary arts.

12. See analyses of popular performances such as public house entertainment and go-go dancing (Gonos 1976; Mullen 1985).

13. Two-thirds of the critics in one study claimed to prefer watching with an audience to see its reactions (English 1979, p. 61).

14. In addition, the audience for live performance, as opposed to movies or television, is typically concentrated in one place.

15. The few sociological studies of reviews have generally focused on the relationship between cultural objects and reviews (Griswold 1986, pp. 171–73) or the reviews themselves, but never on the review as a mediator of the relation between artwork and audience. For example, Griswold (1987) employed an exhaustive collection of reviews of the novels of George Lamming in order to show how critics in different cultures fabricate alternative meanings from the same cultural objects.

16. Where interviews were relatively systematic, as in Chapter 8, there is no attribution of source. Occasionally, I have attributed quotations to particular individuals when they are taken from longer, less focused interviews where explicit permission was granted.

17. Clemens 1968 [1883], p. 243. Twain's second example here was the experience of the shelling of Vicksburg.

18. In the matter of methods it should be noted that the need for manual coding of the data provided a crucial if unanticipated opportunity for observation. This was the necessity to sit for hours and days and weeks in the Fringe office while business in the unpartitioned front workroom took place within audiovisual range. Under the recent computerized system, some of these data could be more readily obtained, but I can think of no adequate substitute for this intensive period of observation that otherwise would not have occurred.

CHAPTER ONE
CULTURAL MEDIATION AND THE STATUS BARGAIN

1. The political nature of such ascriptions is exemplified by events following the unification of Germany. Some West German artists refused to consider the products of East German artists as "art," for, in their view, art was necessarily the product of the creative and unfettered imagination at work in a free society.

2. This parallels recent developments in the sociology of science that expand the boundaries of study so as to include many activities that are not considered "scientific" by scientists.

3. A discussion will be found in the next chapter.

4. Sometimes qualities of their creators are of equal importance to qualities of the object proper.

5. Musical programs might contain Italian opera, devotional songs, and comics, while museums would display fine art along with bearded women and mutant animals.

6. In 1849 a riot occurred outside the Astor Place Opera House in New York City, leaving twenty-two people dead. The cause was a feud between two actors in competing productions of *Macbeth* in which supporters of the popular Edwin Forrest rallied against the cerebral William Macready and the aristocratic sponsors of the Opera House. Three years earlier when Macready was playing *Hamlet* in Edinburgh, he executed a pirouette and was hissed loudly by Forrest for desecrating the scene with a "fancy dance" (Levine 1988, p. 67).

7. This hypothesis regarding the direction of the relation between class and taste is relatively recent. Zablocki and Kanter, in a 1976 review, considered the idea that socioeconomic status affects both life-style and taste, and the idea that socioeconomic and life-style affect taste independently, but not the idea that taste itself is a factor in the maintenance of status differentials.

8. For Bourdieu, this is particularly true for members of the cultural nobility, whose "practices derive their value from their authors, being the affirmation and perpetuation of the essence by virtue of which they are performed" (1984, p. 24).

9. *Letters of Philip Gawdy* (ed. Jeayes, pp. 120–21), as quoted in Harbage (1941, p. 91).

10. A typical article of the period comparing Eduard Thalberg and Beethoven reads much like a contemporary comparison of Beethoven and Elvis Presley (1975, pp. 19–20).

11. In Vienna, the bourgeois elite could also be found at the promenades of Johann Strauss (1975, pp. 110–11).

12. As quoted by Jelavich (1985, p. 243), who goes on to note that it became fashionable for the upper classes, and even the Wittelsbach princes, to attend the Intimes Theater "for reasons that are not entirely clear."

13. Dwight Macdonald's widely quoted statement that popular art lacks even the "theoretical possibility" of being good is quite correct—if quality judgments are based on comparisons across genres, that is, with the kinds of things that popular art is not. It is a particularized usage of the concept, applicable only to works of a certain kind. Of course, they cannot be bad either.

14. Hohendahl remarks that "the dependence of literary criticism on the theory of the trivial novel can be proven paradigmatically" (1982, p. 217). But he is astute enough to realize that another form of discourse arises: "Professional critics, no less than literary scholars, are inclined to see popular and/or trivial literature as separate genres well suited to survey reviews with a bit of sociology of the reading public thrown in. . . . What is not worth discussing aesthetically can still be discussed through criticism of ideology" (p. 219).

15. This is congruent with the philosophical analysis of "good" that restricts its use to adjectival contexts (Danto 1989).

16. The whisky example is telling, since the majority of nondrinkers cannot tell that The Macallan, the "Rolls-Royce of single malts," is better than The Claymore, as deadly as the name implies.

17. Bourdieu himself associates the popular aesthetic with the working class, but the present argument does not require this and indeed assumes widespread distribution.

18. A Harvard Ph.D. and professor at the University of Chicago was on a job interview when asked about the recent symphony season in Boston. After fumbling briefly over the conductor's name, he looked around the table: "Listen, I may as well say, don't ask me any questions about that. I like rock 'n' roll." After this admission, there was laughter all around, and a lengthy, spirited discussion of a recent Rolling Stones concert.

19. This inability to measure or agree on "quality" is functional and applies to entire genres. It is sometimes argued that there is some benefit to all groups, or to the "whole" of society to be gained from supporting resident painters or symphony orchestras—that it is simply "unmeasurable." But the unmeasurability is such that it is difficult to say exactly what that benefit is. The direct "consumers" are those that actually attend performances. The arts audience for museums, theater, classical music, opera, and dance is a good deal wealthier than the average American (Feld et al. 1983; DiMaggio and Useem 1983; Baumol and Bowen 1966). In the contemporary United States, according to Feld et al., "subsidies to the arts, including those financed through the tax system, flow from the very wealthy to the moderately wealthy and the well-educated" (p. 71).

20. The present line of argument suggests that when we say "entertainment" we simply *mean* that critical opinion is irrelevant.

21. As quoted in DiMaggio 1982a.

22. *Majime* is Japanese for "earnest" or "sober." Japanese writers worry that their works are not *majime*—another way of saying that critics do not consider them "legitimate" or "highbrow" art.

23. American drama critic quoted in English (1979, p. xiii).

24. Eugene O'Neill's father, after watching his son's play *Beyond the Horizon* (1920), asked, "What are you trying to do—send the audience home to commit suicide?" (quoted in Rigg, 1982, p. 187).

25. As Adorno would have it, the concept of the popular is "both murky and self-evident" (1976 [1962], p. 21).

26. Curious? The firework does ignite, a few seconds after removal from its aforementioned resting place. Mr. Lynam lives to strike again.

27. That taste in popular art is not mediated by experts does not imply that

it is not mediated at all. Friends are much more significant, but the kinds of arguments for and against artworks that prevail in these networks are beyond the scope of this work.

CHAPTER TWO
CRITICS IN THE PERFORMING ARTS

1. Henderson further proposes that classics are generally taken to be clear and accessible to all, but there is substantial disagreement within the several canonical traditions on this point (1991, pp. 133–35). Note this is the only assumption that pertains to the audience rather than internal properties of the works themselves.

2. The terms "aesthetician" and "critic" are used interchangeably, the terms "critic" and "reviewer" are used interchangeably, but not the terms "aesthetician" and "reviewer." This fact indicates the underlying continuum. In Germany, the term *Literaturkritik* refers both to the academic and popular modes of discourse, with, if anything, a bias toward the meaning of book reviewing (Hohendahl 1982, p. 13). John E. Booth, who views the critical enterprise in portentous terms and refers to reviews as "critiques," does not distinguish between critics and reviewers (1991, p. xiv). Lehman Engel, whose book is entitled simply *The Critics*, begins by owning that "For the most part, I will *not* be writing about *critics*" (1976, p. xv).

3. There is a good deal of movement between these roles in some art worlds (Greenfeld 1989, p. 78).

4. Appendix A provides a typology of the varieties of secondary discourse about artworks commonly found today.

5. Judith Kramer nicely documents this evolution for literary critics through a discussion of the changing media of critical discourse, from prefaces to literary essays, lectures, books, little magazines, and critical quarterlies (1970). There were status similarties as well: "None of the eighteenth-century critics would have been welcomed in aristocratic drawing rooms on the basis of their birth alone; their literary achievements were their 'admittance ticket'"(1970, p. 439).

6. The critics were generally men, except in the case of opera, where ladies were more vocal, especially in their agonistic partisanship for the Italian prima donnas, Cuzzoni and Faustina, brought together by Handel to perform *Alessandro* in 1726 (Smith 1953, pp. 55–57).

7. An extended description of this behavior is given in Charles Bodens's *The Modish Couple* (London: J. Watts, 1732), 4:47–48. Grinly, a self-proclaimed expert, discusses how his friends will clap with the audience for two acts, and destroy it in the third: "We strike up such a Chorus of Cat-calls, Whistles, Hisses, Hoops, and Horse-laughs, that not one of the Audience can hear a Syllable, and therefore charitably conclude it to be very sad Stuff.—The Epilogue's spoke, the Curtain falls, and so the poor Rascal is sent to the Devil."

8. Nor is it required today, since most newspaper and media critics are drawn from the ranks of journalists. Although 80 percent have college degrees in the United States, there is only a small association between a critic's field of study and his or her field of criticism (English 1979, p. 21).

9. In an ironic and self-conscious age, it is difficult to read such statements seriously, but they still appear: "Critics exalt the good and condemn the bad and thus guide the public toward improving its potential for pleasure and civilized progress" (English 1979, p. 3).

10. *Covent Garden Theatre* (1752).

11. From a rejected prologue by Dryden, quoted by Smith (1953, p. 153).

12. In this instance, it may have proved to be a good thing, since the play and staging were substantially reworked, and subsequently enjoyed a very successful run.

13. Dane Farnsworth Smith considers some forty plays from the Restoration through the eighteenth century that discuss critics (1953).

14. *The Way to Keep Him* (1760).

15. *The Rival Ladies* (1664).

16. For the former, see *Covent Garden Theatre; Or, Pasquin Turn'd Drawcansir* by Charles Macklin; for the latter, Henry Fielding's *The Historical Register for the year 1736*. Sheridan's *The Critic* is a veritable catalog of critical "types," designated principally by their occupations: (1) the man of the world, (2) the man of the theater, (3) the theatrical "agent," (4) the envious or offended author, (5) the critic of the pit, and (6) the newspaper critic, a variety that increased in prominence in the late eighteenth century.

17. Notably, Richard Steele's *Tatler* and *Spectator*, established early in the eighteenth century, set no real precedent for theater critics (Gray 1931, p. 1). In the United States, the *South Carolina Gazette* published theater reviews in the 1730s (English 1979, p. 11).

18. The *Morning Chronicle* and the *Morning Post* were the most important (Burns 1972, p. 196).

19. The timing of the review does not necessarily imply the expected relationship between spectatorship and authorship, as Sheridan made clear through his character Puff: "A new Comedy or Farce is to be produced at one of the Theatres. . . . The author, suppose Mr. Smatter, or Mr. Dapper—or any particular friend of mine—very well; the day before it is to be performed, I write an account of the manner in which it was received—I have the plot from the author,—and only add—Characters strongly drawn—highly coloured—hand of a master—fund of genuine humour—mine of invention—neat dialog—attic salt! Then for the performance. . . . We are at a loss which to admire most,—the unrivalled genius of the author, the great attention and liberality of the manager— the wonderful abilities of the painter, or the incredible exertions of all the performers!" (*The Critic*, 1.2. 160–78).

20. The practice persists today, though rare. During the 1989 Edinburgh festival Malcolm Hardee reviewed his own Tunnel Club show, signed William Cook's name, and slipped it under the door of the *Scotsman*, which duly published the notice (19 August 1989). Hardee was careful to include the phrase "Funniest show I have seen in Edinburgh this year," for subsequent use in his 1990 program advertisement.

21. The abuse was often mutual. For all the flattery they received in prologues, critics were not favorably treated in the analogical world of the playwright. They were compared to judges, guardians, soldiers, military engineers, hunters, medical students, midwives, pregnant females, schoolmasters, Calvin-

ists, bullies, bruisers, brigands, plunderers, pirates, barbarians, cannibals, devils, dogs, hogs, vultures, sharks, fleas, bees, locusts, spiders, sands, rocks, and poison (Smith 1953, pp. 159–70).

22. From 1816, quoted in Rigg, 1982, p. 34. Originally *A View of the English Stage* (1818).

23. John Hill, *The Actor* (1750) (Burns 1972, p. 194).

24. Burns 1972, p. 196. John Dennis was probably the first man in England to make a living as a professional critic.

25. Reviewing was emphatically not the province of specialized periodicals only. The addition of a *feuilleton*, or cultural supplement to the daily papers, was common practice on the Continent by the mid-nineteenth century, and the *feuilletonist* was clearly distinct from his academic counterpart (Hohendahl 1982, p. 16).

26. In music, too, criticism began in the eighteenth century in response to the expansion of the market for public concerts across Europe and the new "Italian style" of singing. These critics were professionals, drawn from the ranks of the musical elite who began writing with a "heavy, intellectual and scientific approach" in musical magazines. By 1810 they had switched to a popular style and language, suited to the daily newspapers (Graf 1946, p. 115.). As in the theater world, many critics were themselves composers, writing in defense of their music or a style of music, while other journalist-critics were attuned more to the audience and the formulation of principles of criticism than the composers themselves. There is an association between the shift from amateur associations to public concerts and the origin of "journalistic" criticism in daily newspapers. Instead of an internally oriented specialist, the critic becomes an externally oriented educator and reporter.

In painting and sculpture, critical essays began to appear during the 1740s. These articles commenting on the exhibitions at the Salon in Paris, puffed and condemned anonymously until authors were required to sign their names in an ordnance of 1765. (About thirty such critiques appeared each year by 1783.) Denis Diderot's famous essays, conversational in tone and a far cry from the aesthetic theory that appeared in the *Encyclopédie*, were published in a private newsletter distributed by the Baron Friedrich von Grimm across Europe. The late eighteenth century saw an increase in the number of exhibitions by independent artists outside of the academies. Art reviews, often accompanied by illustrations, appeared in association with these exhibitions to provide visitors with a critical guide to the objects on display (White and White 1965; Holt 1979, pp. xxiv–11).

By the mid-nineteenth century, both the number of works produced and the demand for canvases by the middle class had soared. These conditions undermined the central control of the Academy and encouraged the growth of a "dealer-critic" system marketing the works of painters and schools, notably the impressionists, to circles of patrons. Independent critics, rather than artists themselves, took over the tasks of evaluating work as well as educating viewers and potential buyers. The laudatory review became a substitute for the salon medal (White and White 1965, p. 150). Although American art criticism lagged a half century behind Europe, by the early twentieth century "picture reporting" was no longer found primarily in relatively expensive magazines. Art critics had columns in daily and weekend editions of major newspapers, often adopting both the standards and the prose style of John Ruskin (Olson 1980).

27. Some reviewers have strong negative feelings about this. As one theater critic put it, the judgment should emerge from the totality of the review, without having to come right out and say it; a good critic will never say "Go see this show"; "Give this one a miss"; "Thumbs up." It is in the nature of highbrow discourse that sensibility is differentiated. Cultural objects are not "all" good or bad, but only with respect to aspects.

28. Many cringe at the Michelin Green Guide practice of giving stars to sites of interest. This smacks of reviewing high art in the manner of popular art.

29. This is not to say that criteria cannot be developed, as they have been in international ballet competitions. The obvious similarity between competitions in ballet, generally defined as art, and gymnastics, which is clearly sport, leads to a concern about contamination of the genre. "Competition fever can breed the facile dancer, the equivalent of the anonymous virtuoso of piano competitions" (Anna Kisselgoff, *New York Times*, 23 February 1992, section 2, p. 1).

30. While a majority of critics lamented the lack of attempts on goal and generally uninspiring nature of play in both the 1990 and 1994 World Cup finals, no one disputed that Germany and Brazil won, fair and square. This clarity was applauded by Bertolt Brecht who pinned his hopes on the sporting public.

31. For instance, the *auteur* theory of film employs the distinguishable personality of the director as a criterion of value, or principled standard.

32. Lu Xun, the Chinese novelist, parodied the old notion of the perfect socialist poem: "Oh, steam engine! / Oh, Lenin!"

33. Interviewing Israeli painting critics in the 1980s, Liah Greenfeld found that virtually all were "acutely aware of the relativity of the definitions of art" owing to their exposure to Marxist and structuralist views. Criteria for defining and evaluating paintings were explicitly lacking or simply irrelevant. Critics agreed that there were no properties intrinsic to the artworks themselves that justified a distinction between good and bad works—yet they were constantly required to make such distinctions. Hence, they become "ideologists" and servants of particular artistic circles.

34. Thresholds and variability are related at two levels. At the individual level, variations in judgment can be perceived as implying refinement. In aggregate, there must be judgmental variation but in addition one must ask about consensus over evaluations. For example, when it is said that an academic department must "maintain its standards," it means that there are some students who are passing now that shouldn't be. But there must be an additional agreement over who those students are and why they are inadequate as a precondition for holding there are implicit criteria for performance.

35. Michael Feingold of the *Village Voice*, quoted in English 1979, p. 21.

36. Many critics who hold this view rarely deal with amateurs (e.g., books, architecture). About half the critics in English's study (1979) said they use a "single standard" for all works. When Brown asked, "How should [the work] be evaluated?" only about one-quarter of respondents said using the "highest critical standards" (1978). Both results are based on surveys rather than interviews or content analysis of reviews.

37. In America, William Winter was the dean of the Victorian style critics, along with John Rankin Towse, Henry Austin Clapp, and Lewis Strang. These "scholarly and thoughtful" critics wrote detailed analytical reviews for newspapers that provided ample space, but were uninterested in the new drama and production techniques that began to characterize theater (Wilson 1973, p. 259).

38. The "interactional" phase is not the same as the "informal" aspect or style of criticism. Informality is reflected in what some consider an "English" style of reviewing, the "cocktail party" talk that in a review is a kind of "ultra-civilized amaterism" (Sutherland 1978, p. 92). As Evelyn Waugh put it, "the most acute and influential criticism is uttered in private conversation by people with no identifiable qualifications" (*Spectator*, 24 February 1956). Waugh believed that it was "un-English" to take reviewing seriously (Sutherland, 1978, p. 92).

39. This estimate derives from a Harris poll reported by English (1979).

40. In the early eighteenth century, Daniel Defoe began his career as a journalist writing as the editorial character "Mr. Review."

41. Sutherland discusses the recent "purification" of book reviewing, corrupt from its earliest roots, owing to the expansion of review outlets and the production of a generation of academics since World War II with no prejudice toward reviewing and fewer links to the publishing industry (1978, pp. 86–92).

In a recent month of reviews in the *New York Times Book Review* I counted sixty-five reviewers, 58 percent of whom were authors (generally identified by their last or forthcoming book) and a further 25 percent were scholars or teachers identified by their published books. Eleven reviewers were not specifically said to be authors but nine of these were journalists, editors, or professors. Only one of the reviewers was occupationally identified as a critic. Similarly high proportions are to be found for the *London Review* and the *New York Review of Books*.

42. The shrewd observer will note the difficulty of precise quantification at this point.

43. The role of the critic is now strongly institutionalized as a legitimate occupation. When the Royal Court Theatre considered withdrawing invitations to the press, the Arts Council, an important sponsor of the theater, rejected the idea. When the same theater stopped inviting one particular critic (because of an early departure from a play) subsequent performances were boycotted by other critics (Doty and Harbin 1990, pp. 120, 160).

CHAPTER THREE
DEVELOPMENT OF THE FESTIVAL FRINGE

1. Ben Jonson (1572–1637).

2. David Edge first urged notice of this fact.

3. R. L. Stevenson's *Picturesque Old Edinburgh* (1878), as quoted in Massie (1994, p. 181).

4. The Edinburgh festival is, without exaggeration, the largest festival for performing arts in the world. In addition to the International Festival and the Fringe, there are several other formally organized arts "festivals"—television,

books, jazz, film, and children's, as well as the Military Tattoo. The particular configuration of festivals changes slightly each year. Altogether, the 1990 festival consisted of approximately 2,200 events at 238 venues with an estimated audience of 1.3 million people (Scottish Tourist Board 1992).

5. In 1974 ticket sales for the Fringe surpassed those for the International Festival but the latter has much larger average audiences. In 1990, with only a tenth as many shows as the Fringe, the International Festival sold about half as many tickets. In all, the Edinburgh Festivals that year contributed an estimated £72 million to the Scottish economy.

6. "Fringe" probably does not do justice to the trek required of festivalgoers, since Dunfermline is across the Forth bridges in Fife.

7. To date the best history of the early years is Alistair Moffat's *The Edinburgh Fringe* (1978). Michael Dale's more recent compilation *Sore Throats and Overdrafts* (1988) contains many useful insights. Both volumes are by former Fringe administrators.

8. Edwards mentions that there were up to fifty "subsidiary events" associated with the official festival as well (1990, pp. 17–18).

9. By way of comparison, the New York International Festival, lasting over two weeks in June, hosts about fifty acts.

10. Quoted in Dale 1988, p. 79.

11. Duncan MacRae, speaking to the Fringe Society in 1959 (Dale 1988, p. 41).

12. Quoted in Moffat 1978, p. 38.

13. Jonathan Miller, Alan Bennett, Dudley Moore, and Peter Cook were the coconspirators. The play was revived at the 1990 Fringe by four performers who had never seen the original.

14. The official festival still occupies many of the established performance spaces: Usher Hall, Queen's Hall, King's Theatre, Playhouse Theatre, and the Royal Lyceum Theatre.

15. About one-third of arts festivals in Great Britain take place in a single venue (Policy Studies Institute 1992).

16. In the art world, growth in the number of performers should lead to innovation but not necessarily to the intimate and participatory "style" described here, unless under similar spatial contraints. Whenever there is an increase in the number of performers in a given location and a corresponding need for space, these features of innovation and intimacy should characterize the resulting performances. Chicago experienced such an influx in the 1980s with many of the same consequences. In addition to large professional theaters, an "off-Loop" theater has developed corresponding to off-Broadway theater in New York.

17. This style of naturalism is also associated with film, since close movements are easily followed by camera.

18. In one show, spectators were exhorted to burn their credit cards. In another, the audience was led, piperlike, to the women's toilet before usurping the stalls to sing campfire songs with percussion provided by the sanitary bins. In the opinion of one observer, they "trained a whole generation of Fringe club audiences."

19. In the next chapter the emergence of supervenues, a phenomenon that caters to the desire of critics and spectators for greater predictability, is considered.

20. While high cultural discourse often uses the term "genre," popular discourse prefers the four-letter words "type" and "kind."

21. Discussed in Chapter 1 (see also Wolff 1983, p. 105).

22. Given preferences for particular genres, it makes sense to move beyond considering the statement "I haven't seen it yet, but . . ." as an embarrassment and allow that it is a crucial topic for investigation.

23. As Crane treats it, a style is a cultural network that represents a collaborative effort of artists who work on common aesthetic problems (1987, pp. 19, 22). It may also be defined as a set of cultural objects whose common properties are defined by critics, especially in reinterpretations of older artists in terms of new criteria.

24. Categorizations may change. It is often said that "movies" became art as a result of criticism (Zolberg 1990, p. 7), but critics did not raise the status of an entire medium: they played a role in the process, which involved the differentiation of a new genre of art films.

25. By the twentieth century the distinction between vaudeville and burlesque was drawn, as these two kinds of performers received separate billings.

26. As Lynes demonstrated, objects that are commonplace for one generation can be prized by the highbrows of the next, while prestigious objects can become vulgar (1949). Styles and objects are simply too local and specific to consitute anything but ephemeral carriers of the highbrow/lowbrow distinction.

27. The most popular group, Purves Puppets, has appeared since 1963.

28. The official festival was (and is) criticized for ignoring Scottish theater ("They aren't ashamed of Scotch Whisky or Arthur's Seat, but they seem to be of Scottish Drama"—quoted in Moffat 1978, p. 15), while the Fringe is criticized for being too English ("I don't mind English accents, ken, as long as they're in England").

29. The paradigm here would be a "revue." This genre is on the verge of disappearing at the Fringe altogether, as shown in the next chapter.

30. Comedian Jeremy Hardy once joked that Edinburgh is called the Athens of the North because every summer it's full of students throwing up everywhere (Cook 1994, p. 235).

31. In 1990, eight companies used the name "Cambridge" and four "Oxford" in their titles.

32. As ex-student performer Tim Palmer wrote: "Over the course of the week not once did we contaminate our artistic integrity with the slightest trace of theatrical accomplishment. . . . [the Fringe's] charm lies in its quality as a status symbol. . . . this helps to explain the irresistible attraction that Edinburgh holds for every incompetent thespian in the country. It is, quite simply, the best you can hope to achieve if you're no bloody good."

33. The director of a London theater company defined a Fringe group as something between the amateur and professional: "you've got no one backing you up—you're on your own."

34. Even in the late 1980s, a reviewer for the *Scotsman* claimed that until recently professionals were not allowed at the Fringe.

35. Michael Walker of the Oxford Theatre Group, as quoted in Moffat 1978, p. 93.

36. This statement is less true for new work by known playwrights, insofar as various forms of continuity over an artist's production may be assumed.

37. Nine were awarded in 1973 out of forty-nine eligible shows. The number has dropped as low as four in 1975 but averages about thirteen or fourteen per year.

38. Although Fringe Firsts were the leading form of performance recognition for many years, the number and variety of awards increased in the late 1980s and early 1990s.

39. Quoted in Moffat 1978, p. 26.

40. Gordon McDougall, former Traverse director, exaggerated the local reputation with the remark: "To most people in Edinburgh, the Festival is a bore. To most of them the Traverse [i.e., the Fringe] is a strip club" (Moffat 1978, pp. 62, 74, 101).

41. Rewriting drafts is rare during the festival. This particular reviewer wrote more than thirty that year.

42. As quoted in Dale 1988, p. 93. Sometimes it is argued that the central quality of a Fringe is its peripherality. This is completely mistaken. The most important, indeed defining, feature of a Fringe is lack of artistic vetting.

43. "Punter" is a British term for spectator.

44. The substitution of diversity claims for quality claims only holds for the Fringe administration and not the Fringe performers, who must, of course, make quality claims for their shows.

CHAPTER FOUR
FESTIVALS AND THE MODERN FRINGE

1. A survey of spectators by the Scottish Tourist Board indicates that about nine in ten have a copy of the Fringe program.

2. A Fringe brochure was sold for twenty-five pence in 1972. It ran to 128 pages with a full page for each group, including photos.

3. The record for the most shows ever seen is 169, set by Nigel Tantrum in 1994. Asked why he was willing to spend £1,500, his answer is instructive for the present argument: "In part it's because I long to see the first performance of a potential mega-star. Mostly, it's because there is no other profession that must prepare so thoroughly to give of itself so fully to produce something that when complete is gone forever" (Festival Fringe Society 1995a, p. 50).

4. On distribution systems, see Becker 1982, pp. 93–130, and Hirsch 1972.

5. *Festival!*, a guide to international theater and dance festivals, lists thirty-seven festivals during a recent two-month period in Europe and North America. One indicator of the abundance and popularity of festivals is the annual publication of special sections in the *New York Times* on summer festivals in Europe and the United States. The listing of major summer arts events in Europe usually inventories fifty festivals of which the Edinburgh Festival is only one. The 1992

listing of summer American arts events included 160 classical music festivals and 61 dance festivals.

6. This property, since it is consistent with both the presence and absence of central administration, makes it impossible to determine the number of fringe festivals worldwide. Any uninvited groups appearing in concert with an official festival constitute a fringe, whether organized or not. The Edinburgh Fringe maintains links with more than fifteen relatively organized fringes, including those in Canada, Australia, and France (Avignon). By 1995 there were seventeen organized fringes in North America (twelve in Canada and five in the United States).

7. This open-access type is exemplified by the Adelaide fringe as well, which began as an outgrowth of an official festival in 1960 and was organized formally in 1966. By 1994 there were 306 events at 151 venues.

8. Edmonton hosts the largest fringe in Canada. Its establishment in 1981 heralded the huge growth of Canadian fringes. Their sequential timing allows them to form a summer circuit for many groups.

9. Other fringes, while operating according to this general principle, seek actively to include certain kinds of groups, though not on aesthetic grounds. The Adelaide fringe consciously seeks to include Australian aboriginal work, while some U.S. fringes have ethnic quotas.

10. In 1995 the Fringe Society charged groups a participation fee of £125 plus £100 per show. The rule of thumb often used for renting an equipped venue was £100 per 100 seats per week, for a one-hour performance. Many venues also require 40 percent of ticket sales after this minimum is reached.

11. As Michael Dale wrote, "Any group which comes out of the Fringe with smaller losses than it envisaged can be deemed to have done well. Any group that makes an overall surplus has either done remarkable business or has got its sums wrong" (1988, p. 60).

12. For the years prior to 1970 I have used counts from Moffat's book because no official records were kept prior to the establishment of the Fringe office. For the past twenty-five years I have used Fringe office records where available.

13. In the late 1970s and early 1980s the number of shows per group declined slightly, which accounts for the appearance of a more rapid increase in the number of groups. The average number of shows per group since 1975 is 1.98, but in the early 1990s it has averaged 2.14, higher than any other period.

14. The Fringe now has so many shows beginning before the official start date that Week 0 is now an official designation in the program. One virtue of festival studies is an automatic control for time of year, generally thought to affect the success of shows.

15. Even the local audience appears not to have materialized for venues in such council-estate suburbs as Pilton, Craigmillar, Sighthill, Firhill, and Gilmerton (Moffat 1978, p. 104).

16. An exception is Rosslyn Chapel, a tourist attraction in its own right south of the city, that uses a fifteenth-century chapel as a setting for religious and historical drama as well as music.

17. A separate map is usually provided for these outlying venues but several are still too distant to appear.

18. In Nairobi, I witnessed the performance of a new play entitled *Otongolia* that lasted one hour. The cast took a curtain call, but many in the audience simply retired to the foyer to await the start of the second act. In Edinburgh, a venerable sitarist from India was startled when he was informed on arrival, just prior to beginning his concert at the Assembly Rooms, that he would have just sixty minutes—time for a thorough warm-up.

19. The limited number of central venues does impose serious limitations in terms of scheduling. Stand-up comics sometimes wind up offering their wares to a morning audience.

20. Four administrators have succeeded him: Alistair Moffat, Michael Dale, Mhairi Mackenzie-Robinson, and Hilary Strong, who was appointed with the new title of director in 1994.

21. Participation fees from performing groups together with revenue from program listings represented 28 percent of the annual income of the Fringe Society in 1993, substantially more than that generated by the box office (16 percent).

22. The Fringe Society Internet address is http://www.presence.co.uk/fringe/. Within its first twelve weeks, it had become one of the most popular sites in the United Kingdom, registering over 250,000 "hits."

23. Open access on the Internet means that many—and, for some groups, all—of the reviews posted are by performers or others directly associated with the group.

24. The 1995 edition of *Fringe Safe* details the regulations for the transformation of spaces into licensed theaters and the rules for creating special effects, including explosions and the use of firearms. This document, made essential by the vast range of spaces and performance needs, and regulatory constraints encountered over the history of the Fringe, is a masterpiece of bureaucratic cooperation between the Lothian and Borders Fire Brigade, the Lothian and Borders Police, and the Licensing, Environmental Services and Property Services departments of the Edinburgh District Council. It contains seventy-six pages of instruction on everything from raising the seating to scaffolding, food hygiene, toilets, the stage area, fire safety, dressing rooms, exits, emergency and stage lighting, posters, and security.

25. The number of accredited journalists has grown from 641 in 1992 to 840 in 1994. This number includes not only press from Britain and North America, but also Europe, South America, and the former Soviet bloc countries. Nearly 3,000 press tickets were issued by the Fringe press office alone but some of the larger venues distribute press tickets exclusively through their own press offices.

26. One such individual created and promoted a show that didn't exist simply to promote himself for future work.

27. Quoted from the Fringe Press Office Diary 1994.

28. The 1995 edition, *How to Sell a Show on the Fringe* (fifty-two pages), discusses marketing, print, distribution, advertising, promotions, advance press, press releases, and photography as well as what the media want, the festival press, reviews, and the Fringe press office.

29. Howard Becker (1982, pp. 233–46) defines mavericks as outside the boundaries of the art world, but they are well within the boundaries of the Fringe.

30. The administration provides a discrete number of genres that companies must use to categorize their shows. Such categories are often an occasion for dispute. Over the 1980s the number of genres grew larger to accommodate these demands, with a maximum of twenty-three in 1994. The following year, owing to a decision to restructure the program and list all shows by genre (rather than simply show titles), the number of genres was reduced to eight: children's shows, comedy and revue, dance and physical theater, exhibitions, music, musicals and opera, talks and events, and theater.

31. At the extreme, the 1988 Fringe included two productions of both *The Real Inspector Hound* and *Abigail's Party*. In each case, one company viewed it as "theater," the other as "comedy." Whether the decision was based in any sense on the style of production is unknown. In 1990, the *Canterbury Tales* received two such dissimilar classifications. The director of the "theater" version indicated that his emphasis on the flow of the narrative influenced his choice. It is important to note that companies are almost never aware of competing offerings of the same show until very late in the process.

32. Just as it is easiest for the Fringe office to accept group classifications, this simplifies editorial work. But there are exceptions. The *List* formerly used a slightly different classification system with categories such as "world theatre" and "adaptations." This increased the chance of receiving review coverage since fewer shows fall under these headings. Multiple reviews incorporating similar thematic material can move shows in or out of a genre through comparison.

33. One American comic who first came to Edinburgh in the mid-1990s remarked, "seeing things here, where anything goes, reminds me of the late 1970s in the States." One critic calls it "the most dynamic and influential development in the performing arts since Punk Rock" (Cook 1994, p. 3).

34. On the tenth anniversary of the Comedy Store in London, Simon Fanshawe wrote that the apparent decline of overtly antiestablishment comedy was mistaken. The increase in demand for comedy had simply caused innovation and diversification: "Like the Labour Party, we are no longer playing to rooms full of Labour voters" (*Guardian* 19 May 1989).

35. The significance of the festival is indicated by the fact that in the early 1980s comedians used Edinburgh as a testing ground for new material, while ten years later many were careful to try new material before arriving.

36. In 1994, the Assembly Rooms, the Gilded Balloon I, and the Pleasance each ranked among the top seven venues in terms of the ratio of reviews to shows. The Traverse Theatre ranked first with an average of 4.27 reviews per show.

37. Located on magnificent George Street in the New Town, where Charles Dickens read his novels and Walter Scott made known his authorship of the Waverley books, the Assembly Rooms attracts huge audiences as well as large numbers of journalists and talent scouts. Performers are often nationally known

comics and cabaret artists, and presentations are slick and professional. The club bar is a place for deals and networking.

38. The Gilded Balloon itself had become so large as to require two venues, including the old Traverse Theatre in the Grassmarket.

CHAPTER FIVE
MYTH OF THE FRINGE

1. As noted by the former director of the Adelaide Festival Fringe, Peter Tregilgas.

2. Dale's judgment that "countless thousands of aspiring professionals have had their reputations made or broken at the Fringe over the last four decades" (1988, p. 81) is certainly false but is a pure expression of the ideology. The actual association between reviews and attendance is considered in the next chapter, while the beliefs of performers are the subject of Chapter 8.

3. As quoted in Dale 1988, p. 85.

4. *Sell Out*, a play about an amateur company bringing its first play to the Fringe, depended completely on these shared archetypes (as well as an audience consisting mainly of Fringe devotees) for its success and predicted its own titular fate, but its self-referential aspects could only be meaningful for its first run.

5. Kington penned this sardonically reduced "history of the Fringe" for the introduction to Michael Dale's book (1988), claiming that a three-week stint on the Fringe was like "having an entire show-biz career compressed into one glorious stress-ridden month." I have modified it here slightly.

6. The title of Dale's book as taken from an article by Alec Renton in the *Independent* interviewing the "Hat Factory."

7. McEwan's brewery sponsored ticket printing in the 1970s in return for advertisements on the back of the tickets. At £1.50 per performance, some groups made more money in this fashion than ticket sales (Dale 1988, p. 58).

8. The lowest average audience per performance in the past twenty years is four dozen.

9. The love of diversity is by no means novel. In the seventeenth century and throughout the nineteenth, London theater programs included singing, dancing, and acrobatics. Even the traditional Fringe practice of rushing from show to show has a historical precedent in the eighteenth-century Battle of the Romeos: the savvy spectator would take in the earlier acts with David Garrick at Drury Lane, but rush to Covent Garden, where Spranger Barry's tomb scene was considered superior (Griswold 1986, p. 258).

10. Charles Maclean, as quoted in Dale 1988, p. 83.

11. In 1981, Robin Strapp, with a lilo on his back, was judged the winner, with twenty performances to his credit.

12. In the case of this 1966 Fringe premier, Stoppard was neither unknown (the Royal Shakespeare Company had commissioned the third act of the play), nor were the reviews especially positive. The *Scotsman*, the *Sunday Times*, and the *Glasgow Herald* were lukewarm to negative, and the author of the *Observer*'s positive reviews had both read the script and helped place the piece with the Oxford Theatre Group (Moffat 1978, p. 72). The *Scotsman*, for example,

said that Stoppard asks a thousand questions "without enlightening us in the least. The play is peppered with incriminating phrases that could be taken down and used against it, the saddest confession being that 'We're tied down to language that makes up for in obscurity for what it lacks in style'" (25 August 1966).

13. "They are afraid of missing the messiah. If artists have become obsessed with discovering new styles in painting, critics have become obsessed with discovering artists in the process of discovery" (Moulin 1987 [1967], p. 76).

14. A similar phenomenon may be seen in the tendency for certain television news images to acquire this performance quality. The videotape in the trial of Mayor Marion Barry was reviewed in Walter Goodman's "Critic's Notebook": "The photography, lighting, and sound, which give the illusion of watching and listening through a haze of smoke, are in accord with the cinematic principle that form should follow content. . . . The situation—a bedroom joust between a man with an old-fashioned urge and a woman with ulterior intentions—is inherently farcical. . . . The show ends with humor provided by the FBI agents" (*New York Times*, 2 July 1990, p. C14).

15. According to other London critics, this is why he should be "put out to pasture." The idea that critics are exposed to more performances, while intuitively plausible, is not to be taken for granted, since the average number of hours spent on television and videotaped films is now so high.

16. A famous robbery and murder of a bank currency runner occurred in the courtyard in 1805, precipitating the sale of the building.

17. Quoted in English 1979, p. 26.

18. Broadway theaters once had early curtains, to give the reviewers time to write their pieces. According to Atkinson, *The Iceman Cometh* opened at five o'clock so the reviewers could get out at ten.

19. In 1933, upon learning that *Mourning Becomes Electra* was based on the Greek classics, Brooks Atkinson asked Eugene O'Neill if he should do some background reading in order to review the play properly. O'Neill said no, he should read the manuscript (three plays at the time). Atkinson felt that was unethical ("a reviewer should walk into the theater like a member of the audience"). Most members of the audience do not read Greek classics in preparation, either (Greenberger 1971, p. 165).

20. Sutherland reports that the literary editor of the *Times* received fifteen to twenty novels per week, sent ten to reviewers, and reviewed four to five in the *Sunday Times*. "I sniff them as if they were fish bought on a Monday . . . next I read the first and last pages of the novels still in the running" (1978, p. 92).

21. Up to 200 persons apply each year for five or six vacancies. Thirty-five critics reviewed for the *Scotsman* in 1988, producing over 500 reviews at £15.35 per review.

22. Interview with Allan Wright, former arts editor for the *Scotsman*.

23. Data for all theater, comedy, and cabaret listings were used where the shows ran at least one week (nine theatrical and eleven popular shows). In cases where information for some days was missing, measures were calculated both with and without these shows. Each listing was counted only once regardless of the number of tickets issued since these are generally friends of the reviewer

(e.g., the *Financial Times* would be counted as one case even if two or three tickets were issued). Press passes are given for many reasons: not only for television, radio, and newspaper critics, but to judges (for prizes such as the Perrier Award), promoters, and a miscellany of other characters. For aggregate measures such as total press passes, I simply assume the count is a general measure of "interest" in the show. It is unquestionably true that some listings are not "legitimate" in the sense that the recipient, credentialed or not, does not actually review the show. But that is not an issue to be addressed by the author, who is willing to countenance a lack of fastidiousness on the part of Fringe box offices for reasons best left unstated.

24. This reasoning is supported by the press records at the Pleasance. There, unlike the Assembly Rooms, cabaret/comedy tends to have *longer* runs and, hence, fewer press in attendance on opening day.

25. Throughout the length of the run the average is slightly higher for popular genres (3.6 to 3.3) but, again, is largely due to shorter runs, combined with a rapid decline in media interest after the first week.

26. The lag between appearance at a show and filing copy is generally one day (85 percent, estimated for one of the most prolific reviewers) or two days, rarely longer.

27. About twenty pieces were rejected in 1988.

28. The lag between the time the show is seen and the appearance of the review averages 3.5 days. Ninety percent are printed within five days of the time the critic sees the show.

29. George Orwell described the instructions of English book review editors to their reviewers: "Review this book if it seems any good. If not send it back. We don't think it's worth while to print simply damning reviews." Coser, Kadushin, and Powell assert this remains true to some extent in the contemporary United States (1982, pp. 309–10).

30. Although I was promised access to the unpublished reviews, the files were subject to a rare and untimely cleansing prior to my appearance at the office to obtain them.

31. This example of a "rejected" review is furnished from personal records of a reviewer from the *Scotsman*: "This is a 'one woman show' written and performed by [name]. The title is from a poem which talks of Summers 'washed away' which is fine and comparitively [*sic*] short. The other thirty minutes of this mid-day show in the Chaplaincy centre are relentlessly banal. The monologue opens in London 'Where words were born.' With toe-curling intensity this graduate of Birmingham High, California, tells us 'guys' in the audience about Fred the teacher, William the friend and Sex. A letter to another friend Kate is delivered with a gush of coy self-deprecation that made me wince. 'Primal gestures,' 'Feminism' and other 'American attitudes' ooze across the bare set from this perfomer [*sic*] who bemoans the fact she 'missed out the Sixties.' I regret being so dismissive but this performance made me feel trapped by a peculiarly drab, boring and monotous [*sic*] one-sided conversation." The reader is left to resolve the motives for rejection, but many equally negative Fringe reviews were published.

32. Another offsetting force is the editorial practice of refusing assignments to some reviewers: "If they are too interested in or too close to a show—they

seem to want to do it too much, perhaps for some personal reason—I steer them away from it and won't assign it to them."

33. In the only two instances reported to me, a cut from "engagingly neurotic" to "neurotic" had a significant impact on the review. In another, a word deletion changed a "qualified" good review to a rave. The consensus, however, was that changes were minor, generally unnoticeable, and did not affect the evaluative component of the review. Since editors pass on so many reviews during the festival, this might be thought unusual, particularly since reviewers write very rapidly. For comparison, 95 percent of the critics in English's survey (1979) claimed their editors never or rarely made major changes. About half, however, said that reviews were trimmed.

34. In one major forum, they are even more strongly shifted for highbrow than for popular forms. Two hundred short and long movie reviews from the *New York Times* were paired (selecting cases from June and October for a ten-year period). Summary reviews from the Sunday edition were matched to the longer reviews of the same movies found with the paper's index. While there is a general tendency for most short reviews to be *more* favorable than the longer review from which they are taken, this is more pronounced for drama than comedy (foreign films included).

CHAPTER SIX
DO CRITICS MATTER?

1. "Informal" critics sometimes play key roles even for aficionados, owing to the intensity of their consumption *if* the supply of art is extremely large relative to other demands on the audience. Radway (1984) documents the developing career of one woman from an informal opinion leader in the field of romantic fiction into a critic. She began to publish *Dorothy's Diary of Romance Reading* and eventually became a gatekeeper for several publishing houses. It seems clear, in this instance, that readers needed such selection guidance because of the sheer volume of production.

2. Deviations from established repertoires can be economically disastrous. Zolberg demonstrates that the value attached to originality in orchestral performances is relatively low (1980). Similarly, Martorella shows that standardization of the operatic repertoire occurs because of dependence on subscription sales (1977).

3. To emphasize the point, the arts may be contrasted to the sciences. As Wuthnow and Witten argue, in every sphere of specialization—arts, science, religion—there is a status hierarchy that may be cast as a distinction between the highbrow and the low, an "official" culture and pop culture, a specialist's culture and a lay culture (1988). Even so, there is no direct sense in which science is *for* the lay audience. The public for science "news" is, like the readers of the *New York Times* Arts and Leisure section, interested but uninvolved. Artists, on the other hand, create cultural objects *for* a public, and it is the preferences of this public that are or are not affected by the critics.

4. Blau, for example, demonstrates the importance of living in the city center for arts attendance (1988a).

5. The National Research Center for the Arts conducted a national survey of

3,005 people in 1965 in which 37 percent said that "what critics said about a film" was either very or somewhat important to their decision to go to a movie. Critics were most influential among younger, more educated, and higher-income groups. In one British study 85 percent of respondents said reviews were their main source of information about films, but that the evaluation was not important (Austin 1983b, p. 158).

6. Three findings are noteworthy in the present context. Theater was the most frequently attended genre for virtually all spectators, regardless of which kind of performance they were attending when they were surveyed. Broadway and off-Broadway audiences were similar in social composition to audiences throughout the country, with the exception that there were fewer students. Finally, British audiences were remarkably similar to U.S. audiences.

7. Prior studies of the relationship between critics and public have more to do with the consensus between them than the effects of reviews (Austin 1983b; Brown 1978; English 1979; Levy 1988; Litman 1983; Wanderer 1970; Wyatt and Badger 1984).

8. I refer here to the general public, not those with professional interest.

9. This includes 631 face to face and 973 self-completion questionnaires, but the return rate for the latter was extremely poor (24 percent).

10. Estimates of the proportion of local visitors (i.e., from Edinburgh and the Lothians) vary from 35 percent to 50 percent and the number of Scottish spectators from 45 percent to 65 percent. Visitors from the United States made up only 3 percent of the sample in the Tourist Board survey.

11. The same cannot be said about advance sale tickets, much more likely to be mass-purchased in the case of the official festival than the Fringe. This explains the fact that one may sit in the middle of the audience at an International Festival production surrounded by New York and Californian accents.

12. This percentage is far higher than for any of the seven other festivals studied. (The children's festival was excluded because most visitors are locals.)

13. Personal interviews were conducted at selected performances and at booking offices for (1) the International Festival, (2) the Festival Fringe, and (3) the Film Festival (Macrae 1989).

14. The International Festival estimated that 10 percent of its visitors were from the United States in 1989, down from a peak of 15 percent, but the Tourist Board Survey showed only 6 percent later that year.

15. The Tourist Board found the average Fringe visitor was staying for 7.2 nights in Edinburgh as compared with an average stay in Edinburgh of 4.6 nights for British tourists.

16. Of all Edinburgh festivals the Fringe scores lowest on perceived "value for money" in the Scottish Tourist Board survey (1992), primarily owing to the wide variation in performances.

17. Yet since there are so many of them, there is also ample opportunity for the public to get contradictory advice, as I show in the next chapter.

18. The 1988 Fringe lasted from 12 August through 3 September. Time of year is generally thought to make a difference to the success of shows (Goodlad 1971, p. 150). By restricting our attention to a single period, we automatically take this into account.

19. The published figures for groups are not an accurate count for the following reason: they include only groups with "main listings" in the Fringe program. The use of an umbrella group for several small groups has been a common practice in recent years to save on the cost of listings. The analysis below is based on the *performance* rather than the group.

20. This is based on the results of a survey of groups (n = 129) carried out after the Fringe. Owing to the problem of defining a "group" (see preceding note) and the low response rate (27 percent), these data are to be treated with suspicion (if not outright disbelief), so I have rarely used this survey. Analysis of 1991 Fringe program main headings shows over 50 percent of groups are professionals (69 percent if mixed professional and amateur groups are considered).

21. It should be reemphasized that diversity is not itself novel. As noted in Chapter 2, in the seventeenth century and throughout the nineteenth, London theater programs included singing, dancing, and acrobatics.

22. The paper did not do so in 1988 and was not included as a "comprehensive" paper in the present analysis.

23. In the late 1980s four periodicals attempted to be relatively comprehensive in their coverage: the *Scotsman*, the *List*, *Review88*, and *Festival Times*.

24. In 1988, 92 percent of groups in the postfestival survey said that their shows had been reviewed. Only 18 percent of shows failed to receive a review in any of the four periodicals I considered as major Edinburgh publications. Shows received an average of two reviews each. In 1994, a Fringe press office survey that included all national and Scottish dailies (as well as the *List*, *Stage*, and *Time Out*) showed that only 57 percent of all shows were reviewed. An increase in the number of shows, a decline in coverage by the London papers, and the termination of two of the specialized Edinburgh periodicals largely account for this.

25. As Hohendahl implies in his analysis of Habe's novel *Das Netz*, a "best seller" does not, by that fact, belong to the category of what is in German termed *Trivialliteratur* (1982).

26. See also Goodlad (1971, p. 50). In the London theater, comedy was generally more popular than tragedy (Griswold 1986, pp. 113, 262).

27. Appendix B details the measures used in the analysis that follows.

28. The rationale behind using this measure of popularity will be discussed later. Higher attendance at popular genres is confirmed regardless of the measure used.

29. Popular shows average from 44 percent to 140 percent better audiences. However, if one simply divides estimated total tickets sales by the number of shows (not performances) and simply compares comedy with theater, comedy sells more than 2.5 times as many tickets. Once more I caution that higher ticket sales do not necessarily indicate greater enjoyment for those attending.

30. This view is described for the theater world by Goodlad (1971, p. 137) and sometimes called the "Frank Rich" effect, after a well-known theater critic for the *New York Times*. One version is that the influence of critics is primarily negative. That is, they can kill a play stone-dead, but cannot sustain one over a certain limit.

31. Statistically significant differences exist between these groups and the remainder of the sample in terms of the number of tickets sold, audiovisual and

print media coverage, venue capacity, national visibility, past awards won, past popularity as a Fringe attraction, and even the character of the reviews received.

32. Attendance is transformed logarithmically. As one would expect, total sales and Fringe box office sales are highly correlated: $r = .84$ untransformed and $r = .89$ when reexpressed as logarithms.

33. The definition of review employed here is somewhat narrower than Griswold's, which includes "critical discussions" as well (1987, p. 1088). I did not include Fringe coverage that consisted of such discussions, in which many shows receive a passing mention, or "features" in which artists are interviewed.

34. This is unsurprising, since the model predicting total ticket sales is really a subset of cases from the model predicting Fringe box office ticket sales. However, since it is not a random subset, the latter is preferable as an indicator of attendance.

35. This factor is irrelevant to total sales since complete information is available.

36. To examine the generality of the finding we may ask whether it applies to a genre such as movies. I tested this using the convenient review tables in *Variety*, which break down critical reviews as favorable, unfavorable, and ambivalent. While there is a significant association between total box office receipts after one month and the *sheer number* of reviews, the relationship with their favorability is, if anything, slightly negative. This may fuel the suspicion that film critics despise "commercial" products, but it is doubtful they are better than producers at predicting the movies that will, in fact, make money. Of course, this is not consistent with the idea that the public attends to their recommendations.

37. Raymonde Moulin, quoted in Becker 1982, p. 354.

38. As Gans argues, lower-taste publics become their own reviewers because they are less interested in learning how to respond "correctly" and more interested in entertainment (1974). Lang's work suggests another possibile relationship between genre and review effects, based on a "network" rather than an "aesthetic" concept of social distance (1958). Ties to the network of producers and reviewers (more likely, in his view, for critics in the theater and book worlds than for television and movie reviewers), are associated with positive performance biases, while an absence of ties is associated with audience identification and, hence, public trust. Reviews of *popular* genres should have more impact on attendance than reviews of highbrow performances by this reasoning.

39. Again, venue has a negative effect in the models for Fringe box office sales.

40. The difference would be even larger had I included "children's shows" as a high rather than a popular genre. I discovered after developing the classification system that reviews did affect attendance here, presumably because parents are treating reviewer opinions seriously where their youngsters are concerned. However, it is not true to the spirit of the test to change one's system of classification after the results are in.

41. Here I neglect audience capacity and venue and focus exclusively on Fringe box office sales.

42. The association with total attendance (Pearson correlation) is .49.

43. In Dryden's words: "Fame then was cheap, and the first comer sped; / And they have kept it since, by being dead" (*The Conquest of Granada*, 1670).

44. Another misconception that pervades the festival is the idea, often expressed by performers, that because of the practice of "show-hopping," shorter productions are better for drawing an audience. In fact, the positive association between duration and attendance indicates an audience preference for more "substantial" shows.

45. In this context I note the folk wisdom that the *New York Times* can more easily close a straight play with bad reviews than a musical.

46. "Look at Andrew Dice Clay," notes an American comic. "His reviews said he was racy, told immature jokes, and wasn't funny. He sold out the Meadowlands."

47. This argument does not apply, of course, to social worlds in which stylistic criteria are paramount generally (cf. Smith's 1974 analysis of dandy life).

48. The finding here parallels a difference often noted for the effects of movie reviews, that the impact of critics varies with the type of movie. Mitchell argues that reviews are only important for the reception of the decreasing number of films made for adults (under-25 audiences don't read as many magazines or newspapers) (1990, p. 8).

49. The sociologist in the real-life version of the following exchange is an American, aged forty.

CHAPTER SEVEN
CRITICAL EVALUATION

1. As one of Raymonde Moulin's informants on French painting suggested, critics are the "poor relations" of the family of art: "They have no money, so you can't trust them. They acquire a taste for high living, society, fashionable dinner parties, and scotch" (1987, p. 69).

2. In some segments of the popular music world where periodicals receive large advertising fees, it happens that reviews are always favorable. This is an effect of the editorial selection of reviewers who can be counted on to like what the company produces.

3. The reader's sociological sense will not have failed if she has drawn the conclusion that this behavior is unusual.

4. Occasionally promises of favorable reviews are easier to obtain than the reviews themselves. E. G. Boring agreed to praise Carl Brigham's *A Study of American Intelligence* but then savaged it in print (Stout and Stuart 1991).

5. "Joseph Kell, V. S. Naipaul and Me," *New York Times*, 4 April 1991.

6. Although some famous theater critics (Frank Rich, Brooks Atkinson) have been known to avoid strong associations with the theater world.

7. Coser et al. estimate that only 6,000 of 40,000 books published in the United States each year are reviewed (1982, p. 308).

8. *New York Times* critic John Canaday, whose opposition to abstract painting stirred controversy in the early 1960s, believed one should not leave such preferences implicit: "Fireworks are wonderful to look at but I do not think that

they offer a very profound experience, and I would not want the sky filled with them all night, year after year. Similarly I enjoy looking at abstract expressionist painting, but there is a limit to how much of it one can take, and I am tired of hearing that its skyrockets are cosmic manifestations" (1962, p. 28).

9. There may be more truth to this notion where it applies to editors in deciding which objects to review. In the United States, the *New York Times* selections have a large impact on which books other media choose to review (Coser, et al. 1982, p. 317).

10. This is not to say that reviewers never read the notices. Before departing to write his own piece, I have watched a critic for the *Times* diligently stand and read every posted review after seeing a show at the Traverse Theatre.

11. One reviewer, noting the overwhelmingly positive reviews of the television series *Twin Peaks*, claimed that television reviewers are just so used to reviewing garbage that they rave about anything given the opportunity. Another rails against movie hype, elevating films that are mediocre works of art. Mitchell shares the opinion that in movie reviewing one's standards slowly sink lower over time, finding things praiseworthy after reviewing for some years that initially they condemned (1990, p. 88).

12. Which is why the most peculiar use of reviews must surely be as *indicators* of popularity and success (McGranahan and Wayne 1947).

13. *Rehearsal at Goatham.*

14. The reviews were read by two independent raters and averaged.

15. In statistical terms, all of the bivariate correlations are significant at the .05 level or better, except for the association with older shows (p = .07). That is, if this were a random sample from a population of shows, one would expect a correlation coefficient at least this large to occur by chance about once in every twenty samples.

16. Although it is only significant at the .11 level, a factor indicating whether the group is from the Edinburgh/Glasgow area also reveals a positive effect. This suggests that local performing groups have an advantage when it comes to reviews, though slight.

17. Such a comparison has not been made, but Levy (1979) examined reviews of the Israeli National Theatre from 1918 to 1968, reporting that evaluations became harsher in the poststatehood period as the population of reviewers professionalized and adopted the frame of reference of their peers abroad. Critics ceased to view themselves as helping to create a new Israeli society and began to regard their task as guiding and educating the public. Although the the public preferred even mediocre Jewish plays, reviewers disliked these nostalgic shtetl comedies and melodramas, while holding classical and modern non-Jewish plays in high esteem.

18. Several reviewers suggested a distinction between one's "assessment of artistic quality" and one's personal taste or intuitive preference for the work. The later, however, is almost always elaborated as a genre preference.

19. The reader may be interested to learn that informal opinions of critics are generally expressed in terms of relatively simple likes and dislikes rather than elaborately phrased discourse. They talk about shows in ordinary language.

20. If the respondent could not rate the performance in terms of the five

categories, midpoints were used. When the reviewer did not remember the performance immediately by the name of the show, the performer's name was given. In a few cases where this was still not sufficient, the descriptive summary from the Fringe program was used (never the reviews themselves).

21. The percentage is calculated by squaring the correlation. In this case, $r = .78$ for the combined score, or $R^2 = (.78)^2 = .61$.

22. In the case of the combined scores, values can match exactly, since half points are possible.

23. A different kind of evidence against the characterization of the cruel critic is the fact that when *individual* performers are mentioned in a review, it is generally in a positive fashion. Bad acting is condemned collectively where possible.

24. For each of the four differences, F values show that the variances of the two groups were not significantly different, such that the exact two-sample t-test could be used to test the difference between means. While the difference between informal reviews of high and popular shows is statistically indistinguishable from chance levels ($p = .47$), in each of the other panels it is significant ($p = .01$).

25. The criterion used was a difference score with t-value > 2.

26. In two cases, only the bias for highbrow shows is statistically significant (owing to few popular reviews). In another, only one highbrow review was available. In the final case, the difference is quite small.

27. For this measure I did not include the four main local papers.

28. Any of these factors might affect the tendency of a published review to appear as more favorable than its author felt about the show. In one instance (number of printed lines), cuts by the editors might affect the judgment. In the remainder, lower standards for youth groups, original productions, local acts, or less visible groups might cause a reviewer to exaggerate the quality of a performance. I also tested the idea that the experience of the reviewer, as measured by the number of years he had reviewed for the *Scotsman*, is related to bias, but it had no effect.

29. One could in principle interview the critics *before* they write the reviews, but that procedure would likely be worse in its potential to affect the published reviews.

30. In 1995 the *Scotsman*, for the first time, adopted a rating system in which from one to five stars were affixed to the top of each review. Discussions with numerous spectators revealed a remarkably consistent pattern: scanning the paper in order to pick out and read the "extreme" (one- or five-star) reviews. Although I do not have systematic evidence for this tendency, it would appear that use of such graphics leads to a reduction in the perusal of text.

31. The complete text of the 1990 edition of the volume was used, containing 862 movies. Ebert rates movies from zero to four stars, so this system was used by a coder after concealing Ebert's own ratings. She considered as higher status any films that, after reading the reviews, involved intellectual stimulation (documentaries, espionage films with involved plots) and lower status films that did not (comedies, action films). Differences between ratings occurred in exactly 50 percent of the cases, but were within one star 95 percent of the time. The text

of Ebert's higher-status film reviews is, on average, more positive than the rating, while the text of lower-status film reviews is less positive (t = 1.7, p = .08).

32. Analogous to Benjamin's argument that reproducibility detracts from the sacred essence of an object.

33. Using the "Critical Mass" columns of *Entertainment Weekly* from March through November 1990, movies were classified by genre (using *EW* categories), and the "grades" from A+ to F were coded as a numerical score. The video review score given by the *EW* reviewer was subtracted from the mean rating given by the original film reviewers that *EW* takes from a variety of sources. (*EW*'s own original movie rating was not included.) The average difference for drama and documentary films was −.27, while for the remaining categories it was .95 (t = −2.08, p = .04).

34. Edwards 1991, p. 107.

35. The practice of note-taking during the performance may have been originated by critics who sat on the stage itself and wished to remember certain juicy bits of gossip that had been revealed during the performance (Burns 1972, p. 188).

36. It should be emphasized, however, that in the analysis the effect of reviews was weighted by the time between the review and the closing of the show, in effect controlling for the number of performances "at risk" for the review.

37. The *Exorcist*, for example, is often said to have received universally bad ratings. But in a random survey of forty critics, about one-third wrote favorably about it and only one-half actually wrote negative reviews (English 1979, p. 126).

38. Pearson correlations range from .13 to .33, so the maximum variance that can be explained in any one set of reviews by any other set of reviews is .11 ($R^2 = (.33)^2 = .11$), while the minimum is less than 2 percent ($R^2 = (.13)^2 = .017$). Spearman correlations, based on the rank ordering of observations, are generally smaller. Kendall's tau, shown in the third column of Table 7.5, is based on the extent of *disagreement* in the rankings of each pair of reviews. It may be interpreted as the difference between the probability that any two (randomly selected) shows will have the same order on two reviews and the probability that they will have different orders. So the larger the number, the greater the agreement in rankings.

39. As noted already, small associations render it inappropriate to use reviews, no matter how they are combined, as a measure of the quality of a show.

40. Correlations between reviewer recommendations on journal manuscripts average about .3, according to Fiske and Fogg (1990) who found a correlation of only .20 in their own study of psychology reviewers. Whether this means that Fringe performance critics are almost scientific in their agreement, or that science relies little more on consensually defined performance standards than art is impossible to say.

41. Of course, 25 percent of the time these would be agreements that a work is meritorious, while 25 percent of the agreements would condemn it.

42. Calculated as $(.69)^2 + (.27)^2 = .48 + .07 = .55$.

43. Even this overestimates the agreement of reviewers, since I have counted borderline cases (differences of two points) as agreements.

44. The mean absolute deviation is similar to the variance but takes the absolute value of the deviations from the mean rather than squaring them. The results of the multiple-regression analysis are similar regardless of whether the mean absolute deviation, the variance, or even the range (difference between the highest and the lowest evaluations) of the reviews are used.

45. There is not even a zero order effect of genre, as shown by the nonparametric Wilcoxon rank sum test (p = .52).

46. However, it could also be said that less favorable reviews, on average, are related to lower variability for the same reason (because unless there is some consensus about a show, it is impossible for it to achieve a low overall rating). Since this is not the case, empirically, the finding is not altogether lacking in interest.

47. New shows were defined as those that have not been performed in the United Kingdom more than six times.

48. If we split the population of shows into new and established shows and reestimate the models in Table 7.6, we find that reviews indeed have a larger impact on the audiences for original performances than for older work. For original shows, the standardized effect of reviews is .12 (p = .04), while the effect for established work is not significant. Splitting the population into highbrow and popular genres still shows no effect of reviews for popular shows. A similar analysis shows that reviews have an effect for groups without reputations, but not for groups that were well known. For popular shows, reviews have no effect regardless of the reputation of the group.

49. This depends, in all likelihood, on historical factors as well. During some periods, such as the late eighteenth century, the critical reaction to new drama was almost always unfavorable (Griswold 1986, p. 114).

50. Averages for new work are lower than established work for three of the publications, but differences are not statistically significant. The average score for original work is higher than established work in *Review88*, where critics are more likely to be students.

CHAPTER EIGHT
DO PERFORMERS LISTEN?

1. *New York Times* critic Mel Gussow recounts that a playwright once saved him from choking. Still, he conceals her name in order not to damage her reputation among her colleagues, who assign critics a "special place in hell . . . somewhere between the hypocrites and the spreaders of false doctrine" (16 July 1989, p. 5). Bensman claims that critics and musicians are "institutional enemies" but believes critics rate higher in the esteem of musicians than music historians or musicologists (1967, pp. 56–57).

2. "Lectures on Shakespeare and Milton," 1808.

3. *New York Times*, 21 February 1971, p. 12.

4. Forty-four (54 percent) were conducted with artists associated with "highbrow" shows; thirty-seven with "popular" artists.

5. Two of the theater selections were International Festival offerings. Excluding these shows, approximately equal proportions of highbrow and popular

performances at the Fringe were included: 6.7 percent (29/433) of all dramatic works (or 6.9 percent if poetry and mime are counted) and 7.7 percent (21/272) of shows in the popular genres (comedy, cabaret, revue, children's shows, and musicals).

6. The selection of shows was stratified in the following way: (1) relatively equal proportions of highbrow and popular shows were chosen; (2) special efforts were made to interview a range of artists—including amateurs and professionals, performers based in Edinburgh, London, and the United States, and performers at various career stages. This involved overselection of groups with established reputations.

7. This fact, as well as their propensity to save reviews even when they are negative, allowed Diana Rigg to assemble her book *No Turn Unstoned: The Worst Ever Theatrical Reviews* (1982) partly by writing the best-known actors and actresses in Britain and simply asking them to donate their worst review.

A nice account of the daily preoccupation of artists with reviews is by Peter Whitebrook, himself a reviewer for the *Scotsman*. *Staging Steinbeck: Dramatising "The Grapes of Wrath"* is a diary of a production that won a 1987 Fringe First. After the opening, there are daily entries on reviews that have and haven't appeared ("a wizened paragraph," "generally favorable but contradicts itself in the last sentence") as well as encounters with those in the press, who are now on the other side ("Spot a chap with an AFT Press Pack . . . against my better judgement, attempt casual amiability" [1988, p. 141]).

8. My favorite "recounting" episode occurred in New York City where a director and actors were discussing a reviewer as a robbery developed. Although the other customers immediately gave up their wallets, the listeners were so engrossed in the story that the thief was *unable to get their attention* and left them, still sitting there discussing the review.

9. Groups responding to my survey after the 1988 festival indicated that 59 percent had gone on to produce the same show elsewhere and 64 percent had used Edinburgh reviews for advertising purposes after the festival.

10. About 20 percent of all informants volunteered this point.

11. The show was not in fact reviewed in the *Independent*.

12. A related metaphor was once used by Christopher Hampton, the British playwright, in describing the relationship between performers and critics: "Asking a working actor what he thinks about critics is like asking a lamp-post how it feels about dogs."

13. Arnold Hauser, in his weighty treatise *The Sociology of Art* proclaimed: "Criticism is . . . least intended for the artist, and when it addresses him with objections, advice, and directives, it is generally found to be superfluous" (1982, p. 480).

14. That is, the interview situation may subtly encourage the interviewee to give certain answers.

15. Production contexts away from the large urban markets of New York, Paris, and London are places where performance changes most often occur after the initial rehearsal period (Engel 1967, p. 180).

16. Although not talleyed here, one company that had been devastated by reviews the previous year changed its name to The Beset Theatre Company.

17. Both were directors, and one had just experienced the worst run of reviews in his career.

18. Of course, since my interviews were conducted with a sample of *surviving* professionals, it may also be true that willingness to accept critical advice was a factor in their (successful) careers.

19. Rosenberg and Fliegel, who see critics as the decisive public for artists, suggest that young painters particularly need this confirmation (1965).

20. It will be remembered that the question of standards is crucial to the ideology of criticism and the notion of highbrow mediation because reference to standards legitimates the transfer of judgment.

21. There was variation, just as there is with professional critics, in the extent to which they discussed the performance or the play itself.

22. These included the *Scotsman*, the *Evening News*, *Review90*, *Festival Times*, the *List*, the *Independent*, the *Guardian*, and *Scotland on Sunday*. This list is not comprehensive, but comprises the Edinburgh and national papers with the most complete coverage. The reviews were organized by show. Two researchers read the reviews and extracted all comments (adjectives, sentences, and phrases) that could be considered judgmental. We divided them into positive and negative elements. In this analysis, reviews were not categorized as positive or negative in their entirety, but only insofar as they mentioned grounds, or reasons for a judgment, however trivial.

23. I say "might be" because it may also be due to informal and unreported conversations with the reviewer, a report by a third party, or the devil's disciple, random chance.

24. In all, eighty-seven reviews were dated before my interviews, fifty-nine dated afterward. The six shows for which no review could be found were a diverse group, comprising classic and modern theater, new drama, a musical, and a puppet show. All of them, though, were by youth groups (or for children).

25. This would impact the question of shared standards, since if a script is excellent for a reviewer and poor for a performer, the same standard is not being applied. In the present analysis, I would count this review as similar because the script was mentioned by both. There were nine such judgmental reversals overall, but their exclusion does not alter the results presented.

26. In cases where there was more than one informant present (two leading actors or a director and lead performer), their comments were treated together as judgments of the show.

27. The decision to count both phrasal and conceptual elements *maximizes* the possibility of similarity and does not provide a very stringent test of the claim that there are common performance standards. That is, if both a reviewer and artist referred to the musical qualities of a show in characterizing its excellence, I counted it, regardless of which specific aspect of its music they had in mind. To use the language of statistics (although I use no statistical tests in the present analysis), this increases the likelihood of Type I error (saying there is similarity where there is in fact none) and decreases the likelihood of Type II error (concluding there is no similarity when there is).

The only exclusion here was the reviewer's statement that she or he "liked" or "disliked" it as a whole or its cognates (worked, didn't work, etc.). I did not attempt to address the question of similarity of any *overall* judgment by either the performer or the reviewer. Rarely is the performer's or director's overall view of the show negative.

28. One show was a double bill, counted as half revue (popular) and half theater (highbrow). This was performed by the Cambridge Women's Footlights and was unusual in that there was a large number of reviews (six), but no commonalities. This is attributable to the fact that while the reviews were largely positive, the main actress and the director were reserved about the positive aspects of their shows. The existence of a women's group who dared raise the sacred Footlights banner was enough to occupy most of the reviewers.

29. That is, any point in common.

30. To illustrate, in a production about the life of Vincent van Gogh, the *Scotsman* review described the music as "effective, if at times overpowering." One day later, the director allowed that "(The) danger of this show is that the technical aspect—the music and visuals—will overpower the man the show is about. There's too much distraction."

31. Ratios of positive to negative features range from 2.2 for theater reviews after the interview to 3.2 for those beforehand but these are small differences relative to the number of cases here.

32. One was the equation of the Bacchic frenzy in Euripides with Acid House, while the other focused on class differences in Berkoff's *Decadence*.

33. All of the examples in this paragraph are taken from reviews in the *Scotsman*.

CHAPTER NINE
BEYOND FORMAL EVALUATION

1. Only two of my informants said reviews had no effect. Three of the remainder suggested their effects were small, while forty-seven claimed some significant impact on attendance. I found another question more telling, however. In response to my query "Are critics generally helpful or hurtful?" a large number of artists "heard" the question as referring to the effects of reviews in obtaining an audience. This often required more than one clarification. Some artists, in other words, have trouble thinking of the effects of critics in terms *other than* the potential audience.

2. This number is striking, since I never prompted for any specific effects. Usually the "somewhere else" was London, but amateur groups mentioned their community or city, and several respondents mentioned New York.

3. Only the director of the Traverse Theatre said that reviews were actually *less* potent during the festival. But the Traverse is subject to a special venue effect. Since Traverse productions routinely sell out each August, critics could only have an impact the remainder of the year.

4. Booth's recent study concludes that the testimony of artists offers "indisputable proof of the important, often crucial, impact of criticism on the performing arts" (1991, p. 1). If the testimony of participants alone was conclusive evidence for a phenomenon, sociology would be a good deal easier.

5. This pattern characterizes about 60 percent of my interviews.

6. The director of a group from Moscow University alleged that this effect was strong in the former Soviet Union: "bad reviews, good audience; good reviews, no audience."

7. This was quite positive.

8. "Belter" is a Manchester term for an excellent review. At the 1988 Fringe, the play *Woman of Hiroshima* won a Fringe First, played at the Traverse Theatre, received uniformly superlative reviews, and failed to sell out even one night. Why? The most likely explanation is the content of the show. Reviews informed the potential audience about the show as well as praising it, and few want to be wrenched about by nuclear aftermath stories. The failure of *The Grapes of Wrath* on Broadway has been subject to a similar analysis.

9. Their new American drama had just played to an audience of five.

10. One director said: "Last year I did *Timon of Athens*. It was destroyed by all the London papers and played five weeks to mediocre audiences. Then Germaine Greer did a spot on BBC2 where she said she loved it. Audiences turned around immediately. After that, *20/20*, the *Observer*, and some others printed positive reviews. Reviewers are scared of being out of step. The *Observer* called it 'much acclaimed' but it was really only Germaine Greer."

11. The Festival of Israel is held in May and June each year in Jerusalem and Tel Aviv. It is a prototypical example of the growing number of international festivals that focus on high-status performing arts featuring acts in theater, dance, and music. Popular genres, apart from music, are not represented. Dafna Goldberg collected the survey data on which I base these results.

12. Recognizing the importance of the "potential" audience, a more general study design should also address the comparison of attenders and nonattenders: why did those who *could* have attended choose to remain home?

13. The number of completed surveys was 973.

14. About 70 percent bought tickets before the beginning of the festival and up to 30 percent bought tickets on the day of the performance. Ticket prices are relatively high, but less than 20 percent of our sample paid full price. Half bought a ticket package for several performances.

15. In Baumol and Bowen's study, 3 percent of employed males and 5 percent of females in the performing arts audience were themselves performers (1966).

16. For example, the one-man show by Ray Stricklyn about the life of Tennessee Williams "stole the show at last year's Edinburgh Festival" according to the Israel Festival program.

17. This is the third largest "influence" on decisions to attend. Together with the program and personal recommendations, it is one of only three factors mentioned by at least 10 percent of the sample.

18. Fine (1977) provides a brief discussion of popular culture consumption by groups, but his arguments apply to high culture as well.

19. Fifteen percent of the sample came in groups of three or more. Those who did not themselves play a role in the decision to come were more likely to come with friends or relatives other than the spouse. These figures are roughly comparable to the Fringe statistics reported in Chapter 6, except that Fringegoers are more likely to come alone.

20. Social recommendations are the interactional referent of an "indirect tie." Removed at least one step from the primary viewer, the recommender typically *reports the evaluation but not the source.* For example, "*Lip Service* is supposed to be good." "I've heard Simon Fanshawe is fantastic." "The buzz is good on *Heart of a Dog.* It is remarkable how often the "buzz" is a single person. Ask for the source, and it's a friend or passing associate.

21. Is there a difference between a negative recommendation and no recommendation? Probably not, unless the show is under consideration.

22. I emphasize that the system of giving explicit ratings (e.g., stars) to art introduces a further complexity to the process, offering potential spectators the "pure" (though sometimes misleading) evaluation of the reviewer without the inconvenience of actually reading any of the text.

23. Five major Israeli papers were included in the questionnaire: Maariu, Yadiot, Haaretz, Hadasot, and Hayir, plus an "Other" category, most commonly the Jerusalem Post.

24. This is supported by the fact that there is not much difference between the percentage who had read at least one review and heard a recommendation (31 percent) and those who did not read one but still heard a recommendation (26 percent).

25. Those who had read reviews were also somewhat more likely to have *heard* of reviews they had not read.

CHAPTER TEN
DISCOURSE AND HIERARCHY

1. DiMaggio call this a "robust finding" across a wide range of studies, attributing it to the fact that the social networks of higher-status individuals are larger and more complex, requiring broad repertoires of taste.

2. As in this review of John Cleese by Roger Gellert in the *New Statesman* (quoted in Rigg, 1982, p. 23): "He walks across the stage, rather stiffly, and the audience collapses. He sits down and opens up an *Evening Standard*: loud barks of merriment fill the auditorium like rifle shots. There is, however, something peculiar about Mr. Cleese. He emits an air of overwhelming vanity combined with some unspecific nastiness, like a black widow spider in heat. But nobody seems to notice. He could be reciting Fox's *Book of Martyrs* in Finnish and these people would be rolling out of their seats."

3. Gans does remark on "straddling cultures" by the user-oriented high-culture public, choosing some entertainment from lower cultures (1974, p. 81). The distinction between creator and user orientations captures part of what I intend by the distinction between specialists and aficionados.

4. Some audience research shows that the number watching televised dramas is not correlated with rated popularity (Goodlad 1971).

5. Appendix C contains notes on other approaches to reception and mediation.

6. *Show Boat*, which had a lasting impact on the American musical theater, opened in New York in December 1927 after enormous advance ticket sales. The first-string critics passed it by to attend the opening of Philip Barry's *Paris Bound.* Critics at the time could only be enthusiastic about musicals by examin-

ing features other than those used to measure "serious" theater (Engel 1967, p. 170).

7. *The Idler*, no. 40, 20 January 1759, as quoted in Smith 1953, p. 148.

8. Kerry Shale's *Herringbone* premiered at the Traverse Theatre in 1990, billed as a "surrealistic gothic horror suicide comedy." One critic complained that "it never manages to subvert the genre."

9. "The subjective reactions of a critic . . . are not opposed to objectivity of judgment. They are its premise; without such reactions music is not experienced at all. It is up to the critic's ethic to raise his impression to the rank of objectivity, by constant confrontation with the phenomenon" (Adorno 1976, p. 148).

10. Greenfield interviewed 400 spectators at the openings of exhibitions in galleries and museums during the 1979–80 season.

11. Critics bring artists together and some are quite involved in the development of styles owing to their participation in social networks of artists (Crane 1987, pp. 34, 37–42). For example Clement Greenberg is known for his involvement with the abstract expressionist movement. In the publishing industry, Coser et al. argue that book reviewers, even where they have no personal contact with authors, are often linked to them through a network of intermediaries (principally editors and agents). Over 80 percent of their respondents who were trade-book editors were in touch with specific reviewers (1982, p. 312).

12. This is why the critic is often seen as a caviller or faultfinder.

13. Since advocates of high culture such as Steiner believe that direct perception is sufficient to establish the greatness of the classical canon (or "syllabus," to use his term), it does not occur to them that a prohibition on criticism might lead to radical alterations in the position of various works in the hierarchy.

14. Pursuant to the policy for critics that begins here, our celebration and tolerance of forms should not extend to the practice of iconic labeling, using stars or grading performances, which simplifies, misleads, and corrupts the rhetoric of evaluation.

15. Christopher Fry, the dramatist, agreed when he tried his hand at reviewing: "I could scarcely hear a word of the play for the noise of my own mind wondering how I should write about it" (1952, p. 18).

16. One argument supporting the notion that high levels of participation change aesthetic experience comes from the fact that movie attendance peaked in 1947 while the "agreement" between critics and audiences declines after 1954. Reduced attendance may have led to lower agreement between audiences and critics (Austin 1989).

17. One classic heckle was a retort by a comic in the audience to the question "What d'you do for a living?" "I'm a comedian," said Tony Allen, "what do you do?"

18. Donna McPhail, whose barbed tongue is enough to frighten most would-be wits, complained: "I don't get heckled much. Which is too bad. Sometimes it could turn the audience around."

19. Two cartoon critics of rock music characterized by their phenomenal witlessness.

20. John Gay, *Three Hours after Marriage* (1717), as quoted in Smith 1953, p. 47.

21. At a conference on "Critics and Criticism" at the old Traverse Theatre,

the following exchange took place between an English critic and a Scottish playwright.

> *Critic*: There are no absolute standards, no tape measures of quality. But there are certain objective ways of saying that Sondheim is better than Weber. You might enjoy a play, but still say another play is better.
> *Author*: This is bullshit. If you like something, you're always right.

22. Although there is not room to argue it here, I want to include a negative moral judgment of an artwork that is accepted by a reader of a review who nonetheless appreciates the work for other aesthetic qualities.

23. It is important to keep in mind that negative reactions are rarely reported directly by audiences to artists.

24. In the words of one literary editor, "I have yet to read a contemporary academic critic who could write more intelligently, or read more carefully, than a good book reviewer." Ackroyd, *Spectator*, 6 March 1976, as quoted in Sutherland 1978, p. 90.

25. This implies that *any* continuing discussion will do, positive or negative. Although it is rare, continual negative criticism serves as well as positive for keeping artworks alive. The poetry of William McGonagall is the outstanding example.

APPENDIX A
REVIEW GENRES

1. Assumptions about audience exposure and the occupations of writers, two of the dimensions considered in Chapter 2, are not relevant to the classification of published discourse.

2. This is particularly true for film and television. Nearly three-quarters of television critics preview shows (English 1979, p. 169). In the case of drama, the relationship is reversed: the general public is invited at reduced-rate previews before the critics, who should review the show on opening night.

3. The distinction is blurry because of the practice of "early reviewing," especially common with book reviews (which are mailed for reviewing before the public release), with television reviews (made available to reviewers before the date of the show), and even theater (where reviewers often "jump the gun" by reviewing one of the preview performances). However, in the vast majority of cases, the printed review appears *after* or on the day of release. Prepublication reviews are especially important in book publishing and represent part of a generally successful strategy to bypass the reviewers. Many best sellers do not get reviewed at all (see Coser et al. 1982, chap. 12, for an illuminating discussion).

4. In contemporary movie reviewing, movies are sometimes "hidden" from the critics, who are not given the opportunity to preview (Mitchell 1990). In the summer of 1990, *Problem Child*, *Exorcist III*, *My Blue Heaven*, *Lemon Sisters*, and *Shrimp on the Barbie* were not previewed. At the other extreme, some films have been released only after and *owing to* favorable reviews (e.g. *Brazil*, after it won the Los Angeles Film Critic's Circle award).

5. "Jesus Christ, the same yesterday, and today, and forever."

6. From a 1989 interview with a reviewer for the *Guardian*.

7. While there is never a "theme" as there is for many festivals, a significant part of the job for editors and critics during the Fringe is the attempt to identify common subjects, to reduce the sense of overwhelming diversity and to produce organized discourse ("sex," "politics," "fantasy").

8. Thematic collections should not be mistaken for *group reviews*, particularly for fiction, which are not necessarily thematic, but simply reviews of the week's novels strung together under a byline (Sutherland 1978, pp. 94–97).

9. In the United States, thematic analysis is most likely to appear in large Sunday editions of newspapers, often with special arts sections. These also provide space for art, architecture, and book reviews.

APPENDIX B
METHODOLOGICAL NOTE

1. The parameter estimates in the models refer to the entire population of shows rather than a sample.

2. If two or more separate pieces are included for the price of a ticket, they are considered one "production" by this definition. In such cases the shows are almost always reviewed together.

3. Zolberg published a list of genres in fine and popular art (1990, p. 144). Although her list is more comprehensive, including products such as cemetary gravestones and limited circulation periodicals, it is consistent with Table 6.1 (see Appendix D).

4. This point is worth emphasizing because of the temptation to "refine" dichotomies to fit hypotheses. In this instance, further analysis revealed "Children's Shows," the most "problematic" category, to deviate from the "popular" pattern (i.e., reviews *are* related to attendance). Hence, the test presented in Chapter 6 is conservative.

5. The national newspapers are not included here because they are more selective. Using the review file maintained by the administrative office and a commercial clippings service, I calculated a measure based on the number of reviews in national, local, and Sunday papers (*Guardian, Independent, Times, Observer, Scotland on Sunday, Glasgow Herald, Evening News, Financial Times, Times Educational Supplement, Sunday Times*). This measure is correlated r = .38 with the number of reviews in local papers, but does not contribute significantly to explained variation in the final models that include local review frequency. The London audience is far more likely to read these sources, but if they come to the festival they are subject to the local reviews as well.

6. I have included the primary sources of Festival Fringe coverage in this measure: BBC Radio Scotland (Festival View, Tuesday Review), BBC TV Scotland (Forth Fiesta), and BBC Radio (Round Midnight, Kaleidoscope, Aspects of the Fringe, Cutoff at the Fringe).

7. The five-point scale used is similar to that used by Lang (1958). A simple dichotomous (favorable/unfavorable) code did not do justice to the range of evaluations embedded in the reviews, while a more complex system was too difficult to administer. A Likert-type rating was used, but precise definitions were

264 NOTES TO APPENDIX C

given to aid in coding ambiguous cases. A score of 0 was used if no review was published. Pearson and intraclass correlations between coder ratings are as follows: *Scotsman* r = .93/ρ = .91; *Festival Times* r = .92/ρ = .89; *List* r = .91/ ρ = .88; *Review88* r = .93/ρ = .89.

8. Since the unweighted, zero-order correlations between reviews of the four periodicals are not high, summing would be dubious if they were seen as common measures of an underlying construct (e.g., the "quality" of the performance). This is not the case here. Empirically, we find little consensus *among reviewers* about the merits of particular shows. Their independent judgments are combined to indicate the overall assessment that was publicly available.

9. The number of performances was taken from the Fringe program, then corrected for additional and canceled performances as indicated by the daily update records and checked against the change forms submitted for the daily program guide. The capacity of the venue was given by the District Council or directly by the venue. In thirteen cases of multiple venues, appropriate adjustments were made.

Initially it was thought necessary to control for sold-out shows. Widespread rumors to the contrary, very few shows sell out. Less than 15 percent of shows reported even one sell-out day at the Fringe box office and only 5 percent reported more than three sellouts. These tickets account for fewer than half of total ticket sales, and the average run of a show is nearly two weeks.

10. Nominators included the administrator and assistant administrator of the Festival Fringe Society, the arts editor of the *Scotsman*, the artistic director of the Royal Lyceum Theatre, three critics familiar with the national performing arts world, a playwright, and an actress.

11. This measure must be included in models predicting central box office sales because some large venues are more likely to remove tickets from the box office (which charges 7 percent commission) for weekend shows. Out of 144 fringe venues I have included shows that appear at the Assembly Rooms, the Traverse Theatre, the Gilded Balloon, and the Pleasance (15 percent of the total).

APPENDIX C
NOTES ON THE STUDY OF MEDIATION AND RECEPTION

1. Goodlad's *A Sociology of Popular Drama* is the most thorough and explicit version of this theory (1971).

BIBLIOGRAPHY

Addington, David W. 1974. "Varieties of Audience Research: Some Prospects for the Future." *Educational Theatre Journal* 26: 482–87.

Adorno, Theodore W. 1976 [1962]. *Introduction to the Sociology of Music*. New York: Seabury Press.

Albert, Robert S. 1958. "The Role of the Critic in Mass Communications: I. A Theoretical Analysis." *Journal of Social Psychology* 48: 265–74.

Albert, Robert S., and Peter Whitelam. 1963. "The Role of the Critic in Mass Communications: II. The Critic Speaks." *Journal of Social Psychology* 60: 153–56.

Albrecht, Milton C. 1968. "Art As an Institution." *American Sociological Review* 33: 383–96.

Andreasen, A. R., and R. N. Belk. 1980. "Predictors of Attendance at the Performing Arts." *Journal of Consumer Research* 7: 112–20.

Arnold, Matthew. 1905. *Essays in Criticism: First Series*. London: Macmillan.

Attali, Jacques. 1985. *Noise: The Political Economy of Music*. Minneapolis: University of Minnesota Press.

Austin, Bruce. 1983a. *The Film Audience: An International Bibliography of Research with Annotations and an Essay*. Metuchen, N.J.: Scarecrow Press.

———. 1983b. "Critics' and Consumers' Evaluation of Motion Pictures: A Longitudinal Test of the Taste Culture and Elitist Hypotheses." *Journal of Popular Film and Television* 10: 156–67.

———. 1989. *Immediate Seating: A Look at Movie Audiences*. Belmont, Calif.: Wadsworth.

Austin, Bruce, and Thomas F. Gordon. 1987. "Movie Genres: Toward a Conceptualized Model and Standardized Definitions." *Current Research in Film: Audiences, Economics, and Law* 3: 12–33. Norwood, N.J.: Ablex.

Avery, Emmet L. 1966. "The Restoration Audience." *Philological Quarterly* 45: 54–61.

Baker, Carlos. 1964. "What Are Critics Good For?" *Opinions and Perspectives*. Edited by Francis Brown. Boston: Houghton Mifflin.

Balfe, Judith H., and Margaret J. Wyszomirski, eds. 1985. *Art, Ideology, and Politics*. New York: Praeger.

Barnes, Clive. 1975. "Who Has the Right to Write Criticism?" *New York Times*, 7 December, section 2, p. 30.

Baumol, W. J., and W. G. Bowen. 1966. *Performing Arts: The Economic Dilemma*. Cambridge, Mass.: MIT Press.

Becker, Howard. 1982. *Art Worlds*. Berkeley: University of California Press.

Benjamin, Walter. 1970 [1936]. "The Work of Art in the Age of Mechanical Reproduction." In *Illuminations*, edited by Hannah Arendt. London: Jonathan Cape.

Bennett, H. S. 1964. "Shakespeare's Audience." Pp. 56–70 in *Studies in Shakespeare*, edited by Peter Alexander. London: Oxford University Press.

Bennett, Susan. 1990. *Theatre Audiences: A Theory of Production and Reception.* London: Routledge.

Bensman, Joseph. 1967. "Classical Music and the Status Game." *Transaction* 4: 55–59.

Bentley, Eric. 1964. *The Life of the Drama.* New York: Atheneum.

Berger, B. M. 1971. "Audiences, Art, and Power." *Transaction* 8: 26–30.

Blau, Judith R. 1986a. "Elite Arts, More or Less de rigueur: A Comparative Analysis of Metropolitan Culture." *Social Forces* 64: 875–905.

———. 1986b. "High Culture as Mass Culture." *Society* 23: 65–69.

———. 1988a. *The Shape of Culture.* Rose Monograph Series. Cambridge: Cambridge University Press.

———. 1988b. "Study of the Arts: A Reappraisal." *Annual Review of Sociology* 14: 269–92.

———. 1988c. "The Context of Art Attendance." *Social Science Quarterly* 69: 930–41.

Blau, Judith, Peter M. Blau, and Reid M. Golden. 1985. "Social Inequality and the Arts." *American Journal of Sociology* 91: 309–31.

Blau, Peter M. 1986 [1964]. *Exchange and Power in Social Life.* New Brunswick, N.J.: Transaction Books.

Blau, Peter M., J. R. Blau, G. A. Quets, and T. Tada. 1986. "Social Inequality and Art Institutions." *Sociological Forum* 1: 561–85.

Booth, John E. 1991. *The Critic, Power, and the Performing Arts.* New York: Columbia University Press.

Booth, Wayne C. 1961. *The Rhetoric of Fiction.* Chicago: University of Chicago Press.

Bourdieu, Pierre. 1968. "Outline of a Sociological Theory of Art Perception." *International Social Science Journal* 20: 589–612.

———. 1984. *Distinction: A Social Critique of the Judgement of Taste.* London: Routledge and Kegan Paul.

———. 1985. "The Market of Symbolic Goods." *Poetics* 14: 13–44.

Brantlinger, Patrick. 1983. *Bread and Circuses: Theories of Mass Culture as Social Decay.* Ithaca, N.Y.: Cornell University Press.

Brook, Peter. 1968. *The Empty Space.* Harmondsworth: Penguin.

Brown, Trevor. 1978. "Reviewers on Reviewing." *Journalism Quarterly* 55: 32–38.

Bruce, George. 1975. *Festival in the North.* London: Robert Hale.

Burns, Elizabeth. 1972. *Theatricality: A Study of Convention in the Theatre and in Social Life.* London: Longman.

Burns, Elizabeth, and Tom Burns, eds. 1972. *Sociology of Literature and Drama.* Harmondsworth: Penguin.

Byron, Lord. 1967. "English Poets and Scotch Reviewers." *Byron's Poetical Works.* London: Oxford University Press.

Callenbach, Ernest. 1951. "US Film Journalism: A Survey." *Hollywood Quarterly* 5: 350–62.

Campbell, P. N. 1981. "The Well-Tempered Audience." *Central States Speech Journal* 32: 35–44.

Canaday, John. 1962. *Embattled Critic*. New York: Farrar, Straus and Giroux.

Cantor, Muriel, and Joel Cantor. 1986. "Audience Composition and Television Content: The Mass Audience Revisited." Pp. 214–25 in *Media, Audience, and Social Structure*, edited by Sandra Ball-Rokeach and Muriel Cantor. Newbury Park, Calif.: Sage.

Cawelti, John G. 1976. *Adventure, Mystery, and Romance: Formula Stories as Art and Popular Culture*. Chicago: University of Chicago Press.

Clemens, Samuel L. 1968 [1883]. *Life on the Mississippi*. New York: Dodd, Mead.

Clignet, Remi. 1985. *The Structure of Artistic Revolutions*. Philadelphia: University of Pennsylvania Press.

Coleman, James. 1990. *Foundations of Social Theory*. Cambridge, Mass.: Harvard University Press.

Coleridge, Samuel Taylor. 1909. "Lectures on Shakespeare and Milton (1808)." *Essays and Lectures on Shakespeare and Some Other Old Poets and Dramatists*. London: J. M. Dent.

Connor, John. 1990. *Comics: A Decade of Comedy at the Assembly Rooms*. London: Papermac.

Cook, Ann J. 1981. *The Privileged Playgoers of Shakespeare's London, 1576–1642*. Princeton: Princeton University Press.

Cook, William. 1994. *Ha Bloody Ha! Comedians Talking*. London: Fourth Estate.

Coser, Lewis A., Charles Kadushin, and Walter W. Powell. 1982. *Books: The Culture and Commerce of Publishing*. New York: Basic.

Crane, Diana. 1987. *The Transformation of the Avant-Garde: The New York Art World, 1940–1985*. Chicago: University of Chicago Press.

Dale, Michael. 1988. *Sore Throats and Overdrafts*. Edinburgh: Precedent.

Danto, Arthur. 1986. *The Philosophical Disenfranchisement of Art*. New York: Columbia.

———. 1989. *Connections to the World: The Basic Concepts in Philosophy*. New York: Harper Collins.

DeLaurot, Edouard L. 1955. "On Critics and Criteria." *Film Culture* 1: 4–11.

DiMaggio, Paul. 1982a. "Cultural Entrepreneurship in Nineteeth Century Boston: The Creation of an Organizational Base for High Culture in America." *Media, Culture, and Society* 4: 33–50.

———. 1982b. "Cultural Entrepreneurship in Nineteeth Century Boston, part II: The Classification and Framing of American Art." *Media, Culture, and Society* 4: 303–22.

———. 1987. "Classification in Art." *American Sociological Review* 52: 440–55.

DiMaggio, Paul, and John Mohr. 1985. "Cultural Capital, Educational Attainment, and Marital Selection." *American Journal of Sociology* 90: 1231–57.

DiMaggio, Paul, and Michael Useem. 1978. "Social Class and Arts Consumption: The Origins and Consequences of Class Differences in Exposure to the Arts in America." *Theory and Society* 5: 41–61.

———. 1983. "Cultural Democracy in a Period of Cultural Expansion: The

Social Composition of Arts Audiences in American Cities." Pp. 199–226 in *Performers and Performances*, edited by Jack Kamerman and Rosanne Martorella. New York: Praeger.

DiMaggio, Paul, Michael Useem, and Paul Brown. 1978. *Audience Studies of the Performing Arts and Museums: A Critical Review*. Washington, D.C.: National Endowment for the Arts.

Donohue, Joseph. 1975. *Theatre in the Age of Kean*. Oxford: Basil Blackwell.

Doty, Gresdna A., and Billy J. Harbin. 1990. *Inside the Royal Court Theatre, 1956–1981*. Baton Rouge: Louisiana State University.

Dubin, Steve. 1987. *Bureaucratizing the Muse: Public Funds and the Cultural Worker*. Chicago: University of Chicago Press.

Duncan, Hugh D. 1953. *Language and Literature in Society*. Chicago: University of Chicago Press.

Edwards, Owen Dudley. 1990. *The Edinburgh Festival: A Pictorial Celebration by Robbie Jack*. Edinburgh: Canongate.

———. 1991. *City of a Thousand Worlds: Edinburgh in Festival*. Edinburgh: Mainstream.

Elam, Keir. 1980. *The Semiotics of Theatre and Drama*. London: Methuen.

Ellis, John. 1982. *Visible Fictions*. London: Routledge and Kegan Paul.

Elsom, John. 1985. "The Social Role of the Theatre Critic." *Contemporary Review* 246: 259–63.

Engel, Lehman. 1967. *The American Musical Theater: A Consideration*. New York: Macmillan.

———. 1976. *The Critics*. New York: Macmillan.

English, John W. 1979. *Criticizing the Critics*. New York: Hastings House.

Faulkner, Robert. 1983. *Music on Demand: Composers and Careers in the Hollywood Film Industry*. New Brunswick, N.J.: Transaction.

Feld, Alan L., Michael O'Hare, and J. Mark Davison Schuster. 1983. *Patrons Despite Themselves: Taxpayers and Arts Policy*. New York: New York University Press.

Festival Fringe Society. 1994. *Fringe Press Office Diary*. Edinburgh: Festival Fringe Society.

———. 1995a. *How to Do a Show on the Fringe*. Edinburgh: Festival Fringe Society.

———. 1995b. *How to Sell a Show on the Fringe*. Edinburgh: Festival Fringe Society.

Fine, G. A. 1977. "Popular Culture and Social Interaction: Production, Consumption, and Usage." *Journal of Popular Culture* 11: 453–66.

Fish, Stanley. 1980 [1970]. "Literature in the Reader: Affective Stylistics." *Reader-Response Criticism: From Formalism to Post-Structuralism*, edited by Jane P. Tompkins. Baltimore: Johns Hopkins University Press.

Fiske, Donald, and Louis Fogg. 1990. "But the Reviewers Are Making Different Criticisms of My Paper! Diversity and Uniqueness in Reviewer Comments." *American Psychologist* 45: 591–98.

Ford Foundation. 1974. *Finances of the Performing Arts*. New York.

Foster, Arnold. 1979. "Dominant Themes in Interpreting the Arts." *European Journal of Sociology* 20: 301–32.

Foster, Arnold W., and Judith R. Blau, eds. 1989. *Art and Society: Readings in the Sociology of the Arts*. Albany: SUNY Press.

Fry, Christopher. 1952. *An Experience of Critics and the Approach to Dramatic Criticism*. London: Perpetua.

Frye, Northrup. 1953. *Anatomy of Criticism: Four Essays*. Princeton: Princeton University Press.

Gans, Herbert. 1974. *Popular Culture and High Culture: An Analysis and Evaluation of Taste*. New York: Basic.

———. 1985. "American Popular Culture and High Culture in a Changing Class Structure." *Prospects: An Annual of American Cultural Studies* 10: 17–37. Edited by Jack Salzman. Cambridge: Cambridge University Press.

Gaylord, Karen. 1983. "Theatrical Performances: Structure and Process, Tradition and Revolt." Pp. 135–50 in *Performers and Performances*, edited by Jack Kamerman and Rosanne Martorella. New York: Praeger.

Gerhards, Jurgen, and Helmut K. Anheier. 1989. "The Literary Field: An Empirical Investigation of Bourdieu's Sociology of Art." *International Sociology* 4: 131–46.

Gifford, John, Colin McWilliam, and David Walker. 1984. *Edinburgh*. Buildings of Scotland Series. London: Penguin Books.

Gilmore, Samuel. 1987. "Coordination and Convention: The Organization of the Concert World." *Symbolic Interactionism* 10: 209–28.

Gitlin, Todd. 1989. "The Postmodern Predicament." *Wilson Quarterly*, Summer: 67–76.

Goldman, William. 1969. *The Season: A Candid Look at Broadway*. New York: Harcourt Brace World.

Gonos, George. 1976. "Go-Go Dancing: A Comparative Frame Analysis." *Urban Life* 5: 189–220.

Goodlad, J.S.R. 1971. *A Sociology of Popular Drama*. London: Heinemann.

Gottdiener, M. 1985. "Hegemony and Mass Culture: A Semiotic Approach." *American Journal of Sociology* 90: 979–1001.

Graf, Max. 1946. *Composer and Critic: Two Hundred Years of Musical Criticism*. New York: W. W. Norton.

Gray, Charles Harold. 1931. *Theatrical Criticism in London to 1795*. New York: Columbia University Press.

Greenberg, Clifford. 1984. "Complaints of an Art Critic." Pp. 3–8 in *Modernism, Criticism, Realism: Alternative Contexts for Art*, edited by C. Harrison and F. Orton. New York: Harper and Row.

Greenberger, Howard, ed. 1971. *The Off-Broadway Experience*. Englewood Cliffs, N.J.: Prentice-Hall.

Greenfeld, Liah. 1989. *Different Worlds: A Sociological Study of Taste, Choice and Success in Art*. Rose Monograph Series. Cambridge: Cambridge University Press.

Griswold, Wendy. 1986. *Renaissance Revivals: City Comedy and Revenge Tragedy in the London Theatre, 1576–1980*. Chicago: University of Chicago Press.

———. 1987. "The Fabrication of Meaning: Literary Interpretation in the United States, Great Britain, and the West Indies." *American Journal of Sociology* 92: 1077–1117.

Griswold, Wendy. 1988. "Methodological Framework for a Sociology of Culture." *Sociological Methodology* 17: 1–35. Edited by Clifford Clogg. San Francisco: Jossey-Bass.

Hanna, J. L. 1983. *The Performer-Audience Connection: Emotion to Metaphor in Dance and Society.* Austin: University of Texas Press.

Harbage, Alfred. 1941. *Shakespeare's Audience.* New York: Columbia University Press.

Hauser, Arnold. 1982. *The Sociology of Art.* Chicago: University of Chicago Press.

Hay, Peter. 1989. *Theatrical Anecdotes.* New York: Oxford University Press.

Hebdige, Dick. 1979. *Subculture: The Meaning of Style.* London: Methuen.

Henderson, John B. 1991. *Scripture, Canon, and Commentary: A Comparison of Confucian and Classical Exegesis.* Princeton: Princeton University Press.

Hirsch, Paul M. 1972. "Processing Fads and Fashions: An Organizational Set Analysis of Cultural Industry Systems." *American Journal of Sociology* 77: 639–59.

Hohendahl, Peter Uwe. 1982. *The Institution of Criticism.* Ithaca, N.Y.: Cornell University Press.

Holt, Elizabeth, ed. 1979. *The Triumph of Art for the Public: The Emerging Role of Exhibitions and Critics.* Garden City, N.Y.: Anchor.

Holub, R. C. 1984. *Reception Theory: A Critical Introduction.* London: Methuen.

Hutchison, David. 1977. *The Modern Scottish Theatre.* Glasgow: Molendinar Press.

Iser, Wolfgang. 1980 [1974]. "The Reading Process: A Phenomenological Approach." In *Reader-Response Criticism: From Formalism to Post-Structuralism,* edited by Jane P. Tompkins. Baltimore: Johns Hopkins University Press.

Iwanska, Alicja. 1971. "Without Art." *Journal of Aesthetics* 11.

Jelavich, Peter. 1985. *Munich and Theatrical Modernism: Politics, Playwriting, and Performance, 1890–1914.* Cambridge, Mass.: Harvard University Press.

Johnson, Robert Carl. 1970. "Audience Involvement in the Tudor Interlude." *Theatre Notebook* 24: 101–11.

Kadushin, Charles. 1976. "Networks and Circles in the Production of Culture." Pp. 107–22 in *The Production of Culture,* edited by R. A. Peterson. Beverly Hills, Calif.: Sage.

Kamerman, Jack B., and Rosanne Martorella, eds. 1983. *Performers and Performances: The Social Organization of Artistic Work.* New York: Praeger.

Kant, Immanuel. 1978 [1794]. *Critique of Judgment.* Translated by J. C. Meredith. Oxford: Oxford University Press.

Kemper, Theodore, and Randall Collins. 1990. "Dimensions of Microinteraction." *American Journal of Sociology* 96: 32–68.

Kepplinger, Hans Mathias. 1989. "Content Analysis and Reception Analysis." *American Behavioral Scientist* 33: 175–82.

Kramer, Judith R. 1970 . "The Social Role of the Literary Critic." Pp. 437–54 in *The Sociology of Art and Literature,* edited by N. C. Albrecht, J. H. Barnett, and M. Griff. New York: Praeger.

Kristeller, P. O. 1951, 1952. "The Modern System of the Arts." *Journal of the History of Ideas* 12: 496–527, 13: 17–46.

Kronenberger, L. 1959. "Highbrows and the Theater Today." *Partisan Review* 26: 560–74.

Lamont, Michele, and Annette Lareau. 1988. "Cultural Capital: Allusions, Gaps and Glissandos in Recent Theoretical Developments." *Sociological Theory* 6: 153–68.

Lang, Gladys, and Kurt Lang. 1988. "Recognition and Renown: The Survival of Artistic Reputation." *American Journal of Sociology* 94: 79–109.

Lang, Kurt. 1958. "Mass, Class, and the Reviewer." *Social Problems* 6: 11–21.

Lazarsfeld, Paul F. 1948. "The Role of Criticism in the Management of the Mass Media." *Journalism Quarterly* 25: 115–26.

Levine, Edward M. 1972. "Chicago's Art World: The Influence of Status Interests on Its Social and Distribution Systems." *Urban Life and Culture* 1: 292–322.

Levine, Lawrence W. 1988. *Highbrow/Lowbrow: The Emergence of Cultural Hierarchy in America.* Cambridge, Mass.: Harvard University Press.

Levy, Emanuel. 1979. "The Role of the Critic: Theater in Israel, 1918–1968." *Journal of Communication* 29: 175–83.

———. 1979. *The Habima—Israel's National Theatre: A Study of Cultural Nationalism.* New York: Columbia University Press.

———. 1988. "Art Critics and Art Publics: A Study in the Sociology and Politics of Taste." *Empirical Studies of the Arts* 6: 127–48.

Litman, Barry. 1983. "Predicting Success of Theatrical Movies: An Empirical Study." *Journal of Popular Culture* 16: 159–75.

Lough, John. 1957. *Paris Theatre Audiences in the Seventeenth and Eighteenth Centuries.* London: Oxford University Press.

Lynch, James J. 1953. *Box, Pit, and Gallery: Stage and Society in Johnson's London.* Berkeley: University of California Press.

Lynes, Russell. 1949. *The Tastemakers.* New York: Harper.

———. 1985. *The Lively Audience: A Social History of the Visual and Performing Arts in America, 1890–1950.* New York: Harper and Row.

Macdonald, Dwight. 1957. "A Theory of Mass Culture." In *Mass Culture: The Popular Arts in America,* edited by Bernard Rosenberg and David Manning White. Glencoe, Ill.: Free Press.

Macmillan, Joyce. 1988. *The Traverse Theatre Story, 1963–1988.* London: Methuen Drama.

Macrae, Eric. 1989. "The Nationality and Other Characteristics of the Audiences and Performers at the Edinburgh Festival." Geography dissertation, University of Edinburgh.

Manfredi, John. 1982. *The Social Limits of Art.* Amherst: University of Massachusetts Press.

Mann, P. H. 1966. "Surveying a Theatre Audience: Methodological Problems." *British Journal of Sociology* 17: 380–88.

———. 1967. "Surveying a Theatre Audience: Findings." *British Journal of Sociology* 18: 75–90.

Martorella, Rosanne. 1977. "The Relationship between Box Office and Repertoire: A Case Study of Opera." *Sociological Quarterly* 18: 354–66.
———. 1982. *Sociology of Opera*. New York: Praeger.
Massie, Allan. 1994. *Edinburgh*. London: Sinclair-Stevenson.
McGranahan, D. V., and I. Wayne. 1947. "German and American Traits Reflected in Popular Drama." *Human Relations* 1: 429–55.
McGrath, John. 1981. *A Good Night Out: Popular Theatre: Audience, Class, and Form*. London: Methuen.
Mitchell, C.J.A., and G. Wall. 1989. "The Arts and Employment: A Case Study of the Stratford Festival." *Growth and Change* 20: 31–40.
Mitchell, Sean. 1990. "Moviemakers, Movie Critics, and You." *Los Angeles Times Calendar*, 21 October, pp. 8–9, 88–89.
Moffat, Alistair. 1978. *The Edinburgh Fringe*. London: Johnston and Bacon.
Morton, H. V. 1929. *In Search of Scotland*. London: Methuen.
Moulin, Raymonde. 1987 [1967]. *The French Art Market: A Sociological View*. New Brunswick, N.J.: Rutgers University Press.
Mukerji, Chandra, and Michael Schudson. 1986. "Popular Culture." *Annual Review of Sociology* 12: 47–92.
Mullen, Ken. 1985. "The Impure Performance Frame of the Public House Entertainer." *Urban Life* 14: 181–203.
Mulligan, R. A. and J. C. Dinkins. 1956. "Socioeconomic Background and Theatrical Preference." *Sociology and Social Research* 40: 325–28.
National Endowment for the Arts. 1983. "Audience Development in Four Southern Cities." Pp. 227–40 in *Performers and Performances*, edited by Jack Kamerman and Rosanne Martorella. New York: Praeger.
National Research Center for the Arts. 1975. *Americans and the Arts: A Survey of the Attitude toward and Participation in the Arts and Culture of the United States Public*. New York: National Committee for Cultural Resources.
Olson, A. 1980. *Art Critics and the Avant-garde, New York, 1900–1913*. Ann Arbor: University of Michigan Research Press.
Oxford Companion to the Theatre. 1983. 4th ed. Edited by Phyllis Hartwell. Oxford: Oxford University Press.
Passell, Peter. 1989. "Broadway and the Bottom Line." *New York Times*, 10 December, section 2, pp. 1, 8.
Pedicord, William. 1954. *The Theatrical Public in the Time of Garrick*. New York: Kings Crown.
Peterson, R. A., ed. 1976. *The Production of Culture*. Beverly Hills, Calif.: Sage.
———. 1978. "The Production of Cultural Change." *Sociological Research* 45: 292–314.
———. 1979. "Revitalizing the Culture Concept." *Annual Review of Sociology* 5: 137–66.
Plato. 1980. *The Laws*. Translated by Thomas Pangle. New York: Basic Books.
Policy Studies Institute. 1992. "Arts Festivals." *Cultural Trends* 4: 1–20.
Pollner, Melvin. 1987. *Mundane Reason: Reality in Everyday and Sociological Discourse*. Cambridge: Cambridge University Press.
Radway, Janice. 1984. *Reading the Romance: Women, Patriarchy, and Popular Literature*. Chapel Hill: University of North Carolina Press.

Rich, Frank. 1991. "Previews, That Broadway Malady." *New York Times*, 22 December, section 2, pp. 1, 32.

Rigg, Diana. 1982. *No Turn Unstoned: The Worst Ever Theatrical Reviews*. London: Elm Tree Books.

Rosenberg, Bernard, and Norris Fliegel. 1965. *The Vanguard Artist: Portrait and Self-Portrait*. Chicago: Quadrangle Books.

Ross, Andrew. 1989. *No Respect: Intellectuals and Popular Culture*. New York: Routledge.

Scottish Tourist Board. 1992. *Edinburgh Festivals Study: Visitor Survey and Economic Impact Assessment. Edinburgh. Summary Report*. Edinburgh.

Shrum, Wesley. 1991. "Critics and Publics: Cultural Mediation in Highbrow and Popular Performing Arts." *American Journal of Sociology* 97: 347–75.

Smith, Dane Farnsworth. 1953. *The Critics in the Audience of the London Theatres from Buckingham to Sheridan: A Study of Neoclassicism in the Playhouse, 1671–1779*. Albuquerque: University of New Mexico Press.

Smith, Thomas Spence. 1974. "Aestheticism and Social Structure: Style and Social Network in the Dandy Life." *American Sociological Review* 39: 725–43.

Sobel, Michael E. 1983. "Lifestyle Differentiation and Stratification in Contemporary U.S. Society." *Research in Social Stratification and Mobility* 2: 115–44.

Southern, Richard. 1961. *Seven Ages of the Theatre*. New York: Hill and Wang.

Steiner, George. 1989. *Real Presences*. Chicago: University of Chicago Press.

Stevenson, Robert Louis. 1983 [1878]. *Picturesque Old Edinburgh*. Edinburgh: Albyn Press.

———. 1994 [1882]. *Treasure Island*. London: Harvill.

Stout, Dale, and Sue Stuart. 1991. "E. G. Boring's Review of Brigham's *A Study of American Intelligence*: A Case-Study in the Politics of Reviews." *Social Studies of Science* 21: 133–42.

Suskin, Steven. 1990. *Opening Night on Broadway: A Critical Quotebook of the Golden Era of the Musical Theatre, "Oklahoma!" (1943) to "Fiddler on the Roof" (1964)*. New York: Schirmer.

Sutherland, J. A. 1978. *Fiction and the Fiction Industry*. London: University of London, Athlone Press.

Swidler, Ann. 1986. "Culture in Action: Symbols and Strategies." *American Sociological Review* 51: 273–86.

Templeton, Alice, and Stephen B. Groce. 1990. "Sociology and Literature: Theoretical Considerations." *Sociological Inquiry* 60: 34–46.

Todorov, Tzvetan. 1976. "The Origin of Genres." *New Literary History* 8: 159–70.

Tompkins, J. ed. 1980. *Reader-Response Criticism: From Formalism to Poststructuralism*. Baltimore: Johns Hopkins University Press.

Tumin, Melvin. 1985. *Social Stratification*. Englewood Cliffs, N.J.: Prentice-Hall.

Turner, Stephen. 1994. *The Social Theory of Practices*. Chicago: University of Chicago Press.

Twitchell, James. 1992. *Carnival of Culture: The Trashing of Taste in America*. New York: Columbia University Press.

Tynan, Kathleen. 1987. *The Life of Kenneth Tynan*. London: Methuen.

Walker, John A. 1982. *Art in the Age of the Mass Media*. London: Pluto Press.

Wanderer, Jules J. 1970. "In Defense of Popular Taste: Film Ratings among Professionals and Lay Audiences." *American Journal of Sociology* 76: 262–72.

Weber, William. 1975. *Music and the Middle Class: The Social Structure of Concert Life in London, Paris, and Vienna*. New York: Holmes and Meier.

White, Harrison, and Cynthia White. 1965. *Canvasses and Careers: Institutional Change in the French Painting World*. New York: Wiley.

Whitebrook, Peter. 1988. *Staging Steinbeck: Dramatising "The Grapes of Wrath."* London: Cassell.

Wiley, W. L. 1960 . *The Early Public Theatre in France*. Cambridge, Mass.: Harvard University Press.

Williams, Raymond. 1985. *Keywords: A Vocabulary of Culture and Society*. London: Fontana.

Wilmut, Roger, and Peter Rosengard. 1989. *Didn't You Kill My Mother-in-Law?: The Story of Alternative Comedy in Britain from the Comedy Store to Saturday Live*. London: Methuen.

Wilson, Garff B. 1973. *Three Hundred Years of American Drama and Theatre: From Ye Bear and Ye Cubb to Hair*. Englewood Cliffs, N.J.: Prentice-Hall.

Wolff, Janet. 1983. *Aesthetics and the Sociology of Art*. London: George Allen.

Wuthnow, Robert. 1988. *Meaning and Moral Order: Explorations in the Sociology of Culture*. Berkeley: University of California Press.

Wuthnow, Robert, and Marsha Witten. 1988. "New Directions in the Study of Culture." *Annual Review of Sociology* 14: 49–67.

Wyatt, Robert O., and David P. Badger. 1984. "How Reviews Affect Interest in and Evaluation of Films." *Journalism Quarterly* 61: 874–78.

Zablocki, Benjamin, and Rosabeth Moss Kanter. 1976. "The Differentiation of Life Styles." *Annual Review of Sociology* 2: 269–98.

Zolberg, V. 1980. "Displayed Art and Performed Art: Selective Innovation and the Structure of Artistic Media." *Sociological Quarterly* 21: 219–31.

———. 1990. *Constructing a Sociology of the Arts*. Cambridge: Cambridge University Press.

INDEX

About the Author

WESLEY MONROE SHRUM, JR., is Professor of Sociology
at Louisiana State University.